# POINT OF NO RETURN

# POINT OF NO RETURN

## The Story of the Twentieth Air Force

WILBUR H. MORRISON

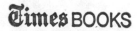

Published by TIMES BOOKS, a division
of Quadrangle/The New York Times Book Co., Inc.
Three Park Avenue, New York, N.Y. 10016

Published simultaneously in Canada by
Fitzhenry & Whiteside, Ltd., Toronto

Manufactured in the United States of America

Dedicated to the memories of Generals of the Army
Henry H. "Hap" Arnold and George C. Marshall,
without whose commitment there would have
been no Twentieth Air Force.

# ACKNOWLEDGMENTS

This book is basically a story of people rather than of events. The history of the operations of the Twentieth Air Force has been told before, including my own personal memoir, *Hellbirds: The Story of the B-29s in Combat*. The complete story, involving world figures and the behind-the-scenes decision-making that changed our world, has never been told in its entirety. I've tried to tell that story while the few remaining decision-makers are still alive.

Without retired General Curtis E. LeMay to guide me through the intricate operational decisions, and provide his intimate thoughts on people and events, and retired Major General Haywood S. Hansell, Jr., who gave unstintingly of his time and recollections, I couldn't have completed the book.

There were literally hundreds of men who provided reminiscences and each one is recorded in the book. Among those to whom I'm most indebted are Denny D. Pidhayny, recording and historical secretary of the 58th Bomb Wing Association, who, without question, is the leading authority on all aspects of the Twentieth Air Force, and retired Colonel Victor N. Agather.

For those familiar with the excellent source materials in the Albert F. Simpson Research Center, Maxwell Air Force Base, Alabama, it will be apparent after reading this book that the facts and figures may be on file there but most of the human element is not because operational records were not designed for such reporting. The courtesies extended to me by James Eastman and his associates at the center are hereby acknowledged with appreciation.

# INTRODUCTION

Japan was defeated by August 1, 1945, before the first atomic bomb was dropped. Her mighty navy had been destroyed by the U.S. Navy, her merchant ships were either sunk or confined to harbors after extensive mining around her home islands, and most of her cities lay in ruins following massive bombing attacks by B-29s of the Twentieth Air Force. By this date, her destruction was almost total as B-29s roamed at will over her main islands.

The war ended so suddenly after the dropping of atomic bombs on Hiroshima and Nagasaki that many people still believe they caused Japan's surrender when, in fact, they merely precipitated that action a few weeks sooner than anticipated. The belief that the atomic bombs won the war caused some decision-makers in the U.S. Government to place a tragic overreliance on nuclear and thermonuclear weapons for massive retaliation in the event of a third world war. I've used the word "tragic" deliberately because the United States has fought two wars since World War II with conventional weapons because use of atomic and hydrogen weapons was inconceivable for moral and political reasons.

After World War II, when the United States had a monopoly on nuclear weapons, the concept of massive retaliation was a deterrent to war. Therefore, the decision to maintain a nuclear and thermonuclear force was not only wise but absolutely essential until all countries agreed to outlaw such weapons with sufficient safeguards to prevent their unauthorized use.

Now that the United States and the Soviet Union are roughly equal in their capability of waging nuclear war, the chances of such a holocaust are remote; not for moral reasons but because there would be no "victor" in the accepted sense. In essence, the use of atomic and hydrogen bombs would devastate both nations.

Due to the huge cost of maintaining a strategic force of bombers and missiles equipped with such weapons, conventional airpower was shortchanged after World War II. As a result, the United States was ill equipped to fight the kind of war it fought in Korea and Vietnam.

In the future, the free world must maintain a nuclear capability to inhibit initiation of nuclear war by those forces inimical to it. It must also provide a capability to wage strategic air warfare with conventional weapons and adequate tactical support of ground troops. The United States has twice fought the kind of war which proponents of massive nuclear retaliation said we'd never have to fight again. Also, the United States Strategic Air Command must retain a nonnuclear capability with conventional weapons. SAC's aging B-52 fleet should be replaced despite the high cost. Total reliance upon ground- or sea-based missiles, or those of the cruise variety, would be disastrous to the free world because they are worthless without their nuclear warheads.

This book tells the story of how Japan was defeated without a costly ground invasion of her homeland, and describes how this was done without the cooperation of the Russians, or the need for the atomic bombs.

WILBUR H. MORRISON

# CONTENTS

CONTENTS

(*Illustrations follow pages 256 and 288*)

PART ONE

# Prologue

"Hap" Arnold squirmed uneasily in his seat as the debate grew hotter. His moon-shaped face was flushed and his thinning white hair was in an unusual state of disarray as a result of the play of nervous fingers. From time to time he glanced at General George C. Marshall but the Army Chief of Staff remained imperturbable throughout the heated exchange between Colonel Harold L. George, head of the newly created Air War Plans Division, and members of Marshall's staff. Arnold had known that this plan for a massive British-American air offensive against Germany and Italy to destroy their war-making capabilities and, hopefully, preclude an invasion would come as a shock because it was such a drastic departure from accepted Army strategy. Still the reaction of some of Marshall's officers seemed unnecessarily harsh. And yet he realized that a proposal to conduct such an air offensive, even before ground forces were involved, was heresy to most of these men. He had listened to such arguments since World War I.

The idea that long-range bombardment aircraft could play a decisive role in war wasn't new. General William S. "Billy" Mitchell had said the same thing for years and finally had resigned from the Army following his court-martial so he could speak more freely. This was the first time, however, the Army Air Corps had formally presented such a plan to higher authorities.

Arnold, as chief of the Army Air Corps, was aware that most Americans still weren't reconciled to involvement in World War II and that such a plan would be anathema to millions if it became known. Personally, he had no doubts after the latest neutrality violations by the Germans; particularly when a Nazi submarine made its first attack on an American warship and torpedoed the U.S.S. *Greer*, and then the merchant ship *Steel Seafarer* was sunk by German aircraft in the Red Sea.

When President Franklin D. Roosevelt called upon the War Department to establish military production requirements "to defeat our potential enemies," an air plan was prepared in August 1941 on an emergency basis. The air portion of the reply to the President, which later became known as Air War Plans Division-1 (AWPD-1), was the direct result of George's request for responsibility to prepare that section involving the Army Air Corps in response to the President's request.

Preparation of such a plan was possible because General Arnold a year earlier had had the foresight to establish an air intelligence division. The correctness of Arnold's decision in endorsing the air plan was fortified when the President issued his "shoot on sight" order. Previously, warnings had been couched in diplomatic language. This time the President was blunt. "From now on, if German or Italian vessels of war enter the waters of the Atlantic, the protection of which is necessary for American defense, they do so at their own peril."


From time to time Arnold's eyes strayed from the proceedings to watch W. Averell Harriman's face for reaction. Although he had made a number of comments, for the most part Roosevelt's personal representative to Soviet Russia gave no indication by word or gesture whether he approved or not. He knew that Harriman's concern for embattled Britain was sincere, and that this August 30, 1941, meeting came at a time when the British had their backs to the wall.

Arnold recalled vividly that such ideas often met with conflict within the War Department during the 1920s and 1930s. He had served in the Army's aviation branch throughout these years of dissension between airmen and the "old guard" of the Army and Navy, and had become indoctrinated with the views of American airmen like Mitchell and Admiral William S. Sims of the U.S. Navy. Although these and other advocates of coequal status for air forces with armies and navies were few, they made up for this paucity by the enthusiasm of their endorsements.

Arnold noted that the questioning was dying down and there was a long pause before the final question was raised by a member of Marshall's staff. He wanted to know if the plan was based on the premise that Germany should be defeated first, with only a holding action in the Pacific if Japan should become involved.

George replied that such an understanding was a basic consideration, and that only a strategic defense was planned in the Far East until Hitler was defeated.

There was a hushed air of expectancy when the questioning ceased. All eyes turned to Marshall. As Army Chief of Staff his support was vital if the plan was to get anywhere. He didn't speak for a moment or two. Then, thoughtfully, he turned to Arnold and his staff. "Gentlemen, I think the plan has merit. I would like the secretary and the assistant secretaries to hear it."

Arnold was elated, knowing that Marshall's approval was a critical milestone in the evolution of American airpower, and crucial to eventual acceptance by the War Department. He hurried over to George and complimented him on the outstanding job his staff had done in preparing the plan. He was warm in praise of Lieutenant Colonel Kenneth Walker, Major Laurence Kuter, and Major Haywood S. "Possum" Hansell, Jr., who had worked so hard to develop the plan, telling them Marshall's words should be viewed as a vindication of their long fight for the advancement of airpower.

Each of these officers was to play roles in the defeat of the Axis powers they never dreamed of at the time. Walker was later killed while leading his command over Rabaul, an action that won him the Medal of Honor. Kuter had a distinguished war record and retired as a four-star general. Hansell, who played such a significant part in developing the doctrine for the strategic phase of the war, little thought at the time that one day he would be called upon to prove the plan in combat.

There was no doubt in Arnold's mind that George deserved credit for the plan's major features. The veteran airman had served as a bomber pilot in World War I and was with Mitchell's First Bombardment Brigade when the Air Corps proved that bombers could sink battleships. George's long personal association with Mitchell and his sincere beliefs in airpower's potential made him an ideal choice to head the Air War Plans Division.

It was Marshall, however, who had the vision and courage to concentrate the Army's aviation units under General Arnold in a separate corps despite the fact that Arnold had been an outcast in the Army ever since his outspoken defense of "Billy" Mitchell. Marshall's action was a complete departure from traditional concepts that aviation should be used only in support of ground troops. He also strengthened Arnold's authority by making him Deputy Chief of Staff for Air of the United States Army.

Marshall's specific reasons for his favorable reaction to the plan are unknown. It is General Hansell's belief that he was most influenced by the plan's thoroughness and clarity, which did not rely merely upon generalities about airpower.

The plan stated a specific objective and that was to bring about victory without invasion, or make invasion of Hitler-dominated Europe feasible. The target systems whose destruction would attain that objective were listed, including details about specific targets within each system, and even specified the number of bomb hits by specific types and sizes of bombers that would be required to bring about such destruction. The plan went even further by estimating not only the numbers of bombers but the bombing accuracy that must be achieved and anticipated losses. Finally, the plan estimated the time required to do the job.

Consideration was given to failure of strategic bombers to bring about victory without invasion, and the plan called for supporting air forces for a combined ground-air effort to bring about capitulation.

The overriding provision in the plan was for the defeat of the German Air Force.

For these reasons, General Hansell said that he believed the meticulous Marshall found the plan persuasive, with its call for destruction of carefully selected targets, and not mass destruction of civilian areas, most appealing of all.

After the meeting with Marshall, the plan was forwarded to Secretary of War Henry L. Stimson rather than to the joint Army–Navy Board where, Arnold was convinced, it undoubtedly would die an early death due to strong Navy opposition.

An additional meeting September 4 was necessary to present the plan to William S. Knudsen, head of the Office of Production Management, and his staff, with Marshall and Arnold in attendance.

Seven days later George and his planners, together with Marshall, presented the plan to Secretary of War Stimson. The latter told the group, "General Marshall and I like the plan. I want you gentlemen to be prepared to present it to the President. I will speak to him about the date."

George and his staff were ecstatic because their plan, which in reality called for a United States Air Force and its strategic employment, had been accepted by the highest government officials.

Later the plan was presented to the President's office along with the War Department's "victory program." The plan called for an Air Force of 3,842 bombers and 2,080 fighters with a monthly replacement of 1,288 bombers and 335 fighters.

Before the President had a chance to review the war plans, an unforeseen event occurred. When the Japanese attacked Pearl Harbor December 7, 1941, most of the War Department's and the Navy Department's plans lost their validity because they called for a major role for the U.S Fleet, which now had lost its backbone. Practically all the strategic plans for the future conduct of U.S. armed forces were nullified by this sneak attack by carriers of the Japanese Navy. One plan still retained its validity, and that was the Air Corps plan. Although there were modifications during the war years, particularly air plans for air operations against Japan that weren't covered in depth originally, there was no alteration whatsoever in the fundamental strategic concept involving the use of airpower.

Arnold and the officers who drew up the plan were aware they had few supporters outside their own ranks. The grossly exaggerated claims of destruction by some of Mitchell's disciples after World War I had hurt their cause, but times had changed. New aircraft in the mid-thirties such as the B-17 Flying Fortress were nearly as fast as fighters with a survivability over enemy territory that was unheard of in World War I.

And now there was the B-29 Superfortress. Although it was still years away from operational readiness, Arnold and his staff had faith it would give them the ultimate strategic weapon airmen had so long sought.

President Roosevelt had written the War Department the previous May recommending a buildup of heavy bombers with a production quota of 500 a month. The new B-29, designed to reach all areas of Germany from England, was still only in preliminary layout. Now the President called for production of 26,000 combat planes and 37,000 trainers by 1944. That was shocking enough to officials of the infant aircraft industry who, in the past, were lucky to count production contracts in terms of a few hundred airplanes a year, but the Air

Corps also recommended production of 17,000 warplanes for the Royal Air Force!

Would the grand designs of AWPD-1 be fulfilled? If they were realized hundreds of thousands of Allied soldiers, sailors, and airmen would be spared maiming or death. Whether the plan was feasible, and fulfillment possible, would be determined by American technological and industrial capabilities that first had to perform a production miracle, and secondly by 2.5 million young men and women who had to be trained before they could be led into combat by 1,200 regular and reserve officers out of a total Army Air Corps of slightly more than 11,000 personnel.

In retrospect, it is regrettable that President Roosevelt never received a formal presentation of the air plan in the manner in which it was presented to General Marshall and Mr. Stimson. It is possible that the President might have gained a better insight into a basic, war-winning air strategy that he never fully understood.

# CHAPTER 1

# The Superfortress

It was the determination of men like Arnold, who were concerned by the growth of Germany's Luftwaffe during the 1930s, that kept the concept of strategic airpower alive. Those who fought in World War I vowed that never again would America's finest be sacrificed in needless trench warfare. They were convinced there had to be another way through the effective use of strategic bombers. Arnold often reminded intimates that Göring had learned his World War I airpower lessons well, and that he obviously had Hitler's trust. The Air Corps chief assured that some of the limited funds available for new aircraft were set aside for research facilities even when it meant a critical reduction in procurement of new bombers.

In 1935, a General Headquarters Air Force was established that gave airmen some measure of autonomy. Up until then Army aircraft had been under corps commanders. This action permitted the small Army Air Corps to draw up its first war-contingency plans.

In that same year, Boeing's prototype for the B-17 Flying Fortress made its first flight in July. Even after it crashed October 30, 1935, these early bombardment pioneers retained their faith and later persuaded the War Department to order 13 more.

Such was the isolationist sentiment in those years that even as late as 1939 the Congress was still refusing to appropriate funds for long-range bombers because they were considered offensive weapons that might draw the United States into war in Europe.

The Army Air Corps was so restricted in its prewar operations that a ruling was passed by the Army–Navy Board that its planes could not fly more than 100 miles from the U.S. coastline.

An earlier requirement to develop a 5,000-mile bomber that could fly nonstop to Hawaii, Alaska, or the Canal Zone from bases in the United States wasn't met satisfactorily. Neither the Boeing XB-15 nor the Douglas XB-19, contracted for in 1934, was suitable because available engines were inadequate to power such huge aircraft and neither met speed or range requirements. However, both proved to be valuable flying laboratories after they flew in 1937.

Major General Arnold, as head of the Army Air Corps, was more than ever concerned about Germany's growing air strength after talking with Charles A. Lindbergh upon his return to the United States from Europe in April 1939 where he had lived for several years.

Lindbergh was given the red-carpet treatment by Germany in an attempt, through him, to influence public opinion in Great Britain, France, and the United States about the overwhelming might of Nazi airpower. Hermann Göring permitted the celebrated hero to fly several German fighters and bombers. Lindbergh was misled deliberately about total numbers of these aircraft, but his evaluation of individual types in relation to comparable British, French, and American airplanes proved amazingly accurate. As for bombers, Arnold was pleased to hear him say that the Germans had nothing to compare with the B-17.

Lindbergh summed up his views by telling Arnold that he was impressed with Germany's military aviation following his tour of airfields and factories. He said that Germany's air strength was greater than all other European nations combined; a fact that was later proved in error.

Arnold sent a report of Lindbergh's comments to Army Chief of Staff General Malin Craig. In one of Craig's final actions, he set up an air board to consider all aspects of hemispheric defense. Headed by Brigadier General W. G. Kilner, the board included Lindbergh at Arnold's request and was charged with the responsibility of recommending the types of aircraft the Air Corps should develop.

When it completed its work, the board reported that Navy ships and coastal defenses no longer were adequate to protect North and South America because air bases could be established in the western hemisphere from which bombers could attack the United States. The board recommended that several long-range medium and heavy bombers be developed to counter such a threat.

General Marshall took over as Army Chief of Staff on September

1, 1939, the day Hitler invaded Poland, and the day the air board's report was delivered to the Chief of Staff's office.

With typical decisiveness, Marshall quickly realized the validity of the recommendations. He endorsed them, saying, "This establishes for the first time a special mission for the Air Corps."

Later, however, Arnold was appalled to receive orders from the War Department to cancel the B-17 Flying Fortress program. With that program dead as a dodo, he knew that strategic air warfare had received its worst setback in years. His instructions now were to concentrate on a smaller, shorter-range airplane. Later, the program was reinstated.

Acceptance of the Kilner report resulted in appropriation of large sums of money for hemispheric defense. Specifically, $4.7 million was set aside to procure five experimental bombers, which permitted Arnold to go ahead with plans for a very long-range bomber.

The war in Europe added impetus to buildup of America's armed forces. On November 10, 1941, Arnold asked for authority to contract with aircraft firms for preliminary studies of a new four-engine bomber. It was granted December 2, and he sent instructions to the Air Technical Service Command at Wright Field to prepare specifications.

Colonel Oliver P. Echols and his staff went to work to draw up requirements for an all-weather bomber that would use a new radar and would operate both day and night without fighter escort, and under all weather conditions.

Meanwhile, the Boeing Airplane Company had made several design studies of its own. The first was an updated XB-15; then came an improved B-17 with a pressurized fuselage and tricycle landing gear.

After the Kilner board's report, Boeing's design studies went through a series of proposals with different engines and wing arrangements but all were discarded because they lacked range. None of these models looked like the eventual B-29, and it wasn't until a bomber with Wright radial engines was proposed that the familiar shape was discernible in the full-scale mockup Boeing built in December 1939 with its own funds.

As reports filtered out of Wright Field about what was an acceptable configuration for the new bomber, Boeing proposed still another design longer than its predecessor, with a shorter wing and a speed of 405 mph, or 15 mph faster than all previous models. Gross payload was 10 tons more than earlier models because of its 2,000-horse-power Pratt and Whitney engines and a new wing design to give it greater lift.

Arnold's own requirements for the new bomber stressed superiority in every way over the B-17B and the B-24. A request for proposal was circulated among four manufacturers on January 29, 1940. To quiet the isolationists, the bomber was presented as a defensive weapon to provide long-range reconnaissance and to make strikes against the fleet of a possible invader. With officers of the Air Corps indoctrinated for years with the philosophy of offensive warfare, the new bomber obviously was initiated under false pretenses.

Arnold's Chief of Staff Colonel Carl A. Spaatz expressed the views of most Air Corps officers when he said privately that such an airplane could be used against Japanese industry in the event of war in the Far East by operating out of bases in the Philippines, Siberia, or the Aleutians.

The Army's specifications called for a bomber with a speed of 400 miles an hour, a range in excess of 5,000 miles, and a payload of one ton of bombs. It was later conceded that the bomb load would have to be increased at some sacrifice to range to make the airplane an effective weapons system.

These "specs" were changed again, after British wartime experiences against the Luftwaffe, to include better crew protection, more defensive armament, and self-sealing fuel tanks.

Boeing refined its previous proposals and submitted its Model 345 to Wright Field May 11, 1940.

Hitler, meanwhile, had conquered Denmark and Norway and in May his armies were rolling through Holland into Belgium. France was next.

On May 16 Roosevelt reacted. He sent a message to the Congress asking for production of 50,000 warplanes a year.

Boeing's efforts to produce a new bomber, expending its own funds for the most part, now paid off. It was selected along with Lockheed to continue development and many considered Boeing far in the lead. At Wright Field, Colonel Echols chose Captain Donald L. Putt, test pilot and engineering officer, as project officer. Putt had survived the crash of the B-17 prototype in 1935 and had much experience in the heavy-bomber field. He was an excellent choice to handle the new program.

The original Boeing proposal had been designed for a gross weight of 85,700 pounds, but with the addition of armor plate, and more and heavier guns, the XB-29's weight rose to above 100,000 pounds, particularly after a longer fuselage was approved.

Until now, these designs were only on paper. When Boeing was declared the winner of the competition, it was awarded an $85,652 contract to continue engineering design and wind-tunnel studies. On September 6, 1940, Boeing received a $3.6 million contract to build two prototypes, later increased to three, plus a static-test article. The Consolidated-Vultee Aircraft Company received a similar contract for parallel development of the XB-32, and Douglas and Lockheed withdrew from the competition.

Earlier, the XB-15 had been seriously underpowered at 92,000 pounds. The XB-29, however, would have the new 2,200-horsepower Wright Duplex Cyclone engines, each with two superchargers instead of one, and with more than twice the engine power of the XB-15. The XB-29 also had a different wing location resulting from its being moved from a low- to a mid-fuselage position. Another important change was incorporation of a nose wheel.

The engine, largest ever hung on an airplane, was unique because Wright Aeronautical Corporation attempted to build it at a weight of one pound for each horsepower. In attempting to reduce its weight, an unusual amount of magnesium was used because it is one third lighter than aluminum. Along with its relative lightness, however, magnesium has the unfortunate characteristic of breaking up under certain vibration conditions, and it burns with an extraordinarily hot temperature. Initially, engines were built with magnesium crankcases and housings. Although the problem didn't appear serious during ground tests, in flight crankcases lasted only a few hours before they broke up and the engine came apart. Thereafter, crankcases were made of aluminum.

During this phase of development Arnold had to counter his critics in the War Department who objected to the huge allocations of funds and resources for one Air Corps project. In a letter to Robert A. Lovett, Assistant Secretary for Air, Arnold stressed that the B-29 was the only weapon which the United States could use against Japan without costly preliminary operations in the event of war.

Marshall, who was under pressure to consider the B-29 for other possible wartime use, including operations in China, was told by Arnold that their employment in other areas would drastically reduce their effectiveness because the element of surprise would be lost. Arnold said the Japanese would inevitably attempt to neutralize potential bases, particularly on the Chinese mainland.

By early 1941, the XB-29 project was in limbo because American officials were concerned whether Britain could hold out. If she didn't, Arnold told his staff, an entirely different long-range bomber would be needed: one with a 10,000-mile range and a five-ton bomb load capable of hitting targets in Germany from American bases. Even though two years of design studies were behind the B-29 project, and a nine-foot wind-tunnel model already constructed, it was touch and go whether the program would continue. When Britain held, the program was put into high gear.

A mockup was approved in May 1941 and later that month Boeing received a letter of intent for 250 airplanes. The contract required that they be built in the new government-owned facilities at Boeing's Wichita, Kansas, plant. It wasn't signed until September and later was increased to 500 airplanes in January 1942. This decision to go into mass production was made a full year before the first airplane took to the air!

The Army specified that additional manufacturers should be added to hasten production so Bell Aircraft Company at Marietta, Georgia, North American Aviation at Kansas City, Kansas, and the Fisher Body Division of General Motors at Cleveland, Ohio, were given production contracts. Such action was almost unprecedented. Only the Martin B-26 had been ordered in quantity right off the drawing boards. Again a "paper" airplane was being ordered into production but this time on an industry-wide basis. For General Arnold it was a momentous decision that, if the program failed, could well destroy the work of a lifetime, and that of many of his loyal associates.

From the start, Boeing had insisted that the design should be "frozen" prior to the start of production, but changes in range, bomb load, and defensive requirements made that impossible.

While Boeing engineers fumed, Air Corps officials insisted that the wing be enlarged because it was carrying too many pounds of weight for each square foot of surface. Such action, Boeing's "Ed" Wells pointed out, would reduce speed and range.

A compromise was reached when Fowler-type flaps, larger than the wings of most fighter planes, were approved to increase the wing area by 20 percent. Wells assured project officials that these flaps, when extended, would sharply reduce takeoff and landing speeds.

While wind-tunnel testing went on day after day, the fuselage of a

Fairchild PT-19A trainer was fitted with a quarter-size B-29 wing and tail and valuable information was gained during flight tests.

It was apparent early in the development phase that individually manned gun turrets would not work satisfactorily in the pressurized cabin contemplated for the B-29. Incorporation of General Electric's fire-control system, instead of the Sperry, added more than 200,000 engineering hours in structural changes to the airframe. The ever-patient Wells reminded the Air Corps that such a change would further delay completion of the first airplane by several months even though he personally felt such action was justified. There was no question that the bomber's ability to fly unescorted missions would be improved because the new system enabled gunners to concentrate firepower from one or more gunners' stations on an attacking fighter. Also, the smoother lines of the new turrets would add to the bomber's speed.

Ed Wells and his Boeing engineers recognized early that it would be impossible to pressurize the entire fuselage without excessive engineering cost. After much discussion, he reached a compromise with his counterparts at Wright Field whereby only the crew areas would be pressurized. A pressurized tunnel over the two bomb bays would connect the forward and central crew areas. The tail gunner would have a separate system but he could leave his position only if the aircraft were unpressurized.

Fortunately, the B-29 went through most of its basic changes on the drawing boards before it went into production. The bomb load was set at 200,000 pounds or 10 times the amount initially prescribed by Arnold. Of course, range was reduced to keep the airplane's maximum weight at 135,000 pounds.

The addition of more guns and ammunition, armor plate, and other changes considered mandatory after British experience against the Luftwaffe inevitably affected performance by reducing speed and range.

Wellwood Beall, Boeing's vice president of sales, put it succinctly when he said, "I've often thought a new airplane is like a Christmas tree. People are tempted to keep hanging things on it, and changing things around." In sheer exasperation, when Wright Field officials complained to him about reductions in the plane's performance, he explained, "When you fly a mass weighing nearly twice as much as the B-17, 30 percent faster than that airplane, and with only an 83 percent increase in horsepower, serious aerodynamic problems are bound to develop."

Wells's engineers consistently faced the task of keeping the airplane as aerodynamically "clean" as possible. The original lines were incredibly good for that era but breaking up those sleek lines with more guns and turrets, and the radar antenna, made it necessary to increase the wing loading to 70 pounds per square foot. That was double the wing loading of the B-17 and of increasing concern to Air Corps officials because of the higher takeoff and landing speeds which the higher wing loading required.

After the United States became involved in World War II on December 7, 1941, following the surprise Japanese attack on Pearl Harbor, Arnold's greatest concern was the B-29's progress, or lack of it. Oliver Echols, now a general on Arnold's staff, was particularly upset about the problems with the engines and persistent troubles that had developed in the electronic systems.

Echols called Beall to Washington to ask some blunt questions. He reminded the Boeing vice president that the U.S. Government was spending more money on the B-29 than on any other project, and, "We haven't even flown an airplane so we're worried about the tremendous risk. Do you believe in your heart that it will be a good airplane?"

The rotund Beall didn't hesitate. "Yes. It's really going to be a good airplane. If you'll give us first priority on test facilities and let us do all the testing we want, and when we want to do it—flight testing, systems testing, all kinds of testing—I'll guarantee that we'll get successful, operating airplanes."

Echols knew he had to talk to Arnold because Boeing was insisting on top priority over every other project. Arnold's neck already was out as far as it could go. Echols excused himself and went into Hap's office.

Beall looked at him anxiously when he returned. "We'll do what you ask," Echols said.

Between them they later proposed a production program that eventually cost $3 billion.

# CHAPTER 2

# A Wing on Fire

With Allied problems mounting daily in the Pacific as the Japanese made deep thrusts into southern and eastern areas, the B-29 program was pushed to the limit. Normally, it took five years from submission of preliminary designs to operational readiness. There was no such time now so an arbitrary goal of four years was set.

Consolidated's XB-32, which was in parallel development, was the first to fly July 2, 1942. There were so many design changes, however, that development was retarded; particularly after the first airplane crashed May 10, 1943. Only in the closing days of the war were a few B-32s used against Japan.

The B-29, hopefully the Army Air Force's most potent offensive weapon, flew for the first time September 21, 1942, with Boeing's veteran test pilot Edmund T. "Eddie" Allen at the controls. After a 75-minute uneventful flight, he told the waiting throng that the plane was excellent.

Captain Putt, the Army's project officer, took her up the next day and confirmed Allen's findings: "It's unbelievable for such a large plane to be so easy on the controls. It's easier to fly than the B-17."

Arnold relaxed for the time being.

Two weeks after the Japanese attack on Pearl Harbor, Prime Minister Winston Churchill felt it imperative that British staff committees meet with their counterparts in Washington. Roosevelt agreed because ironing out an acceptable British-American strategy was of overriding importance.

Although there had been some agreement on joint strategies prior to America's entry into the war, only the air plan for actions against

Germany and Italy was still workable. This plan for a strategic air offensive was acceptable to both sides. For actions against Japan, however, the original plan had dealt only in broad generalities. There had been mutual agreement in the spring of 1941 to concentrate an air offensive against Germany first and to transfer such an offensive to Japan only after Hitler's defeat. After Pearl Harbor, it was generally agreed that the capture of suitable air bases in eastern China, the Philippines, and Formosa was a necessary first step before attacks on Japan could begin. Planners hoped that mass air attacks against the industrial heart of Japan would so weaken her that she would capitulate without an invasion. Or, if her surrender wasn't forthcoming, that she would be in such a reduced military state that invasion forces would not encounter effective resistance.

The Joint Chiefs of Staff first set up four committees, including a strategic committee to finalize agreement on prosecution of the war. At first, there was vigorous dissent among members of the Joint Strategic Committee. The Joint Intelligence Committee had presented its estimate that Russia would collapse within six months; that the Germans and Japanese would join hands in the vicinity of Karachi, India, within the year; and that Europe was hopelessly lost. This estimate fortified the contention of the Navy, which was burning for revenge after its humiliating defeat at Pearl Harbor, to advocate a change in grand strategy and it proposed a defense of the western hemisphere and an all-out offensive against Japan at the earliest practicable time.

The initial vote of the Joint Strategic Committee endorsed this position by a vote of six to two. However, after further arguments, and second thoughts, the committee finally endorsed the initially agreed upon strategy that Germany be defeated first and that the Far East be defended by minimum forces until an all-out assault could be made upon Japan's armed forces. Their reasoning was that a Europe dominated by Hitler was considered more dangerous for the United States than a Far East dominated by Hirohito. Basically, Far East forces would safeguard the lifeline to Australia and New Zealand and other vital areas then held by the United States. Of specific necessity was the determination to pursue efforts that would deny Japan access to raw materials vital to her war effort.

The Joint Strategic Committee made this recommendation to both the Joint and Combined Chiefs of Staff December 31, 1941, and it was accepted.

However, the U.S. Navy never really embraced the decision that an offensive against Japan should await Hitler's downfall. Although the Joint Chiefs of Staff approved top production priority for the war in Europe, with the air offensive against Germany as the initial effort, the Navy insisted on equal priority with the Army Air Forces, even though the Navy forces were destined primarily for the Pacific. The Navy went ahead with production of a fleet of more than a hundred aircraft carriers with double-crew complements for each.

By the summer of 1942, Japan's conquests had brought her halfway across the Pacific to the east, almost to Australia on the south, and to the borders of India in the west. Fortunately, her eastward advances were halted by the battles of the Coral Sea and Midway; the latter decisive victory the turning point in the Pacific war.

The United States Army Air Forces, which at last came of age following its new designation March 9, 1942, developed a master plan in continuing response to President Roosevelt's request of August 25, 1941, for an estimate of future aircraft requirements. The President asked Arnold to submit, through General Marshall, his estimate of the number of combat aircraft, by type, which should be produced for the Army and other Allied nations in factories in the United States during 1943 in order to have complete air ascendancy over the enemy.

Hansell was called back from his command with the Eighth Air Force in England and directed to prepare the answer for Arnold, who placed the full resources of the air staff at Hansell's disposal.

The new plan, given the designation AWPD-42 for the year in which it was prepared, like the first was an "airman's plan" which received little contribution or interference from those outside the Army Air Forces.

The first plan, which Hansell also helped to prepare, called for a combined bomber offensive against Germany. That plan encountered stiff resistance from the Army and Navy. It called for deployment of 24 B-29 groups against Axis Europe, with 12 groups based in northern Ireland and another 12 in North Africa in the vicinity of Cairo.

AWPD-42 recommended that all B-29s be deployed to the war against Japan because they would not be available in time for a knockout punch against Germany. Furthermore, the plan pointed out that B-17s and B-24s were doing very well because their shorter range wasn't a factor in Europe such as it would be in the Far East where the longer-range B-29s would be essential.

The new plan stated succinctly, "Considering the great distances involved, it is apparent that the majority of the bombing effort against Japan must be carried out by long-range bombers of the B-29 type. And these will not be available in quantity until late in 1944." The President's inquiry had specifically asked for the number of combat aircraft to be produced in 1943, but the plan didn't specify the number of B-29s to be produced since none could be put into operation that year.

At this stage of the war, Allied air intelligence about Japan was almost nonexistent. Therefore, the plan listed primary target systems but was less precise about individual targets. It called for a strategic air offensive, such as was getting under way against Germany, to destroy the will and resources of the Japanese people to wage war.

Planners were realistic in their appraisal of early efforts to bomb Japan itself until very long-range aircraft such as the B-29 were available. Even Boeing's most optimistic reports indicated there would be no airplanes available for combat before late 1943. Also, the stepping stones had to be established in the Pacific. It was agreed that only after bases for heavy and very long-range bombers were established, and the successful conclusion of the war in Europe assured, could consideration be given to a full-scale aerial attack on Japan.

Although the plan was approved with modifications September 9, 1942, the Combined Chiefs refused to go along with the top priority requested by the Army Air Forces. One modification was a clarification of the roles the Royal Air Force and the Army Air Forces would have in the bomber offensive against Germany. It was decided that the British would concentrate on night area bombing, while the USAAF would be responsible for daylight precision bombing of selected targets. As it eventually turned out, AWPD-42 became the basic concept upon which all strategy was based for the employment of strategic airpower.

Meanwhile, development of the B-29 was more and more beset by problems. The cabin pressurization system alone had innumerable failures because of production defects in riveting the cabin and bursting of blisters at the gunners' stations. The airplane was so new that everything had to be developed from scratch, but the "bugs" were ferreted out one by one and the pressurization system eventually became so effective that the same basic system was in use in jetliners of a much later era. The air-position indicator, although crude by later standards, was the forerunner of the inertial navigation systems that helped to place astronauts on the moon. The B-29 system was developed to navigate over vast expanses, under conditions of radio blackout and overcast skies, when celestial navigation was impossible. Many electronic, radar, fuel, and safety systems in common use decades later were developed at high cost and with great ingenuity for the B-29.

It was one of those rare days in Seattle, Washington, February 18, 1943, when the sun was shining and visibility was better than five miles.

At noon, the second B-29 test airplane with Eddie Allen at the controls reported everything going normally. Then, at 12:21, as the controller in the Seattle tower listened carefully, Eddie reported he was south of Renton at 2,400 feet. In a calm voice, he asked for landing clearance because the number one engine was on fire. The controller, knowing how serious such a fire could be in a B-29, listened in growing amazement as Allen reported the engine's prop had been feathered but that the trouble wasn't serious. The controller immediately warned other planes to leave the vicinity of Boeing Field and gave Allen clearance for an emergency landing.

The tower controller listened anxiously for further word. He was shocked to hear one of the crew members call the pilot and say, "Allen, better get this thing down in a hurry. The wing spar's burning badly."

Still in that unhurried voice, Allen called the tower again, requesting that fire equipment be on hand. "I'm coming in with a wing on fire."

Those were his last words. Observers on the ground looked up in horror as the plane, flames streaking back from the wing, crashed into the fifth floor of the Fryer Packing Plant, killing not only all on board but a number of employees and firemen. On the way in, the plane had struck high-tension wires and, adding to the confusion, all electric power at Boeing Field went out.

Flight tests were suspended while Boeing engineers sought to find the source of the trouble. When they did it was identified as inadequate engine cooling, and "fixes" were made which, unfortunately, didn't resolve the problem completely until long after the B-29s were in combat.

The watchdog Truman committee in Washington took up the matter. It had harsh criticism for the engine's manufacturer, Wright Aeronautical, accusing it of having produced many defective and substandard parts. With the program on an unprecedented time schedule, some of the accusations were unfair. The Army Air Forces didn't emerge unscathed. The committee blamed it because inspection of completed engines had not met their own standards.

The engine was designed so compactly, with front and rear rows of cylinders, that there was an insufficient flow of air around the cylinders to properly cool them. Every conceivable form of engine cooling was considered because time didn't permit a major engine redesign.

Engine fires later caused many of the operational losses during early combat months. In preflighting the airplane, it was normal procedure for a crew member to be stationed at each turbo exhaust during prop "pull through" to listen for the telltale "swish" that indicated an exhaust valve was unseated. In time, a bad exhaust valve could cause the engine to "swallow" the valve. When this happened, the cylinder had to be replaced.

Boeing engineers determined that when an exhaust valve became unseated during chamber combustion, the leak at the valve created a "blowtorch" effect on the valve's stem which caused the stem to warp and eventually break off. Once this happened the engine rapidly broke up and a fire could be expected.

Later, a "fix" was designed to resolve the basic problem of overheating. Oil flow to the exhaust valves was increased, the engine cowl flaps were redesigned to bring in more cooling air through the nacelle, and baffles were installed to direct a stream of air on the exhaust valves to keep them cooler.*

In later engine fires, the most intense portion of the fire was caused by the magnesium accessory housing because this metal burns at an extremely hot temperature. Once a fire started, and extinguishers failed to contain it in the forward section of the engine, it was impossible to stop. Therefore, when the magnesium housing caught fire it usually burned through the engine's firewall into the wing, which caused the wing to break off. Once that housing caught fire, the crew had one and a half minutes to bail out. The few survivors of such crashes said that the gyrational forces of the spinning airplane pinned them to a given spot and they were unable to move

---

* Also, "cuffs" were added to the propeller blades near the hub to act as fans to drive more air into the engine cowling.

and escaped only if the airplane broke apart at their station and they were hurled out of the airplane.

Until mid-1944, the upper five cylinders had to be changed every 25 hours, with a complete engine change every 75 hours. Gradually the time was built up between engine changes so that an average of 400 hours was common by the end of the war.

Arnold pressured Boeing constantly to get airplanes completed faster because he had assured President Roosevelt that B-29s would be deployed at the earliest possible time. In retrospect, Boeing did a remarkable job in developing such an advanced airplane while training housewives and men with no previous aircraft experience as skilled production personnel.

The first B-29 remained at Boeing's Seattle plant when the third test airplane, incorporating extensive engine and equipment changes, was prepared for a flight to Wichita, Kansas, May 29, 1943. Colonel Leonard F. "Jake" Harman was in the pilot's seat as it roared down the runway. Suddenly, the right wing dropped sharply and Harman pulled back the power on all four engines as the huge plane careened off the runway and came to a shuddering stop behind some flight-line buildings. Shaken, but unhurt, Harman and the crew piled out of the airplane, noting with relief that it appeared to be undamaged.

Later inspection showed the aileron control cables were reversed because they had been installed improperly.

At the Casablanca Conference in January 1943, President Roosevelt insisted that China be given sufficient support to keep her in the war. Japan's armies in Burma had isolated China except for aerial supply from Assam, India, over the Hump to Yunnan. China's plight, he knew, would be desperate by summer.

Agreement was reached on a number of actions and the Combined Chiefs were directed to reestablish land communications with China and somehow step up the flow of military supplies. Such actions were complicated by the North African campaign, which had weakened USAAF's ability to conduct operations simultaneously from England and the Mediterranean.

A combined bomber offensive was approved in principle, under the direct control of the Combined Chiefs of Staff, and it was decided that B-29 groups should be assigned to England. Air Staff planners objected, asking that B-29s be assigned instead to Tunisian bases and shuttled from North Africa to targets in Germany and then on to England.

It was at this conference that the bombing of Japan was discussed in more detail. General Marshall expressed the views of the AAF that Japanese industries were vulnerable to air attack, and that heavy, sustained attacks would drastically reduce Japan's war effort.

Roosevelt agreed because he viewed even limited bombing of Japan as having a great uplifting impact on the Chinese people. He suggested sending 200 to 300 planes to China, not necessarily B-29s. He said he was aware of the problem of supplying them, but he thought by operating out of rear bases in India, then refueling in China to and from targets in Japan, that such missions would be useful.

Marshall's views were not of that magnitude at that time. He interjected with words of caution, emphasizing that supplying bombers in China would be terribly expensive and a further drain on transport aircraft needed elsewhere.

Roosevelt refused to be put off. At the close of the Casablanca Conference he wired Chiang Kai-shek that Arnold would come to Chungking as his personal representative to discuss further U.S. aid. He said he was determined that Chennault's newly designated Fourteenth Air Force would be increased so it could take the offensive against the Japanese in China.

On April 1, 1943, Chiang wrote Roosevelt asking him to invite Major General Claire L. Chennault to visit Washington so he could personally present his ideas for an air offensive by the Fourteenth Air Force. Roosevelt, who believed sincerely in helping China out of her dire straits, agreed because until now nothing that he had wanted to do could be accomplished without disrupting European operations.

Roosevelt's problems with the Generalissimo were largely due to his inability to carry through on unrealistic promises he had made. They were compounded by the quarrels between Lieutenant General Joseph W. Stilwell, U.S. theater commander and Chiang's chief of staff, and General Chennault, who couldn't agree on overall strategy. They had one belief in common and that was that China was necessary if Japan was to be defeated. "If we are going to bomb Japan we will have to have China bases" was their constant refrain. As later events were to prove, both were wrong.

At that time, however, the ambitious Chennault had developed effective tactics for limited support of Chinese ground troops, and had been most successful in strikes against Japanese shipping from bases in eastern China. He believed strongly that his command should be built up, and that with a greater airlift tonnage allotted to it he could drive the Japanese out of China.

It was decided to broaden the scope of the meeting into a full-fledged conference called Trident, which would include Churchill, Roosevelt, their chiefs of staff, and Chennault and Stilwell.

The latter proposed that a major effort be made to recapture Burma, and the road to China be opened so that practically all its tonnage could be used to equip an expanded Chinese Army that would clear China of Japanese troops.

Meanwhile, Chennault's plan called for increased airlift from India to augment his Fourteenth Air Force. He said existing Chinese armies could hold back further Japanese intrusions into China if the Fourteenth Air Force were able to cut the Japanese supply lines. Simultaneously, he said, his bombers would harass the enemy's sea lanes off the Chinese coast and thereby contribute to all Allied operations in the Pacific.

Stilwell's plan was completely unacceptable to the British, who opposed such a massive Burma effort at the time.

Chennault's plan was looked upon with favor because Roosevelt had decided in advance that some kind of air effort out of China had to be started, and this plan called for more immediate aid to Chiang than any other. The basic strategy called for greater efforts in China and Burma and plans to carry the war to Japan. Chennault's long-range plan called for the recapture of Hong Kong as a coastal supply base to service bases in eastern China for eventual attacks on the Japanese home islands.

The most obvious disadvantage of this approach was that operations against Japan would have to await Allied control of the China Sea, and that wouldn't be possible until U.S. forces in the Central and Southwest Pacific moved up into the Philippines and Formosa. The timing to start bombing of Japan from these bases was set for 1947.

More transport aircraft were assigned to Hump operations after the conference, and it was agreed that the aerial route would carry 10,000 tons a month. It was also decided to take the offensive in Burma after the fall monsoon.

Dislodging the Japanese in Burma proved more difficult than was visualized at the time. Even with the transfer of the Chinese 22nd and 38th divisions to the front, it wasn't until after a series of bloody battles under intolerable jungle conditions, ending in January 1945, that the Japanese were forced to retreat.

Even so, the limited resources that could be allocated to the China-Burma-India theater made it impossible to prevent a series of Japanese drives in the spring of 1944 that overran Chennault's easternmost China bases and gave the Japanese a land communications link from North China to French Indochina.

The Chennault plan was refined so it could be formally presented to the Quadrant Conference in Quebec August 14–24, 1943.

Although it had been conceded that B-29s would not be ready in time for effective operations against Germany, Major General Ira C. Eaker, responsible for development of Eighth Air Force bomber operations, wasn't so informed until December 1943.

Once the introduction of B-29s into the Pacific became a foregone conclusion, several commands sought them. Major General George C. Kenney, commander of General MacArthur's Fifth Air Force, wrote to Arnold July 26, "I hear the B-29 is flying again. I assume that I am still to get the first B-29 unit." Evidently his assumption was based upon the fact that he had helped to develop the new bomber while assigned to the Materiel Division at Wright Field.

Three months later Arnold sought Kenney's advice about possible use of the B-29. In response, Kenney recommended striking at Japanese petroleum installations, shipping, and military bases from airfields at Darwin and Broome in Australia. "If you want the B-29 used efficiently and effectively where it will do the most good in the shortest time," he said, "the Southwest Pacific area is the place and the Fifth Air Force can do the job."

There were those in Washington who agreed with Kenney, but such a limited role for the Superfortresses was not in keeping with Arnold's overall plans. Furthermore, the crisis evolving in the CBI effectively precluded any talk about using B-29s in the Southwest Pacific.

Even the U.S. Navy got into the act, putting in a request for B-29s to operate with its antisubmarine command. Although the airplane would have been suitable for such work, production was too limited to divert combat airplanes from their primary task of strategic bombing of Japan.

# CHAPTER 3

# Matterhorn

When the Quadrant Conference met at Quebec in late August 1943, General Arnold submitted an outline plan that called for air operations against Japan from advanced bases in eastern China which would be supplied by air from the vicinity of Calcutta, India. It met stiff opposition from the Joint Logistics Committee but at Arnold's insistence it was forwarded to the Combined Logistics Committee, which also declared it unfeasible. The plan resulted originally from studies made by Major General Laurence S. Kuter in March of that year under Arnold's direction. The Air Force chief had asked the Committee of Operations Analysts to identify the strategic Japanese targets that B-29s, soon to start coming off the production lines, could reach from bases in China. Kuter's plan was later called Setting Sun. It called for a sustained bombing campaign against the Japanese war-making industries such as aircraft and engine plants, naval and merchant-shipping bases, aluminum factories, iron and steel mills, and oil and chemical installations. According to the plan Chinese bases within 1,500 miles of these targets could send B-29s to bomb the majority of them with 10-ton bomb loads. Japanese electric-power systems, and Japan's transportation system, were overlooked. This later proved to be a costly oversight. Planners didn't consider the Inland Sea Transportation system, they said later, because they believed that was a job for the Navy. Major General Curtis E. LeMay later corrected this oversight.

The plan contemplated use of some B-29s as tankers with bomb-bay tanks to help carry fuel from India to China, and specified Calcutta as the port of entry.

Two factors created interest within the Combined Chiefs. The first was projection of the start of operations by October 1944. The second was the self-contained nature of the operations, which wouldn't need a port of entry on the China Sea.

There was a basic weakness to the plan. The assumption that the Chinese Army and Chennault's Fourteenth Air Force could protect bases in the Kweilin area wasn't valid because retaliation by the Japanese was not taken fully into account.

Planners were amazingly accurate in predicting the effectiveness of B-29 operations for they estimated that 780 B-29s, flying five missions a month, could destroy Japan in six months. Thus, it was predicted that Japan could be occupied by the end of August 1945.

The Combined Chiefs were sufficiently interested to seek further analysis by their own planners, who were told to report back September 15. The plan was also given to Chennault and Stilwell for their comments.

Stilwell reported that such a time schedule was overly optimistic. He said planners hadn't fully considered the logistical difficulties of supplying such a string of air bases as were contemplated north and south of Changsha. He knew what he was talking about because he had learned through bitter experience how impractical it was to try to get supplies from India to China in acceptable quantities. He also pointed out the limited port facilities at Calcutta.

Stilwell and his staff proposed an alternative plan designated Twilight, which recommended advance bases along the Kweilin-Changsha railroad. Unlike Setting Sun, Stilwell's plans called for rear bases in the Calcutta area. Under his proposal, much of the fuel would be transported in the B-29s themselves, and the rest by cargo carriers over the Hump. The plan specified that operations could be started in April 1945 with 10 B-29 groups flying an average of 500 sorties a month. Stilwell's insistence on 50 U.S.-trained and -equipped Chinese divisions to protect the airfields, and a great number of fighters for defense, made his proposal unfeasible.

A reorganization of the Far East Command structure was agreed to at Quadrant. To assure maximum use of limited resources, a Southeast Asia Command was established under Vice Admiral, the Lord Louis Mountbatten. Lieutenant General Stilwell was appointed his deputy but the Combined Chiefs retained general jurisdiction over all operations.

Further complicating an already unwieldy command structure, Stilwell was given command of all U.S. Army forces, ground and air, in the China-Burma theater. Royal Air Force units in India and Burma and the Army Air Forces, including the Tenth Air Force operating over the Burma front, were formed into the Eastern Air Command under Major General George E. Stratemeyer.

Once these commands were functioning they were given the task of undertaking an offensive in North Burma and extending the Ledo Road from Assam to China. As if this undertaking by American construction engineers wasn't enough, it was proposed that a pipeline be built from Calcutta to Assam, with another alongside the Ledo Road to increase the flow of fuel to China.

Another goal was to double the capacity of the airlift over the Hump to 20,000 tons a month. It was hoped that the ground and air routes to China would permit delivery of 85,000 tons of general supplies, and 54,000 tons of petroleum products could be sent through the pipelines.

A limiting factor was the single railroad line from Calcutta to Assam which changed from broad to meter gauge en route, and whose trains had to be transported by ferries across the Brahmaputra River because no bridge could withstand the monsoon floods.

Before the Quadrant Conference ended, agreement was reached about specific ways to prosecute the war against Japan. With resources under the reins of the Combined Chiefs, and Pacific operations tightly controlled by the U.S. Chiefs of Staff, General MacArthur was directed to continue operations up the New Guinea coast and reach the Philippines by the fall of 1944. Further, new operations were planned against the Gilberts, Marshalls, and the Marianas. The major goal was to obtain bases on Japan's doorstep in the Ryukyus by the spring of 1945. U.S. Navy Chief of Operations expressed confidence that a decisive battle would be fought between U.S. and Japanese fleets sometime during this drive up the Central Pacific and eliminate the latter from further effective operations.

Admiral Nimitz, Commander of Naval Forces in the Pacific, was directed to continue his independent operations in the Central Pacific under the Joint Chiefs.

Seizure of the Marianas for a naval base was suggested at Quadrant as a possibility for early 1946. Later, after the Quebec meeting, the AAF recommended in September that D-Day be moved up to the middle of 1944 so that eight B-29 groups could be stationed in the Marshalls or Carolines and stage through the Marianas to strike directly at Japan by March 1945 or even sooner. The air staff considered such a move feasible if other Pacific islands were bypassed.

Arnold established a special board to review the latest B-29 proposals and, on September 20 a modified Twilight plan was proposed by members of the board. It reaffirmed the earlier decision to concentrate Allied power against Japan as soon as Germany surrendered, and called for another appeal to Soviet Russia to permit American bases in Siberia for B-29 operations. The first such appeal had been made the day after Pearl Harbor, and had been turned down because the Russians weren't anxious to draw the Japanese into the war against them at that time.

After revision, the plan tended to look like the one proposed by President Roosevelt at Casablanca, particularly the part concerning bases in Calcutta and operating in and out of forward bases in China. The decision to use rear bases would assure easier maintenance of the airplanes and provide for better ground security.

Arnold accepted the board's report and asked Brigadier General Kenneth B. Wolfe to draw up the operational plan to bomb Japan with the maximum number of available B-29s at the earliest possible date. The choice of Wolfe for the job was understandable because he had earlier been responsible for the production of the B-29 at Wright Field, and later he had organized the 58th Wing.

Wolfe had no illusions about the plan's shortcomings such as the vulnerability of advanced air bases in China and the long supply lines. He submitted his plan to Arnold October 11, 1943, using portions of Twilight as a guide. An important change was the advance of D-Day for the start of operations to June 1, 1944. By March of that year, the plan called for 150 B-29s and 300 crews at bases north of Calcutta, with twice that many planes and 450 crews by September 1. They would be controlled by a bomber command with two wings of four groups each. When one of Wolfe's advisers pointed out Stilwell's insistence that 50 Chinese divisions be trained to protect bases in the Kweilin area, Wolfe decided to move the forward bases farther inland to the Chengtu area where additional ground and air defenses would not be required.

Arnold approved Wolfe's plan in principle October 12. Inasmuch as it was basically an American operation, approval was needed only by the U.S. Joint Chiefs once Churchill and Chiang Kai-shek authorized construction of bases in India and China. Arnold's acceptance didn't rule out later use of the Marianas, but he agreed to use the China bases for a year. In fact, Arnold didn't have much choice because Chinese bases were the only bases available for B-29 missions against Japan.

Stilwell went along reluctantly because he had no faith that Japan could be knocked out of the war by airpower. Arnold had no illusions that the job could be done from China, and neither did anyone else in a high-command position.

General Arnold, who had earlier promised Marshall that the B-29s would go to China by January 1, 1944, now faced the unpleasant duty of informing the President about the true status of B-29 deployment. In a letter in early October, he told Roosevelt that he wouldn't be ready to go with the B-29s until March or April of 1944.

Roosevelt was incensed. He wrote General Marshall October 15, 1943, that he was upset with Arnold's letter that the B-29s wouldn't be sent to the Far East until March or April of the following year. In expressing what he called his disgust with the India-China situation, and Arnold in particular, he wrote, "The worst thing is that we are falling down on our promises to China every single time. We have not fulfilled one of them yet. I do not see why we have to use B-29s. We have several other types of bombing planes."

Arnold prepared a reply for Marshall's signature. He reminded the President there were always unforeseen problems in getting a new airplane into combat. "This time," he said, "our problems have been aggravated by labor difficulties in the Wright engine factory." As an alternative, he said B-24s could be sent to China but only B-29s could hit targets on the Japanese mainland.

Roosevelt declined the offer of B-24s and reluctantly agreed to the later date for overseas deployment of the new Superfortress.

The Wolfe operational plan to carry out Project Matterhorn was endorsed in Arnold's own handwriting. "I have told the President that this will be started on March 1. See that it is done. H.H.A."

While Roosevelt prepared for an Allied conference in Cairo, to which the Generalissimo was invited, he sent Churchill a message November 10, 1943. "We have under development a project whereby we can strike a heavy blow at our enemy in the Pacific early next year with our new heavy bombers. Japanese military, naval and shipping strength is dependent upon the steel industry which is strained to the limit. Half of the coke for that steel can be reached and destroyed by long-range bombers operating from the Chengtu area of China. The bombers can supply themselves by air from bases to be constructed near Calcutta without disturbing present airlift commitments.

"In order to expedite this project I ask you to arrange for the Government of India to render every possible assistance in the construction of these four air bases for long-range bombers.

"This is a bold but entirely feasible project. Together, by this operation, we can partially cripple the Japanese naval and military power and hasten the victory of our forces in Asia."

He wired Chiang the same day to request construction of five bomber fields in the Chengtu area for use by the end of March 1944. He told the Chinese leader that the United States would supply the engineering advisers but that the Chinese Government must furnish labor and materials.

In conclusion, he said, "I am personally convinced we can deal the Jap a truly crippling blow."

After Churchill and Chiang Kai-shek responded promptly that they would provide the necessary B-29 bases, movement orders were issued November 14 to aviation engineer battalions by the War Department that they proceed to India to start constructing the fields. The first contingent arrived ten days later.

The die was cast for B-29 operations but production problems escalated, and mandatory changes further delayed delivery of the first airplanes. Brigadier General Hansell, who had been assigned to the Eighth Air Force as commander of the 1st Air Division, returned to the States to become the air member of the Joint Plans Committee. He told them he was convinced that the B-29 would be extremely vulnerable to head-on attacks with only two .50-caliber guns in the top forward turret. He recommended that the number of guns be increased to four in this turret. He chaired a committee that agreed such a change was desirable despite the increased weight and the added clutter of the forward compartment that would result from installation of a larger ammunition drum in an already tight situation.

Once the 14 YB-29 service-test airplanes were modified at Wichita, some of them became available for checking out pilots. From the beginning Arnold had insisted that only pilots with at least 400 hours of four-engine time be selected for the B-29 program. Captain James Pattillo, an instructor pilot in B-17s and B-24s, was one of those chosen in the summer of 1943. He was assigned to the 468th Group at Smoky Hill Army Air Field, Salina, Kansas, and checked out first in the B-26 because it was the only bomber available. Originally, it was selected to give pilots with only B-17 time a chance to fly an airplane with a tricycle landing gear like the B-29.

It wasn't until October 4, 1943, that he got a chance to fly a '29. Unlike later airplanes that were bare aluminum, this one was dressed in the olive drab of early Army Air Force planes.

While waiting for their squadron commander, Lieutenant Colonel James B. Edmundson, Pattillo and Clarence C. "Shoes" MacPherson and Harold Brown walked around the airplane. He was impressed by its size, with a 141-foot wing and a 99-foot fuselage, and intrigued by its bulbous nose and the majestic sweep of its vertical tail that soared to a height of almost 28 feet.

Once the colonel arrived they boarded up with Edmundson in the left seat and Shoes in the right. At the north end of the field, Edmundson ran up the engines. To Pattillo he seemed to take an agonizingly long time to check out the airplane. Later, he learned that preflight procedures required the adjustment of the superchargers on the ground to get the exact power settings before takeoff. At the time, however, he noted with concern that the engines were heating up. After takeoff, Edmundson explained some characteristics of the plane and came back in and landed.

On the ground, he and Shoes changed seats. Each of Edmundson's students was told to make three landings. On the first, Pattillo noted that while Shoes was lined up properly on approach, the airplane seemed to drift to the left just before touchdown.

When it came his turn, Pattillo was apprehensive while the engines were run up at the end of the runway. Some of his misgivings resulted from the lack of several instruments which, in the B-29, were on the flight engineer's panel. The "greenhouse" effect of the pilot's compartment pleased him because he had never seen such visibility from a cockpit.

During takeoff he was disturbed to suddenly realize that he didn't have the usual flat windshield to look out. Instead, most of the Plexiglas panels in the nose were curved except for two flat panes directly in front of each pilot. The fact that no two were mounted at the same angle caused him to shift from one panel to another to orient himself properly, thinking to himself that one could soon get stoop-shouldered and develop a twitch flying such an airplane.

During the first landing approach he found it difficult to figure out which of these separate panels one should use on landing and, as he flared the airplane for touchdown, he noted that it was again drifting left on the runway despite an approach that he thought was perfectly aligned.

On the second landing, he dropped the plane a good 50 feet, jarring it so hard that the bombardier's gunsight, which had been in a stowed position, bounced out of its restraining socket and was thrown violently forward. He didn't dare to look at Edmundson, figuring the colonel would think he had lost his mind, or send him back to the Training Command. The colonel didn't look pleased but he didn't say a word, so he took off for a third time. On this landing he managed to get the aircraft down without bouncing and, when each had made three landings, Edmundson told them they were now checked out as B-29 pilots.

For days afterward Pattillo tried to figure out why he and so many others had difficulty holding the airplane to the center of the runway. He theorized that when sitting on the far left side of the cockpit, with the left side of the fuselage looming in one's field of vision, that when one searched for the ground out of the corners of his eyes, unconsciously he tended to lift the right side of the fuselage so as to bring his perspective into balance.

Two nights later he made his first night landings and discovered another problem. He found it difficult to adjust to the many reflections from ground lights that radiated and bounced off the Plexiglas windows in the cockpit. At first, he and the others "up front" were jumpy because the reflections made it appear they were on a collision course with first one airplane and then another.

The 792nd Squadron had only one B-29 during October 1943 so none of the pilots got much time in the airplane. By the end of the month he was most fortunate to have 25½ hours because so often when a flight crew reported to the airplane some mechanical malfunction caused the flight's cancellation.

During the first few hours he noted fear of the airplane was strong until the preflight check had been completed at the end of the runway. Once the decision was made to "go" those fears disappeared and it was thrilling to maneuver the huge aircraft as it roared down the runway.

The first time his entire crew flew together was on a night flight several months later when they were to help check out another pilot. Lieutenant John W. Sims sat in the pilot's seat as they took off to the north with Pattillo in the right seat. They had just broken ground when right gunner Eric Tidy called, "Fire in number three!"

He turned to look because that engine was on his side. He couldn't see it at first. Unlike a B-17 or B-24, in which a pilot could look directly at an engine and not have to rely upon others to describe what was happening, in the B-29 the pilot was lucky to see the outboard engine on his side. He had to lean way over to the side and then crane his neck to look back before he could see the inboard engine. What he saw froze him with fear, because inside the engine cowling everything was white-hot with fire. He thought, "This is it!" Momentarily in panic, he thought no fire extinguisher or prop-feathering system could possibly stop that fire. Turning away in horror, he expected that the wing, on which their lives depended, would explode and the aircraft cartwheel into the ground.

"I'm feathering number three!" he yelled to Sims and flight engineer James P. Smith, although he felt this was a useless gesture because he expected the wing to explode.

In a state of shock, Pattillo almost casually moved his fingers to the aisle stand on his left, lifted the plastic cover on the prop-feathering buttons, and fumbled across them as he counted "one, two, three." He pushed the third button. He still had a feeling that it didn't matter one way or the other which button he pressed because he considered they were all doomed.

Dimly, he heard the flight engineer, Lieutenant James P. Smith, report, "Roger. Feathering three."

"Hold her nose down!" he shouted to Sims in the pilot's seat.

As the plane descended, he glanced at the tachometer needles and saw one going down to zero. Again, he didn't believe it mattered whether the correct engine was feathered or not. After a few moments, he screwed up his courage, turned, and went through the contortions necessary to look at number three engine. He couldn't believe his eyes! The fire was out!

He called the tower. "We've had an engine fire. Get others out of the traffic pattern. We're coming in on the first available runway."

Sims racked the '29 around into a climbing turn to the west and, at 500 feet off the ground, turned to his final approach. Pattillo glanced nervously at the blackened engine, fearful it would erupt in flames again but all was dark so he lowered the landing gear and flaps and they touched down with instructions to park in front of the squadron hangar.

He was still shaking as he walked up to Chief Warrant Officer Alfred J. Ortiz. "What's the problem, Pat?" the engineering officer said.

"We've had an engine fire, Chief."

Ortiz ordered the plane into the hangar where mechanics found that a portion of the exhaust collector ring had fallen out. The engineering officer theorized that because they were taking off with superchargers on, the hold in the exhaust collector ring had permitted exhaust flames to escape through this hole into the engine nacelle, instead of out through the tail pipe.

When Pattillo asked why the fire had quit so suddenly, he was told that because the engine was shut down before the exhaust flame had ignited something else there was no fire left when the engine stopped. He'd had his first experience with an uncontrolled "blowtorch" in a B-29 nacelle. It was not his last.

Later in the month Pattillo was made an instructor. On his first flight to check out other pilots, several landings were made more "sporty" by a half inch of snow that had fallen. Upon return to the ramp he was met by a line man. "Captain, the engineering officer wants to see you."

Pattillo walked over to Ortiz. "Pat, what have you done to the radar system?"

"Hell, I haven't done anything to it. What's the matter, Al?"

"You've destroyed the radome and beat hell out of the radar antenna inside."

Pattillo couldn't believe it. The dome was located underneath the airplane between the bomb bays. While he mulled over the information, he was called on the carpet by Colonel Pearl Robey and other engineering specialists from Wright Field. When they demanded to know what he had done to the airplane, he grew angry. "I've done nothing but fly it!"

Finally, they decided he was telling the truth. After investigation it was realized the radome was crushed when the nose wheel touched down on each landing and a jet stream of snow and slush rushed out between the two nose-wheel tires and was hurled back against the radome. Once the radome housing was stove-in serious damage was done to the antenna.

Late in October, while Pattillo was on duty as tower officer, he watched an old friend, Captain Warren Chittum, take off. Although he didn't notice it at first, he learned later that his blond friend was making three-engine takeoffs although they had been expressly forbidden. Flight crews were told that this was such a new airplane that they were not to experiment but "fly it by the book. Don't play around," Edmundson had cautioned. "There's enough war and enough flying left for all of us." Edmundson knew whereof he spoke because he had flown B-17s in the South Pacific, and was one of the Air Force's finest officers. Edmundson constantly reminded pilots that these early B-29s had carburetors that tended to malfunction. "Wait until they are changed," he said. "Remember, the B-29 hasn't been proven like the B-17. Save it for the Japs."

Pattillo watched Chittum, admiring the sure way he handled the airplane, knowing he was probably one of the most experienced four-engine pilots in the group.

On the ground, Chittum called the tower to ask for clearance for a second takeoff. Corporal Chester L. Villinas, controller, gave it.

Pattillo watched casually as Chittum's plane seemed to hug the ground longer than usual.

Villinas interrupted his thoughts. "Captain, he's taking an awful long roll."

"No. That's just old Warren Chittum. He's all right. "

The airplane broke ground near the tower with its right wing down slightly. Pattillo watched as the plane slowly climbed to the north in a shallow right turn.

Villinas' voice reflected his nervousness. "Captain, I think he's in trouble. Shouldn't I call the crash wagon?"

"No. Don't bother." He had such confidence in his friend that he couldn't conceive Chittum would ever get in trouble he couldn't get out of.

The plane was now in a 35-degree bank, and Pattillo began to be concerned because the B-29 was lower than safety permitted. He watched the plane as it turned through 90 degrees. It seemed to fly almost in slow motion. By now the corporal used his common sense and called the crash wagon on his own. Chittum's plane kept turning slowly to the right back toward the base. Suddenly, it stalled and plunged to the ground. Pattillo was dumbfounded by the suddenness of the end. With a roar the plane exploded, tearing itself apart. Obviously, only a miracle could save anyone aboard. Miraculously tail gunner Staff Sergeant Oscar H. Bolt survived, although injured, because the fuselage acted as a shock absorber, and the tail section broke off from the fuselage.

After investigation, it was learned that Chittum had been making unauthorized three-engine takeoffs. When the other engine on the right side quit, the engine that had been deliberately shut down on the same side was too cold to accelerate fast enough to save the plane.

# CHAPTER 4

# The Battle of Kansas

Arnold laid it on the line to his staff that at least 150 B-29s must be deployed to India no later than April 15, 1944, for operations out of China against Japan in May. Again he pleaded with the Joint Chiefs to get priority for the program, but an investigation showed that delays were caused primarily by introduction of a radically different airplane into the inventory and not because of material or manpower shortages. His request was denied.

The first B-29 wing, the 58th, had been organized June 1, 1943, at Marietta, Georgia, but later was transferred to Salina. It was authorized four groups of 30 aircraft each by its table of organization but only one B-29 had been delivered. The XX Bomber command was established at Smoky Hill Army Air Field, Salina, under Brigadier General Kenneth B. Wolfe, and another wing, the 73rd, was placed under its jurisdiction along with the 58th. To command the 58th, Wolfe selected his special project deputy Colonel Leonard Harman, and placed Colonel Thomas H. Chapman in charge of the 73rd. The latter wing was transferred from the XX Bomber Command later and assigned to the XXI Bomber Command, which later went to the Marianas.

In a declaration issued December 1, 1943, at the Cairo Conference, it was publicly announced for the first time that an invasion of Japan's home islands was under consideration at an unspecified future date. Not announced, but agreed to previously, was Stalin's promise at the Teheran meeting in November 1943 that Russia would enter the war in the Far East after Germany's surrender. At that time Arnold had argued with Russian generals about disposition of B-29s that might be forced to land in Siberia but they were evasive. They consistently replied that any such agreement would jeopardize their peaceful relations with Japan. After the Teheran meeting the Combined Chiefs had returned to Cairo to refine earlier plans. Consideration was given to the possibility that an invasion of Japan's main islands might not be necessary if bombing and blockade measures were effective. Long-range plans, however, continued to contain provisions for invasion because it had yet to be proved that airpower could force a country to surrender.

Wolfe sent Colonel William F. Fisher to China to obtain firsthand knowledge of conditions the B-29 organization would face. To prevent the Japanese from learning his real purpose, he was assigned temporarily as commander of the Fourteenth Air Force's 308th Bombardment Group. He actually flew combat missions as he visited the various bases. After talks with Chennault and Stratemeyer, his reports were sent through normal mail channels to Washington.

Wolfe sent another advance party of five officers to India in November 1943 to check on base construction progress. U.S. Army Aviation engineers had started work with the Central Public Works Department under Mountbatten.

Two of the party flew to Kunming to consult with Fisher and Chennault on operational matters. Important groundwork for later missions was established through arrangements to procure escape and evasion materials for crews who might have to bail out.

Early in 1944, Chennault deliberately went over the heads of all his immediate superiors and wrote directly to President Roosevelt and asked that B-29s be assigned to his command. Later, on January 26, he wrote separately to General Arnold saying that the air commander in China must be given complete control of all air operations, including those of the B-29s. However, Arnold was in no mood to grant such a request from the overly ambitious Chennault.

In India, Mountbatten also sought control of the B-29s to support his operations in the Burma-India theater. Although he didn't question that B-29s would be used primarily against Japan, he hoped to gain some measure of control over their use while they were in his theater.

General Marshall sharply disagreed. In response to their appeals, and speaking on behalf of the Joint Chiefs, he said these new bombers would not be economical for limited use by theater commanders.

While Arnold was on a visit to the Boeing plant at Wichita, he asked how many B-29s would be delivered that month. To the consternation of company officials, who already were hard pressed to meet the contract, Arnold walked down the line in final assembly and picked an airplane that was just down the line from that goal and wrote his name across the fuselage. "This is the plane I want this month." It became known as the Gen. H. H. Arnold Special,* and its checkered career and ultimate end would have shocked Arnold if he could have foreseen the future.

By now Bell was in production at Marietta, Georgia. The Martin plant at Omaha, Nebraska, was selected to replace the Fisher Body plant at Cleveland, which thereafter produced only subassemblies. And the North American plant at Kansas City was traded for the Navy's Renton plant at Seattle for production.

As Arnold studied reports from the Far East, he became more and more concerned about meeting his latest commitment to the President for operational use of the B-29s. His concern deepened after a December 21 meeting with Wolfe. When he found there were only a small number of men assigned to the China-Burma-India theater, he told Wolfe to "get over there yourself, with some of your staff."

Wolfe reached New Delhi January 13, 1944, with a small staff. In China he wasn't at all satisfied with progress and, meeting with Lieutenant Colonel Waldo I. Kennerson, he made arrangements for extending the existing airstrips at Hsinching, Pengshan, and Kiunglai, and construction of a new base at Kwanghang.

Kennerson, the officer in charge of base construction in China, and Wolfe were on hand at Hsinching when work began the 24th. Wolfe watched in amazement as thousands of blue-clad men and women crushed rocks with hammers while others carried pails of sand and crushed rock suspended from shoulder poles. Kennerson noted that Wolfe was gazing at the high peaks that loomed to the west over the valley, and reminded the general that Tibet wasn't too far beyond those mountains.

A similar situation existed in India. Wolfe met with Colonel L. E. Seeman, who was responsible for base construction there. At

* A painting of this aircraft hangs in Mahan Hall, U.S. Military Academy, West Point.

firsthand Wolfe learned that Seeman's units, which had arrived without their heavy equipment, had to move 1.7 million cubic yards of earth, more than half of it for runways. Seeman told him some of his problems in building the 10-inch-thick runways. Indian cement, he said, was of such poor quality that he had to import American cement from the United States at enormous cost.

Wolfe stood looking silently at the choking red dust, and the heat waves radiating from the parched soil, and sympathized with the colonel. It was an incredible scene as thousands of the lowest class of Indians, mostly Untouchables, worked under supervision of American Army engineering troops. Due to the lack of heavy equipment, Indian women were carrying dirt in baskets carefully balanced on their heads. Many chewed betel nuts that stained their mouths red but helped to deaden their hunger pains. Each wore a garment wrapped around herself and up over her head and across her face as a sort of veil. The garments had once been white but all bore a grimy red hue because of the ever-present red dust. To Wolfe, they looked stunted and half-starved, and he didn't doubt that they were. He had heard that up to a million had died of starvation in Bengal the previous year. In the best of times, they seldom had an adequate minimum diet.

Wolfe realized that the bases would never be built in time unless something drastic was done. He flew to Stilwell's jungle headquarters. A reluctant Stilwell agreed to a temporary assignment of several Army construction battalions to help build the bases even though top-priority work on the Ledo Road would have to be slowed.

In one of the most colossal construction projects ever attempted in such a short span of time 700,000 native laborers, and 6,000 U.S. Army construction engineers, worked around the clock in India and China without modern equipment. Rocks were broken by hand and earth moved in pails and wicker baskets. In China, huge stone rollers, each weighing up to 10 tons, and pulled by hundreds of Chinese laborers, smoothed the runways after they were topped by a heavy coating of tung oil to partially seal them. Occasionally, one of the blue-clad figures wasn't nimble enough and stumbled in the path of one of the huge rollers where his body was crushed and became part of the runway's fabric over which heavily laden bombers would soon head for Japan. Once these rollers were moving, they weren't easy to stop in a short distance. Americans stared in bewilderment when the Chinese roared with laughter when one of their number became a casualty. Such a casual attitude toward death was unbelievable to Western minds. There was a constant stream of blue-smocked Chinese coming from nearby streams as they carried thousands of tons of rock, gravel, and sand to build the 8,508-foot runways to a depth of 19 inches. In addition, they also helped to construct strips for Chennault's 312th Fighter Wing, which was assigned to protect the bases.

Despite Arnold's request to the War Department the previous November that a minimum number of construction battalions be diverted from other projects, the Joint Chiefs had cut the number in half. Even so, to get these units to India, shipping priorities were rearranged and vitally needed supplies for Stilwell's army, already pared to the bone, were cut even further.

Stilwell had been given the responsibility of building the fields at Dudhkundi, Piardoba, Kharagpur, Kalaikundi, and Chakulia. This area of southern Bengal was selected because of its direct air relationship with the forward bases in China, and because of its proximity to Calcutta's port facilities. These Indian bases would be relatively free from attack by Japanese bombers, or so it was felt.

Accommodations for living quarters were adequate on the bases, but primitive by standards in some other theaters. By the time work was completed in September 1944, months after the first B-29s were operational, $20 million was spent. This was a drop in the bucket compared to costs in China where everything had to be flown in, and Chiang Kai-shek attempted to raise costs to astronomical heights.

While Seeman had his problems in India, they were nothing compared to what Kennerson had to deal with in China. The Min River Valley in the Chengtu area for generations has been one of the most fertile in the world. Centuries ago the Chinese diverted the river into a series of canals to irrigate the land and prevent flooding in the spring. The delta-type plain, 70 miles long and 1,700 square miles in area, lies at the foot of huge 20,000-foot-plus mountain peaks to the north and west. This rich rice-growing farmland then supported 2,200 persons to the square mile. When farmers first learned that thousands of small farms would be plowed under to build the bases, an explosive political situation developed. Fortunately for the Americans it never became a serious problem despite the fact that the Chinese in this area were strongly isolationist and anti-Chiang Kai-shek; their war lords paid only lip service to the Generalissimo.

Kennerson worked closely with the governor of Szechwan, who agreed on January 11, 1944, to draft men to build the bases. Two weeks later 200,000 were on the job. When this number wasn't sufficient to meet the schedule, the governor drafted another 60,000 in mid-February.

Officials in Washington, who well knew Chiang's propensity for driving a hard bargain, tried to get an estimate of the final cost. When he finally did so, he asked for $2 billion in Chinese currency and a personal guarantee from Roosevelt that it be paid. Roosevelt was agreeable if the amount was charged at the current rate of exchange of $100 Chinese to one American dollar, or $20 million American. When the Generalissimo set the rate at 20 to one to help, so he said, to control inflation in his country, U.S. officials refused to honor such a commitment because the cost would be prohibitive at $100 million American. When Chiang refused to compromise, Stilwell had to guarantee payment at a rate to be decided later just to keep the bases under construction.

The Chinese claimed there was a shortage of their currency so funds were frozen in China. Minister of Finance, Dr. H. H. Kung, continued to insist there was a shortage despite U.S. claims that $10 billion in Chinese funds were available. With funds frozen, however, there was no money to pay for supplies or the wages of Chinese workers so $200 million was shipped by the Air Transport Command from India. Inasmuch as the money was in small denominations of Chinese bills, its weight was a serious problem to transport by air and many needed supplies had to be temporarily left behind in India.

Stilwell was not convinced the Chinese were short of money because Chiang had turned down a $1 billion loan at the Cairo Conference. He believed the request was a matter of prestige rather than actual need. The price for the bases wasn't settled until July 1944 when a lump-sum payment of $210 million in American money was paid to China, but this amount included funds for other things and not just for the bases. To this day no one knows if any of this money was pocketed by bureaucrats, but few officials in Washington at the time had any doubts. Certainly, Chinese landowners didn't receive much of it because they were paid a pittance for their ancestral farms. Chinese laborers got $25 Chinese a day, which hardly paid for food because inflation had risen to $270 Chinese to one American dollar. Their families helped to feed them while the bases were built. At first, their anger about loss of their farms, and their conscription at starvation wages, almost led to revolt but the bases were completed without serious incident. When the B-29s arrived with bombs for Japan, they took pride in their contributions.

When some members of the 462nd first arrived at their base at Kiunglai, adjacent to one of China's oldest cities that dated back almost 5,000 years, they were intrigued by the fact that it was called the "city of free love." They were quickly disillusioned because the words "free love" had a different connotation in China than they did in the United States. They stood for a city where hundreds of years ago young people were given freedom to marry partners of their choice instead of having their parents decide whom they should marry.

Back in the States only 67 first pilots had been checked out by the end of 1943. B-29s were so short that other airplanes were still used for training. The B-26s, which supposedly had somewhat similar takeoff and landing characteristics to the B-29, proved to be an unwise choice. Most of the B-26s had the shorter wing of the early models which many pilots dubbed "The Baltimore Whore," claiming she had no visible means of support. Dozens were destroyed and many crews were lost during the early transition stages. Later models of the B-26 served with distinction in Europe.

The original plan was to train 452 crews. Brigadier General La-Verne G. "Blondie" Saunders, a veteran combat officer who had led the 11th Bombardment Group during the battle for Guadalcanal, was made Wolfe's operations officer with responsibility for training air crews under auspices of the Second Air Force.

The complement of each wing was set at 3,045 officers, eight warrant officers, and 8,099 enlisted men. The large proportion of officers was due to the fact there were double crews for each airplane.

In mid-January of 1944, the number of airplanes available was still critical to complete training. There were 97 off the production lines but only 16 in a flyable condition. Therefore, it had been possible to check out only 70 first pilots. The schedule always had been unrealistic, and the pressure unrelenting. After the second B-29 was lost, it had been considered necessary to "freeze" design changes, and make necessary modifications only after each B-29 came off the production line. Soon there were so many mandatory changes that the modification line at Kelly Field, Texas, could not handle them all, so, in an attempt to bring order out of chaos, modification centers were established at each base in Kansas, the Bell plant in Marietta, and the Martin plant at Omaha, with Colonel Carl Cover, a former Douglas vice president, in charge. Despite the best of intentions, not one Superfortress was ready for combat by mid-January 1944 because of the time lag in training inexperienced people, matching modification kits with each aircraft, and completing mandatory safety changes. The problem was compounded at the bases because ground crews had to leave for India by ship and air transport so as to arrive in time to service the B-29s when they flew over. Arnold learned that any thought of deploying 150 planes to India by early March was clearly out of the question unless drastic measures were taken.

Initially, Wolfe believed that B-29s could be "debugged" during the production and training phases and thereby save at least six months. He learned to his regret how wrong that assumption was as the program almost collapsed. However, the airplane proved to be so totally different from all previous bombers that the problems mushroomed out of control. There were over 2,000 engineering changes to the Wright engine alone. The centralized fire-control system that operated the guns and the APQ-13 radar-bombing system caused endless problems and proved baffling to air crews. Costs rose to $600,000 for each airplane, which was extremely high for that period.

Arnold was most concerned about two problems that developed early in the flight-test program. The first, and most difficult, was engine overheating, particularly when above 32,000 feet. The second was the inability of B-29 bombardiers to bomb accurately because early B-29s had bomb-bay doors that opened electrically. While the doors opened slowly, airplane speed would drop as much as 15 mph, and it was almost impossible for the pilot to hold a constant airspeed required for accurate bombsight synchronization. The latter problem was overcome by introducing pneumatic pressure to snap the doors open during the last minute of the bomb run. Overheating of the engines was partially solved by drastically reducing the length of the cowl flaps and additional baffling inside the nacelles to direct more cooling air onto the cylinders. Until both problems were resolved, Arnold knew the B-29 was worthless as a high-altitude bomber.

Thomas R. Vaucher, a young captain from the 462nd Group at

Walker Army Air Field, Victoria, Kansas, was assigned to fly a modified B-29 to check out the latest changes. Vaucher became an airplane commander at Pratt after only three and a half hours in a B-29 but he had accumulated more than a thousand hours in other four-engine bombers, which was far above the average. Still in his early twenties, Vaucher was selected as the pilot to accept the first B-29 on behalf of the Air Force and fly it back to Pratt from Wichita because he had 30 minutes more flying time than the other pilot assigned to the flight, who outranked him.

When Vaucher took the airplane up from Walker, it was just another flight to him because he didn't realize how crucial this test was to Arnold. At 38,000 feet, he made a bomb run and the engines maintained their cylinder-head temperatures and the new doors snapped open properly, and the bombardier made a good run.

Later, in Operations, he reported they had made a successful flight. Then, much to his surprise, he was told that General Arnold was on the phone and wanted to talk to him.

"I've just heard about your successful flight at 38,000 feet. Were you able to hold your airspeed on the run?" The general's voice was well modulated and pleasant as Vaucher listened, assuring Arnold that he had been able to do so.

"Did the cabin pressurization hold?" Arnold said.

"Yes, sir," Vaucher said. "There was no problem with it whatsoever."

After thanking him, and asking Vaucher to convey his congratulations to the crew, Arnold hung up. Only then did it sink in that he had actually talked to the head of the Army Air Forces, and he was amazed that such a busy man would take time to talk to him personally.

Major Victor N. Agather, associated with the B-29 project office at Wright Field, had been working on the engine fire problem, but early in February 1944 he received a call from Colonel Erik Nelson at 2 A.M. "Vic, get your tail in the saddle and get out to Salina immediately with a list of all aerial numbers of B-29s and the modification required. General Bradshaw's airplane is standing by at Operations to take you."

After he arrived in Salina he quickly learned there was ungodly confusion at all four bases, and that nobody knew exactly what modifications were needed in any given aircraft. As a result, all airplanes were grounded.

He was assigned to Pratt, Kansas, where the 40th Group was stationed. There Agather checked each aircraft and made a complete list of modifications that were necessary to get the airplane flying. For five days he and a special crew went without sleep but by the end of that time they knew exactly what had to be done to each airplane. That was a good first step. Now they had to identify the kits for each aircraft and locate them.

They flew to Boeing in Wichita one night and walked down the production line. When they saw an individual who was doing similar work that was required at Pratt, he was pointed out to his supervisor and immediately taken off the production line and driven to the airport and then flown to Pratt. Meanwhile, a car went to his home to advise his family and pick up his clothes, which were sent separately. In all, 400 individuals were taken off the Boeing lines.

At Pratt, as at other B-29 bases, there were only two hangars so the bulk of the work had to be done in the open on the ramps. It was midwinter, snowing much of the time, and bitter cold. Crews could work on the airplanes under such conditions for 20 minutes at most before they had to go inside and be replaced by others. It was a frustrating period because there was inadequate housing for all, but Arnold had given priority to the job and everything that was needed was somehow made available.

At Pratt, 100 engines had to be changed as the airplanes had outmoded engines. No engine slings were available but an enterprising individual located some in Erie, Pennsylvania, where an American airliner was ordered to unload its passengers and the engine slings were cut to size with torches to fit on top of the passenger seats of the DC-3. The next morning the pilots and stewardess, red-eyed from flying all night, arrived with their unusual load. The slings were welded back together and, when engines were flown in, the changes were made.

During this trying period, the bases were overrun with armchair generals trying to get into the act and impress General Arnold with their abilities to solve all the B-29's problems. Within one three-week period more than 60 general officers arrived at Pratt to offer their services. To Agather and project heads they were more of a nuisance than a help because they had no conception of what needed to be done.

One day, while Agather was in the bowels of a B-29 sweating over a problem, a lineman sent word that a general wanted to talk to him.

"If he wants to talk to me, tell him to climb up here!"

Agather, dirty and unkempt from days of exhausting work without sleep, peered out through the Plexiglas, noting the general's beautifully pressed uniform and all the characteristics of a dandy except a swagger stick. Agather brushed his hair back with a greasy hand, chuckling to himself, because from the general's appearance it was obvious he didn't know how to climb into the nose of a B-29 without a ladder, and there was no way he was about to soil his tailor-made uniform anyway.

The general stalked off after he got Agather's message. Shortly thereafter, Agather was told he was being cited for insubordination and a possible court-martial. He reported the matter to his boss, Colonel Nelson, who told him not to worry. Whether Nelson, an early intimate of General Arnold, went directly to the top or not, Agather never found out. He did hear that the general was relieved of duty and sent to Greenland to cool off.

Arnold felt confident now that with the emergency measures under way B-29s would be able to depart on time. He wired Wolfe in India March 1 that they would start to leave Kansas March 10.

When Arnold and his assistant, Major General B. E. Meyer, went to Salina March 9 to watch the B-29s depart, he was shocked to find that not one airplane was ready to leave. He found the modification program still a shambles. He was blunt in denouncing what he called a complete lack of organization and managerial leadership. With thoughts of how he would explain this latest fiasco to President Roosevelt, his wrath turned on Colonel I. W. Stephenson, who happened to be the highest-ranking officer present. He accused the Technical Service Command colonel of failure to coordinate the work properly between the Boeing factories, the modification centers, and the bases. When he demanded to know about shortages, no one had any idea of where parts were or when they would be delivered.

The more he reviewed the situation the madder Arnold got, insisting on knowing who was running the show. "I'll do it if no one else is!" he shouted, an angry flush suffusing his face.

To Stephenson, he said he wanted a shortage list of everything by the next morning. "I want to know where each item is and, if it's in the factory, when it will be delivered."

Stephenson was as shaken as he'd ever been as Arnold stormed out of his office. He and his aides worked through the night to prepare a status sheet on each aircraft, and the next day sent them to Pratt, Kansas, where Arnold was staying.

When Arnold saw the report, he told Meyer to remain behind as his special project coordinator with full authority to act on his behalf.

A period of frenzied activity began to complete the 150 B-29s so they could be on their way to the China-Burma-India (CBI) theater by the middle of April at the latest. The "Battle of Kansas" had begun and would continue until it was won.

Despite frantic efforts, a week later not one B-29 was ready for dispatch overseas.

General Orval Cook, production division chief of the Air Materiel Command, hurried to Wichita to talk to Boeing officials. He didn't mince words and demanded five to six hundred Boeing mechanics to work on the planes at the bases. He told them, "Come hell or high water the last plane has got to leave April 15." Boeing acted quickly and the men were working on planes the next day.

Colonel C. S. "Bill" Irvine was placed in charge as Meyer's deputy and ace troubleshooter. He quickly found one large source of the trouble. There had been so many changes to the wiring diagrams that they bore no resemblance to the plane's 15,000 feet of wire. Irvine ordered each wire system traced so accurate drawings could be made on the spot.

With Major Thomas Gerrity as Meyer's top man to expedite the modifications, it was soon apparent that more people were needed if the job was to be done on time.

Meyer again turned to Boeing. Even at the risk of slowing production, he insisted that experienced production people be lent to work on planes already at the bases. Subcontractors were told to concentrate on finding missing parts at the expense of future production.

To complicate matters, a raging snowstorm and bitterly cold weather lashed the Kansas bases and men and women on the flight lines fought to keep their tempers under control.

In the middle of this frantic activity Boeing workers from the southern states threatened a walkout because their wages were below the level of their northern counterparts. Meyer appealed to their patriotism and they went back to work.

By some miracle the B-29s of the 40th Group were ready to go overseas by Easter. Along with Major Agather, Lieutenant Colonel

Harry Hubbard, Lieutenant Colonel Mark Maidel, and Captain Arthur Borden were shifted to Great Bend to continue the job. Eventually they went to each base to get the last of the B-29s ready for overseas. Their work didn't end there because they ended up in India and China when engines continued to cause problems in combat.

There were many who disagreed with Matterhorn and alternative plans were offered for use of the B-29s but none was accepted. The Joint Chiefs did reduce Matterhorn to one wing—the 58th. It was decided that the 73rd Wing would become part of a XXI Bomber Command to be based later on Saipan.

Arnold personally selected the commanders for each group. After the 58th Wing was activated instructions were issued to the 40th Bombardment Group under Colonel Lewis R. Parker to transfer two squadrons, plus necessary headquarters personnel, to the new 462nd at Victoria, Kansas, under Colonel Richard H. Carmichael, a veteran combat officer from the early days of the war in the Southwest Pacific. The split-up was ordered because the 40th had a high percentage of experienced flying personel who had served with the Sixth Air Force in Central and South America flying combat patrols to guard the Panama Canal, and with an unusual background in the use of early radar equipment. Colonel Alva L. Harvey, B-29 project officer at Boeing's Seattle plant during 1942 and 1943, was given the 444th at Great Bend, and Colonel Howard F. Engler from North Africa was assigned the 468th at Salina, Kansas. Harvey was the senior officer in the 58th Wing.*

Once they were selected Arnold sent Colonels Harvey and Parker to England to study combat operations at firsthand with the Eighth Air Force. Each of them flew missions over Germany and, on their fifth, the first daylight raid on Berlin, Colonel Parker was shot down and ended up in a German prisoner-of-war camp. Harvey was returned to the States to take over his group. To replace Parker, Wolfe moved Colonel Leonard F. Harman from wing headquarters to command the 40th. Harman was a top selection because he had been associated with development of the Wright R-3350 engine.

What with the lack of available B-29s, training was limited. Most of the longer flights involved transporting the airplanes to and from modification centers. At least it was some minor preparation for the

* A painting in honor of Harvey hangs in Arnold Hall, USAF Academy, Colorado Springs, Colorado.

11,530-mile flight ahead of them from Kansas to India. Although over-water flights were limited prior to departure, some managed to fly to Cuba and back. Such a flight, however, hardly qualified as a long over-water flight.

In reality, most crews were about as ill equipped to fly combat missions as any ever sent overseas. Few crews had tested their guns in flight, and none of them had dropped anything but practice bombs. The Army Proving Ground had set up targets in northwest Florida, but not enough crews were able to participate in simulated missions to give many gunners experience in tracking targets.

Ready or not, Brigadier General LaVerne G. "Blondie" Saunders, wing commander of the 58th, took the first airplane off in late March and headed for India with stops at Gander; across the route's longest over-water stretch of 2,700 miles to Marrakesh; then on to Cairo; Karachi; and its base at Chakulia.

Earlier that month Colonel Frank Cook flew a B-29 to England as a decoy gesture that fooled no one. It was dutifully inspected by Generals Eisenhower and Doolittle and top British officials. It was parked so it would be spotted by German reconnaissance planes, and it was, and controlled leaks were made in hopes the Japanese would be deceived. Those long runways in Bengal and the Chengtu area in China were dead giveaways, and the Japanese were not misled by such artless subterfuge.

# CHAPTER 5

# B-29s Arrive in the Far East

General Wolfe and British and American officials were on hand at Chakulia, India, awaiting the appearance of General Saunders' airplane March 30, but it failed to show up. It didn't arrive until April 2 when it swept over the field in salute while cameras recorded the event.

Four days later, the B-29 that had been sent to England as a decoy came in. There was finally evidence in the Far East that the B-29s were about to start their long-delayed operations.

Meanwhile, other planes left the States for the long, dangerous flight to India, and many crews had anxious moments en route before it was completed.

Early in April, Captain Pattillo was assigned a B-29 that first had to be taken to Oklahoma City for a final modification.

Back in Operations at Salina, Pattillo met Edmundson. "Pat, that's your airplane. The one you're going to take to combat. Go out and change all four engines with your crew."

"Yes, sir." And that's what they did because all crews were trained to maintain their airplanes without benefit of ground crews because, Arnold knew, there would be times when it would be necessary overseas.

After the third engine was removed, the airplane began to settle on its tail. Technical Sergeant Harry Chatham rushed back with another crew member to try and hold the tail up while another ran for a tail jack. They learned a valuable lesson—that you don't remove that forward weight without a tail jack!

After the engines were changed Edmundson told Pattillo, "Get your orders and get going."

Pattillo looked questioningly at the colonel, hoping he would reveal where they were going. All Edmundson would say was, "Your first stop is Presque Isle, Maine."

"My God," Pattillo thought, "that means we're going to England. I volunteered for the wrong war." He had requested combat to fight the Japanese because his older brother had been killed in the Pacific while flying as a navigator.

With a spare engine in the bomb bay, they started on their way April 12. The sun was shining, and the air was crisp and cool. After they had been airborne for a while, they heard by radio that they should land at Wright Field because Presque Isle was socked in by bad weather.

The next day they headed for Presque Isle and the flight was uneventful. In Maine it was cold and snowing. On landing, Pattillo came in high but hadn't counted on a strong crosswind and almost ended up in a snowbank. He poured the "coal" to her and went around.

Next time the landing was made routinely, and when he went into the bar he met Edmundson, who said, "I thought I saw one of our white nose wheels trying to land and figured it might be you. Sure enough it was."

Pattillo was embarrassed and made no comment. In the back of his mind, he tucked away a reminder that he wouldn't ever again bring a B-29 in so high and burn up the runway going around.

They arrived at Gander at 2 P.M. the following day. Pattillo was surprised to see so many B-29s parked against snowdrifts, undergoing repairs.

The long flight ahead of them the next day, on a route that would take them 100 miles north of the Azores, was the longest over-water route.

Fortunately, their B-29 had no problems, so the following day, while the engines were run up, he listened to them critically. Each engine had 25 hours flying time but the average life expectancy of a B-29 engine at this stage was 15 hours!

Once they reached the sea their eyes watched with wonder as blue-green icebergs, some of huge size, floated beneath them out in the

Atlantic. They had taken off at 4 P.M. so night settled down quickly as Pattillo kept a lonely vigil on the instruments in the pilot's compartment. Whirls of what appeared to be fire swirled around the propellers, and even flickered around the frame of the cockpit. The crew, always concerned about fire, questioned Pattillo, who assured them it was only St. Elmo's fire, which was harmless.

It was a long night but an uneventful one. Once they made landfall on the coast of Africa, navigator Lieutenant Richard L. Cournoyer got them oriented by identifying specific points on the coast and they headed for Morocco.

On the approach to the base at Marrakesh, he was astonished by the number of Allied planes parked around the perimeter and Pattillo decided they must be on their way to England and Italy.

Major repairs delayed them for two weeks before Pattillo received clearance for the next leg of their journey. When he found their destination was Cairo, he was sure they were on their way to the Far East to fight the Japanese.

All B-29s were designated M-10s to keep their true identity as secret as possible for the time being. Pattillo and the other pilots jokingly referred to the "M" as meaning "modified."

In late April, they took off for Cairo, still hugging the ground as thousands of sheep dashed around in panic below them. Pattillo tried to gain some altitude but the airplane refused to climb. With the Grand Atlas Mountains towering to the east, he was desperate. He called the flight engineer. "How are the cylinder head temperatures?"

"One is at 310. Two are at 320, and another is 340."

Pattillo winced. The engines were redlined at 290 degrees. Anything could happen with those temperatures and no engine could long stand such heat.

Smitty called, "What do you want me to do?"

"Button 'em down." He referred to the cowl flaps, which had been opened to cool the engines but which were causing so much drag on the airplane that it couldn't climb.

In 30 seconds, as cylinder-head temperatures soared higher, the airplane's speed rose to 190 mph and they started to climb.

"Crack cowl flaps," Pattillo called. This action opened them slightly so cooling air could get to the cylinders, and the temperatures started to drop.

In the third week of April, five B-29s with overheated engines crashed near Karachi. Two were demolished, and five crewmen were killed. Wolfe grounded all B-29s so an investigation could be made. It was established that engine failures were due to the high temperatures in India, and the inexperience of crews who were flying with higher loads than they were used to. In a letter to General Arnold, he said that it was imperative to find some means to cool the engines, and cited the need as urgent.

Arnold put his experts from Wright Field to work to study the problem anew with orders to find a quick solution. Their investigation confirmed that overheating of the exhaust valves on the rear row of cylinders was causing complete engine failure. The top cowl flaps, originally designed for a fixed position, were made operable from the cockpit, and shortened by three inches to allow more air to cool the cylinders. Through the use of crossover tubes, more oil was brought to the top engine cylinders to reduce overheating of the valves. Major Victor Agather and members of the special group that had helped to modify the engines in the United States were sent to India to lend their expertise.

Pattillo's crew arrived in Cairo shortly after sunup, confused at first by the many branches of the Nile in the delta region, while getting a breathtaking view of the pyramids.

From now on the flight was routine. After a night in Cairo fighting fleas, and being warned the next day to stay away from the Suez Canal, which was guarded by British fighters with orders to shoot first and ask questions later, they took off to the north and turned east. After marveling at the greenness of the countryside around Jerusalem, they turned southeast and made their way across Abadan, and then flew across the Red Sea. It was hot as they flew at 6,000 feet across the Indian Ocean south of Afghanistan to Karachi.

There, the base was exotic in one sense because of the varying contrasts, and the colorful turbans of some of the people. Pattillo thought what a miserable place for human beings to have to live with poverty evident everywhere along with the suffocating heat and humidity.

One of the planes that was lost at Karachi was flown by John Blackwood when he ran out of gas on approach during a thunder and lightning storm with blowing sand. He was killed along with some members of his crew.

Pattillo, who was short a right gunner, acquired Gordon Prestodak from Blackwood's crew.

Their flight to Bengal brought varying scenes of India's differing landscapes. First, a desert country was crossed as they headed east. Then, villages and cities began to appear but they wondered how so many millions could survive in the parched country unfolding beneath them.

When they circled their new home at Kharagpur, noting the straw-roofed buildings and the dirt streets below them, they were almost ready to turn back and head home to the States.

On the ground, the incongruity of loading their heavy winter flying gear into a truck struck Pattillo with amusement as he wiped the sweat from his face in the stifling heat.

They were exhausted by the time they arrived at their quarters and Pattillo slumped down on the rack laced with manila ropes that passed for a bed. Looking up at the bamboo and thatched roof when he heard a rustling noise, he saw an 18-inch, beige lizard strike at something. Out of the ceiling tumbled a 9-inch black centipede with yellow legs that took off for the door with a snakelike motion. One of the crew killed it with a shovel.

Pattillo glanced at his copilot, Lieutenant Geoffrey Matthews, wondering if he felt as he did, saying, "What a rat hole." He was dispirited and, to add to his miseries, he felt the first twinges of dysentery as he rushed to a nearby latrine with a roll of toilet paper, an action that became all too familiar in the days ahead.

They had been warned about cobras but they didn't take the warning seriously until one of the squadron commanders killed one of the deadly snakes inside his room a few days later. After that, a flashlight was mandatory equipment after dark.

Pattillo's plane still had the spare engine so they were told to fly it to their A-7 base at Pengshan, China. They took off early in a brilliant, blood-red sky as the sun came up out of the east.

They gazed with wondering eyes as they flew northeast over a countryside of small lakes and rivers, with countless villages on higher ground. The Ganges, flowing sluggishly beneath them, was heavily impregnated with mud. Over Assam, the Shillong Hills stood out as bright-green oases in the otherwise water-soaked countryside.

After they passed Chabua the mountains rose spectacularly with deep, swirling rivers like the Yangtze and Mekong as they headed down their tortuous ways to the sea. They shuddered at the thought of bailing out, and prayed those Wright 3350 engines would hold out even though they were overdue for replacement.

In China, the scenery changed again as more brilliant colors of brown, green, and red appeared at the higher elevations, while the lowlands were a lush emerald green from the thousands of rice paddies.

Near their base at Pengshan, Pattillo looked with awe at the rugged Himalayas that half circled the valley, with their snowcapped peaks glistening in the clear air at altitudes above 25,000 feet.

The cool air of China and the rich farmlands around their China base were a welcome change, but they spent only one night before they headed back for India.

Pattillo was relaxed as they neared Fort Hertz in Burma. The flight had gone well and his admiration for the scenery had reduced his fear of flying over this rough country. They were at 22,000 feet when the airplane received a rough jolt that sent quivering shocks through the airframe. He realized that the number four engine had failed, and he quickly feathered the propeller. He decided to land at Chabua in India and sent a message to home base of his intentions, and the need for a new engine.

They spent five days waiting for the new engine, and changed it themselves before they took off for Kharagpur. En route, he tried to avoid a huge black cloud formation soaring thousands of feet in the familiar anvil shape of a thunderhead. It was impossible to avoid and the airplane was torn from his grasp as it rose and fell with express-train speed thousands of feet at a time. He couldn't imagine any plane able to stand such a pummeling, and he thought they'd pop rivets from the control surfaces. During severe down drafts, they would have been pinned to the ceiling without their seat belts, and during upward escalation they were slammed hard into their seats. After Pattillo landed, he surveyed the airplane for damage and found it unbelievable when none was discovered.

Generals Wolfe and Saunders also flew over the Hump, a distance of more than 1,000 miles, April 24 and, after landing at Kwanghan, were met by General Chennault and Chinese officials while thousands of men and women who had so torturously constructed the runway stood silently on the sidelines.

April 26 two more B-29s flew to the forward bases. Major Charles E. Hanson's plane was sighted by 12 Japanese Oscar fighters. They were 2,000 feet below when they were sighted by the crew, who watched six climb toward them. Hanson warned the crew to be ready but the fighters remained out of range of the bomber's guns.

Instead, they flew alongside the Superfort while the Japanese pilots studied her.

Just as the crew was relaxing, figuring they wouldn't be attacked, the fighters formed a circular formation. Suddenly, the lead plane dove at the bomber, breaking away at 400 yards, after firing and scoring hits on the left side of the airplane and wounding the gunner.

Now that the situation was developing seriously, the gunnery system broke down. The tail gunner's 20-mm cannon, and three of the four top guns, jammed and remained out of commission. Hanson expected the worst now that they were practically defenseless but the Japanese made two single attacks, both of which failed to score hits. A fourth and final attack came in low from behind and the tail gunner caught it with several bursts from his .50-caliber machine guns, and it broke away smoking.

Hanson, once they were on the ground, demanded an explanation of why the guns failed. He learned that the cannon in the tail didn't work properly because the armorer had failed to wind the spring-loading mechanism. The other guns jammed because their rapid-firing mechanism wasn't working properly.

Throughout the month of April many B-29s were stripped of all unnecessary equipment to carry fuel and supplies to China. When only 1,400 tons of fuel were delivered, Wolfe realized he couldn't launch his first strike on May 1. Instead of the 660,000 gallons needed for two large strikes that he had promised Arnold, he had only 380,000 in storage. Even more of the bombers were stripped for tanker use, with the average hauling seven tons of gasoline each trip.

Despite the early problems of getting the B-29s to India, by May 8, 145 had reached Marrakesh, and 130 were in India to continue their training, as well as hauling gasoline and supplies to the forward bases in China.

The Air Transport Command had been given responsibility to get the planes to the Far East. Five airplanes were lost, and four others seriously damaged. For an airplane with the problems and deficiencies the B-29 had at the time, and the inexperience of the crews, the ATC's efficient handling of the move was commendable.

# CHAPTER 6

# Twentieth Air Force Formed

After General Arnold completed a tour of Pacific bases in the fall of 1942, he was convinced that he should maintain control of the B-29s because there was no unity of command in the Pacific and neither Nimitz, MacArthur, nor Stilwell were strong enough advocates of strategic air warfare to use the new bombers effectively. Also, the rivalries within the CBI, and between Nimitz and MacArthur, would make it difficult to move B-29 organizations from one command to another as strategy dictated. Although Arnold claimed after the war that he was reluctant to retain command of the Twentieth Air Force, his personal papers and the reminiscences of his intimates indicate no such reluctance. On the contrary, it appears that he enjoyed an opportunity to command a large air force in the field.

Now that the Superfortresses would be used only in the Pacific under American organizations for administration, supply, and defense, Arnold was determined that the Joint Chiefs of Staff would have final control despite the directive agreed upon at the Casablanca Conference January 21, 1943, that a bomber offensive would be under the direct control of the Combined Chiefs of Staff. On April 10, 1944, a plan was adopted for the strategic bombing of Japan under control of the Joint Chiefs instead of the Combined Chiefs. The latter would be used only for directives to instruct British commands to make available such facilities and services that were needed in the Far East.

Some officers, mainly in the U.S. Navy, opposed such control because they were trying to block the Matterhorn project. Arnold listened to arguments from both sides, including his own staff officers who initially favored establishment of a Headquarters Strategic Air Force which would be administered by the Army Air Forces' member of the Joint Chiefs.

A number of conferences were held between February 11 and 19, 1944, until agreement was reached, with the President's approval, that control of all very long-range forces would be retained by the Joint Chiefs with Arnold exercising "executive direction." Hansell had obtained Admiral King's agreement to a proposal to centralize command of the B-29s directly under the Joint Chiefs, an arrangement similar to King's retention of the U.S. Fleet command and functioning as executive agent for it under the Joint Chiefs. General Handy, chief of the Operations Plans Division, concurred for General Marshall.

This was not the end of the conflict about control of the new bombers. On March 2 the Joint Planning Staff came up with another version that kept in language about control by the Joint Chiefs but made no mention of Arnold as executive director. Arnold quickly proposed a paragraph that would delineate his responsibilities according to the earlier agreement.

Chief of Naval Operations Admiral Ernest J. King came up with a different idea that would drop the use of the word "control" and substitute "strategic deployment and designation of missions." Under such a proposal the theater commander would coordinate activities at the local level. The Joint Planning Staff accepted King's amendment but still didn't take up the matter of Arnold's status as executive agent. They did recommend that Arnold be authorized to communicate directly with B-29 forces in the field to coordinate missions with other operations.

Such recommendations were contrary to the original agreement, and Arnold considered them unworkable. When the report was submitted to the Joint Chiefs March 28 with its chairman Admiral William D. Leahy recommending approval, Arnold offered another proposal that surprisingly was suggested by Admiral King. In an attempt to resolve a situation that was becoming difficult, King recommended that a Joint Chiefs of Staff Air Force be created under Arnold as Commanding General Army Air Forces, and that he be named as executive agent for the Joint Chiefs. He said Arnold would determine employment of the very long-range bomber force, and that as its agent he would command under specific directives from the Joint Chiefs. Finally, a more equitable solution to a thorny high-command problem was resolved by the man whom many AAF officers believed was their strongest opponent to strategic air warfare. The Joint Chiefs informally accepted the recommendation and told their planners to come up with a definitive proposal. King personally helped to draft many of the basic ideas that, upon approval April 10, 1944, became the official charter for the Twentieth Air Force. The plan designated the Twentieth as a strategic Army Air Force, operating directly under the Joint Chiefs with Arnold as Commanding General Army Air Forces acting as executive agent to implement their directives. It was agreed that major decisions about deployment, missions, and target objectives would be made by the Joint Chiefs. Theater commanders obtained one of their objectives. In an emergency, theater or area commanders were authorized to divert VLR bombers from their primary strategic warfare mission to assist in a tactical situation, with the stipulation that the Joint Chiefs must be informed immediately. Theater commanders were charged with the responsibility of providing bases and their defense, as directed by the Joint Chiefs. Under the circumstances, it was the best possible agreement and Arnold was appreciative of King's assistance. He now had authority to communicate directly with Twentieth Air Force officials in the field without first going through theater and area commanders. It was a crucial step in establishing a strategic air command for the eventual destruction of Japan.

Although no public announcement was made at the time, the Twentieth Air Force was activated in Washington April 4 with Arnold as commander. He designated each member of his staff to perform his normal role for the Twentieth as well as the Army Air Forces.

Brigadier General Haywood S. Hansell, Jr., was the named chief of staff. A strong backer of strategic warfare, Hansell had steered the Matterhorn project through the most difficult period just prior to overseas deployment. Colonel Cecil E. Combs, who had fought against the Japanese in the Philippines and the Southwest Pacific, was named deputy for operations.

Organization of the Twentieth Air Force was an almost impossible job because there was no precedent, but with the assistance of AAF's Management Control the task was accomplished and functioned well until war's end.

Stilwell wasn't advised of the establishment of the Twentieth by the Joint Chiefs until April 3. In the past, during informal discussions, the British had not objected, but when they were briefed on the new air force April 19 they sought control by the Combined Chiefs. They didn't object to Arnold's control but after VE-Day the British wanted Royal Air Force units assigned to the Twentieth. Arnold's position, under such a revision, then would be comparable to that of Sir Charles Portal, who was executive agent for the Combined Bomber Offensive under the Combined Chiefs. The American Joint Planning Staff was opposed to such a change because they were convinced that the air war against Japan would be completely different from the one against Germany. They explained that the present four groups would ultimately expand to 49, all of which would be in areas controlled by American commanders. They voiced other objections with the main one being that the British couldn't possibly send planes until mid-1945 and, furthermore, the RAF didn't have a very long-range bomber comparable to the B-29 that could operate at the distances contemplated in the Far East. The Joint Planning Staff filed a negative report May 31, and the Joint Chiefs declined the British proposal. It wasn't a flat refusal because the British were told that the matter would be reconsidered when British squadrons became available.

The arguments over command responsibilities in the China-Burma-India theater were due largely to the uniqueness of a huge land area with masses of people and extremely poor lines of communication. The Chinese, in particular, often felt alienated from the war efforts outside their own country. They were not represented on the Combined Chiefs of Staff so Chiang used his direct contact with Roosevelt to keep in touch. Chiang Kai-shek's main objective was to oust the Japanese from his country, but his problems were aggravated by the Communist Chinese in the north under Mao Tze-tung who were disputing Chiang's shaky control of large areas of China. The British in India, however, had their own objectives, which as a colonial power were not necessarily the long-range objectives of the United States. They were interested in defending India from invasion by the Japanese, and in reconquering Burma and Malaya and regaining their former prestige in those areas.

Stilwell's primary mission was to keep China an active and effective ally. After the Japanese cut the Burma Road, his problems mounted because supplying the Chinese in 1943 had to be done entirely by air transport over the Hump. The primary mission of the Tenth Air Force in India and the Fourteenth Air Force in China was to defend this air route, while the Ledo Road was given high priority to serve future operations in northern Burma. One of the basic reasons why control of the Twentieth Air Force was maintained in Washington was Arnold's conviction that neither Stilwell, with his preoccupation with the recapture of Burma, nor Chennault, with his close association with Chiang Kai-shek and his China-first policy, was capable of carrying out the Twentieth's strategic goals.

Mountbatten, Chiang Kai-shek, and Chennault were not happy with the decision to control the Twentieth from Washington, where all major decisions would be made by the Joint Chiefs. Mountbatten, in particular, resented the direct line of communications between Arnold and Wolfe without going through him as theater commander. As a face-saving gesture, President Roosevelt cabled Chiang April 12 to say that he personally would command the Twentieth from Washington, but that the Generalissimo would have the responsibility of coordinating all its missions with other operations in China. He assured Chiang that he would be kept informed by directives from Washington.

Most of the nonflying personnel, and even some flying personnel, had been sent to India by ocean transport. High-priority men were shipped from Newark, New Jersey, to Casablanca and then flown by Air Transport Command to Calcutta. The majority of men and supplies went by ships and were at sea by the end of February. Some were taken to North Africa where they were transferred to British ships for transport through the Suez Canal. Most supplies and personnel departed from West Coast ports on the long journey around Australia and through the Bay of Bengal to Calcutta. For them the journey lasted 8 to 10 weeks. One service-group man, William H. Chiesi, traveled 12,000 miles by ship and it took him and his 462nd Group comrades 98 days to reach India before being delivered by Indian Railway cattle cars to their base in Piardoba.

Before the B-29s left Kansas all ground school was completed by the end of January 1944, but not more than half the scheduled B-29 flying was completed. Crews were particularly inexperienced in high-altitude formation flying, long-range simulated combat missions, and gunnery and bombing practice because such flights were almost negligible in number. Wolfe's first task overseas was to complete the training in India before the first mission.

In Kansas, a fifth group was formed at Smoky Hill to train crews for the second wing. The 472nd Bombardment Group thus became the nucleus around which the 73rd Wing was formed.

Wolfe established his Indian command headquarters at Kharagpur, an important junction with rail lines to the other bases, and 65 miles from Calcutta on the main Bengal-Nagpur Railway. A large new building that had been designed as a political prison in the adjoining village at Hijili was set up as headquarters. In addition, the base was assigned the 468th Group, with the 40th Group and wing headquarters at Chakulia, the 462nd at Piardoba, and the 444th temporarily assigned to Charra until it could move to its permanent base at Dudhkundi.

Wolfe's engineers installed a six-inch fuel pipeline from the Hooghly River to Dudhkundi, with four-inch lines to the other fields so great quantities of fuel could be stored in tanks readily available for missions.

General Kenney, head of MacArthur's Fifth Air Force, earlier had requested that Superforts be based in Australia so that petroleum targets in the Netherlands East Indies could be bombed. Arnold resisted such a suggestion and told his planners to find a way to bomb Sumatra's chief oil center from Indian bases by staging out of Ceylon. The suggestion had been made at the Sextant Conference with a target date of July 20, 1944, but that proved to be an unrealistic date because the base at China Bay wasn't finished that early.

Arnold arranged with the Navy for use of an escort carrier to transport two fighter groups with P-47s from North Africa to Karachi. He had little fear for the Bengal fields because they were isolated at the extreme range of Japanese bombers in Burma. China was another matter, and he fully expected attacks on those forward bases in the Chengtu area. One hundred of the fighters were delivered fully assembled by late March and ready for service with the 312th Fighter Wing under command of Brigadier General A. H. Gilkeson. The wing commander welcomed the modern fighters because they replaced P-40s, which long since should have been replaced.

Arnold wrote to Wolfe April 26. It was an understanding letter of Wolfe's difficulties that said, "The airplanes and crews got off to a bad start due to late production schedules, difficult modifications, inclement weather, and the sheer pressure of time necessary to meet the early commitment date." It was one of the last communications Wolfe was to receive from Arnold in such a friendly vein.

The Matterhorn project had been approved by the Joint Chiefs, with concurrence of the Combined Chiefs, because officials of the XX Bomber Command said they could supply their forward bases by using stripped-down B-29 tankers equipped with four bomb-bay tanks, plus 20 C-87 cargo aircraft. In late April, it was apparent to Wolfe that the command's ability to sustain itself was impossible to achieve. All too often the five-and-a-half-hour flight to the forward bases used so much fuel that little or none could be off-loaded for storage. By May 1, there was only enough fuel in China to fly one B-29 to Japan with sufficient gasoline to get it back to India. Wolfe had to admit that self-sufficiency could not be attained so he had to turn to the Air Transport Command for assistance. C-46 cargo planes were turned over to the command in late April. This action antagonized other commands which also needed the transport aircraft. Wolfe had no choice because it was evident that future operations would be dependent upon cargo aircraft, and a greater use of B-29s as tankers. Wolfe informed Washington of the situation and told Arnold that he was stripping B-29s of their combat equipment except for tail guns and a minimum of radar so they could haul seven tons of gasoline each trip instead of three tons in combat-ready B-29s. When Arnold demanded a further explanation, particularly about readiness of these B-29s for a combat mission, Wolfe assured him that they could be reequipped within a week. Furthermore, he told his boss, there wouldn't be any combat missions until fuel was stockpiled in China. Arnold was upset because Wolfe's comments completely negated the very essence of the Matterhorn plan.

By mid-May, Wolfe's plans for his first two missions called for 4,600 tons of fuel to be transported to China by the cargo planes, plus whatever the B-29s could bring. He informed Arnold that he could stage two strikes of 100 Superfortresses each with the first about June 20, and the second in July.

The Japanese upset his plans by their drives into eastern China. General Shunroku Hada had launched a strong ground offensive in April to capture the bases at Kweilin and Liuchow before they could be used to bomb the home islands of Japan. Although Wolfe had rejected these bases because of Stilwell's insistence on extensive ground-defense forces, and placed his forward B-29 bases in the Chengtu area, these eastern Chinese bases were used by Chennault's Fourteenth Air Force. Chennault had recommended their use originally for B-29s because the huge bombers would be within range of Kobe, Osaka, Tokyo, and most other major cities in Japan. Arnold had always doubted the Chinese could hold these forward bases, and now his assessment was proved valid. As the Japanese drove toward the Canton-Changsha railroad, Stilwell diverted some of the cargo tonnage previously guaranteed to the XX Bomber Command to the Fourteenth Air Force. The Joint Chiefs in Washington agreed because of the tactical emergency, but refused the Generalissimo's request, which Stilwell also endorsed, to turn the entire Matterhorn fuel stockpile over to Chennault. General Marshall, who replied for the Joint Chiefs, said that the early bombing of Japan would have a far more beneficial effect on the situation in China than the transfer of such stocks to Chennault.

Chinese troops never fought better than they did against the Japanese as they retreated to Hengyang and, with support from Chennault's fighters and bombers, held on for 49 days. The end was inevitable because they were so ill equipped, and August 8 Hada's army captured Changsha. In November, the Japanese captured the Kweilin and Liuchow fields and, before the drive was over, Nanning fell to the enemy. Wolfe's earlier decision to establish bases farther inland now paid off. Although the Japanese had made a successful drive into eastern China, it had no long-term effect on B-29 operations.

With the shortage of fuel in China, a mission out of the forward bases wasn't possible. Wolfe proposed a shakedown night mission to Bangkok, Thailand, and signed a field order for a mission on the 27th. His request was denied. Arnold insisted on a daylight, precision-bombing mission to give crews experience in the type of operations they would conduct later. Wolfe, knowing that crews averaged only two training hours under simulated combat conditions, postponed the strike until an intensive program of formation flying could be completed with bombing runs on the British Halliday Island range. Time didn't permit an extensive program but a limited number of formation training flights were flown, and some of the crews dropped their first practice bombs from a B-29. Pilots and navigators benefited by the experience of flying to China on fuel and supply missions, but this was inadequate training for other crew members.

Wolfe wired Washington that he would make a trial run against an enemy target June 5 to coincide with the D-Day landings in Europe. As it turned out, the mission was flown that date but, due to weather conditions, Eisenhower delayed D-Day to the following day. The Makasan railway shops at Bangkok were selected as the primary target because their destruction would seriously impede Japanese operations in north Burma. The shops at Insein had been damaged by the Tenth Air Force, and there had been a concerted campaign by this air force against rail communications in the area. Wolfe reminded Arnold that such a mission wouldn't cut into fuel stocks in China, and the 2,000-mile round trip would test the readiness of the command against a target that was not heavily defended. Secondary targets included the Malagan rail yards and the Central Station at Rangoon, Burma.

The Army Air Forces Proving Ground at Eglin, Florida, had been directed by Arnold's staff to run a simulated mission. Wolfe disregarded some of their recommendations because they conflicted with his own staff's views and reduced bomb loads to five tons, and increased fuel loads.

Although the maintenance departments had worked overtime to get 112 B-29s in commission by June 4, only 98 took off the following morning at dawn in a slight mist.

The early takeoff was considered necessary to avoid the higher ground temperatures later in the day, and to get the planes back in daylight. Tragedy struck quickly at Chakulia as Major John B. Keller's airplane crashed on takeoff killing all but one person.

En route, 14 others aborted the mission and returned to base. As the weather thickened crossing the Malay Peninsula, the ineffectual training of the command's crews was apparent. The mission was to be flown by four-plane elements in diamond formations but some B-29s went to the target alone, others joined the wrong formations, and chaos reigned supreme. There were repeated runs over the target as crews tried to line up, and runs were made from every direction so that the feeble opposition by nine Japanese fighters was nothing compared to B-29s on collision courses. Out of the 77 planes that released bombs, 48 were dropped by radar despite the fact that crews had been adequately trained for such bombing.

When the B-29s headed home, the weather worsened because this was the eve of the monsoon season. Mechanical problems multiplied as crews anxiously watched their fuel gauges. One plane ran short of gasoline after dropping its bombs and headed for Kunming, China, because it was the closest friendly area. Their engines started to run dry near Yuchi, 60 miles short of Kunming, and 10 crewmen hastily bailed out. They were greeted warmly by the Chinese and brought in by Captain Frank Mullen of the Air-Ground Aid Service.

Back in India, another Superfort crashed at the British Dum Dum base near Calcutta, two others ditched in the Bay of Bengal, and 30 B-29s landed on fields outside the command.

Captain J. N. Sanders' B-29 headed for Chittagong en route back. When his engines coughed in protest at their lack of fuel, he ditched in the sea. Within minutes, Spitfires from the Air-Sea Rescue Squadron were overhead and within 45 minutes motor launches picked up nine survivors from rafts. Two other crewmen were never found even though the B-29 incredibly floated ashore the next day.

Malfunctioning of the fuel-transfer system, a common problem at this stage, brought disaster to a crew from the 40th Group. The pilot and radio operator were killed when the pilot set the airplane down in a rough ditching. Ten others, one a nonmember of the crew, crawled or were blown out of the airplane when it exploded. Some were seriously burned but eight of them spent the night in two rafts. The next day, they picked up two buddies who had been supported only by their Mae Wests. Both were seriously wounded and one was so badly chewed by crabs that he was delirious. His companion, Sergeant W. W. Wiseman, kept his nonswimming comrade alive during a wild night of heavy seas through heroic personal efforts. Their ordeal didn't end with daylight because they had to spend another day and night at sea until they were washed ashore June 7 near the mouth of the Hooghly River. After some of the crewmen contacted natives, they were picked up by an Air-Sea Rescue PBY. All agreed that the wounded recovered because of the contents of a homemade survival kit designed by Lieutenant Louis M. Jones, the squadron intelligence officer, which carried supplies and drugs. The latter were sealed in rubber condoms. The ingenious kit was found to be more practical than the standard-issue kit.

Publicly, Arnold called the mission an operational success, but the loss of five B-29s and 15 dead crewmen with two missing hardly justified such a classification because only 18 bombs hit in the target area. A few bombs hit right on the aiming point but some were 10,000 feet from the target. With tongue in cheek, the command said the damage caused no appreciable decrease in the flow of troops and supplies to north Burma. It was not an auspicious beginning for the much-vaunted Superfortresses, and Arnold privately was not at all pleased with the results.

# CHAPTER 7
# Superforts Bomb Japan

The next day Wolfe received an urgent message from Arnold that the Joint Chiefs wanted an early mission against the Japanese homeland to help relieve the pressure of the Japanese drive into eastern China which was threatening Chennault's airfields. Such a mission, Arnold said, also was important because it was needed to coordinate with an important operation in the Pacific. Wolfe learned later that the latter was the invasion of the Marianas scheduled for mid-June.

After Wolfe was questioned about the number of aircraft he could commit to such a mission, he told Arnold that he would be unable to get more than 50 over a Kyushu target. He explained that he had delayed the first strike against Japan, now tentatively set for June 23, until the fuel stockpile at the Chengtu bases would support a hundred-plane mission.

Arnold insisted on June 15, indicating that an emergency existed, and demanded to know how many airplanes Wolfe could send on that date, or the 20th at the latest.

Wolfe was in a quandary. He tried to explain his problems by telling his boss that the Bangkok mission had diverted some Superfortresses from tanker operations, and Stilwell had appropriated B-29 fuel stocks normally carried by the Air Transport Command for Chennault's air force. Now, he said, gasoline supplies were too low for such a mission. Wolfe agreed to put 50 planes over the target June 15, or 55 on the 20th.

With growing impatience, Arnold insisted on at least 70 planes over Japan on June 15, saying that even greater transport efforts were needed, implying that Wolfe had been negligent in that respect.

Wolfe's immediate problem was to increase fuel stocks in China. Drastic economies were initiated in the forward area so that nothing but fuel was carried by B-29 tankers and cargo aircraft.

After the war, Chennault charged that members of the command airlifted unnecessary luxuries at the expense of gasoline and bombs. Such a charge was unfounded. Food was provided by the Chinese, and it was purchased in the area and supplemented only by packaged K rations that combat crews brought with them, and post exchange supplies were completely eliminated.

Despite strenuous efforts, it was quickly apparent that a 70-plane mission was impossible by June 15 unless drastic measures were taken and Arnold was so advised. Stocks became so low that transport planes in the forward area had to wait for gas to return to India. To help make up the deficit, Arnold reassigned the 2nd and 3rd Air Transport Squadrons to the bomber command, and Wolfe increased the number of B-29 tankers flying the Hump. Even the 312th Fighter Wing, assigned to defend B-29 bases, was placed on a dangerously low ration of fuel.

Lieutenant Leslie J. Sloan and his crew took off for India from their 468th base at Pengshan June 6 after off-loading fuel. Once they were at cruising altitude, they gazed in awe at the towering peaks that soared at dizzying angles while rivers chiseled their way through the mountains. They were over the upper reaches of the Yangtze River where the dreaded Lolo or Yi people, who had experienced little contact with civilization for thousands of years, inhabited the winding valleys miles above sea level. They lived in the wild mountain area between the provinces of Szechwan and Yunnan, and they were violently opposed to the Chinese.

Since they arrived in China crewmen had been intrigued by one legend that if a white man was captured he would become the father of the tribe's children.

Lieutenant Robert F. Casey left his flight engineer's panel momentarily and stood behind the pilot to get a better look. The currents of the rivers were so fierce he almost felt as if he could hear the thundering waters as they cascaded between wall-like cliffs and leaped into the misty reaches of canyons thousands of feet below the soaring peaks.

Shortly after he sat down before the engineer's panel, the airplane shook violently, and he and Sloan exchanged startled glances. They realized immediately they had blown a cylinder head on one of the engines. Hastily, Sloan tried to feather the "prop." It started to feather but then reversed itself. Someone yelled, "Fire," and now, to add to their troubles, an engine flared brightly and extinguishers failed to put the fire out. With the propeller refusing to feather, and acting like a brake on the airplane, they started to lose altitude.

At 22,000 feet, Sloan gave the order. "Bail out!"

Without panic, they exited the airplane—all but one gunner who for some reason didn't make it—and each left the airplane through his prescribed hatch.

Casey dropped through the nose-wheel opening and for the first time worried about the spare chute he was wearing. His regular parachute was being repacked at the base. He pulled the rip cord but it stuck. Somehow the tubing had been jammed through careless use and now the rip cord wouldn't fully pull out to release the parachute. Fortunately, they had bailed out 10,000 feet above the mountains but he was near panic as he took both hands and yanked mightily on the rip cord. This time it came loose and the parachute blossomed above him and his precipitous descent was slowed.

Tail gunner John Moore managed to get out of his tight quarters but his chest chute failed to open despite frantic efforts. Tumbling toward the earth, he clawed at the outer covering until it ripped open and then he pulled the chute out by hand.

Casey noticed one of the men streaking earthward, passing them on his rapid descent because one of the man's chute panels had torn. He learned later that gunner Virgil Bailey somehow survived his swift drop.

Casey watched the rocky ground coming up toward him with anxiety. A quick glance revealed that he was alone in that area. He hit hard but he was able to collapse his chute quickly to avoid being dragged across the rough terrain.

He spotted a group of rifle-carrying natives climbing toward him and his concern mounted as the Lolos made threatening gestures. When one motioned to his .45 automatic, he gave it up without argument.

They didn't all get rounded up until the second day when the natives brought the last man of the crew in.

Once Casey was over the initial shock of the bailout, he glanced at his rescuers noting they were a dark brown, and much darker, shorter, and stockier than the Chinese. Each wore a heavy cloak or robe of goat hair and it was obvious by their smell that water was something used only for drinking and cooking.

The Americans were housed with the chief in a rectangular thatch building coated with mud and divided into three parts: one for sleeping, another for cooking, and a living area in the middle. Entrance to the building was gained through a door in the middle.

They had bailed out in short-sleeve shirts and light pants and gave thanks to the squadron's flight surgeon who had insisted they fly with GI shoes.

Evidently in their honor, the chief ordered a goat to be brought in and he indicated that one of them should slit the animal's throat. The goat bleated in protest and none of them had the heart to use the knife thrust at them by the chief. One of the natives cut the goat's throat and caught the blood in a pan.

Two hours later they were invited to eat boiled goat but the smell turned them off. In part, they refused because they were still in shock and no one was particularly hungry. The next day hunger overcame repugnance and they ate the pot of goat to which chicken had been added.

As it grew dark the first night, a chill descended on the valley with its ever-present rain and fog. Some of the parachutes had been retrieved so they used them to cover themselves.

The next day, they noticed that the five-year-old son of the chief had a deformed arm. Apparently he had been thrown from a horse. Typically American, and with no other thought at the moment, they made a fuss over the young lad because he was a bright-eyed youngster with appealing ways. After that the chief personally took them under his protection and some of the hostility evaporated.

As one day followed another with no indication of when they would be returned to civilization, they became more and more disturbed. The Lolos, whom they learned later spoke a Tibeto-Burmese tongue, couldn't understand anything until the two groups devised recognizable hand signals. Each day the chief indicated they would leave the next day but, when that day came, they were put off again.

Casey managed to hide a ring and a watch in one of his pockets but everything else was taken. One crew member had a canteen hanging on his belt. A Lolo indicated that he wanted it but the gunner refused and started to walk away. Quick as a flash a 10-inch knife slashed the man's belt a fraction of an inch from his body and the canteen tumbled to the ground.

After almost two weeks, they were filthy and lousy with bugs so they decided to bathe in the nearby stream. The Lolos lined the bank in perplexity until the men removed their clothes and started to scrub themselves with sand. They roared with laughter as the "silly" Americans hurriedly cleaned themselves in the frigid air.

At last, the chief indicated they would leave the next day. He gave them a 12-inch plate filled with a black, gooey substance that they learned was raw opium. It was for barter with other tribes to pay their way out.

It was raining as they bid the chief good-bye and walked up a stream bed to the top of a mountain. There, below them, a meadow glistened in the morning sun. It was difficult walking but they hurried on their way, stopping the first night to sleep in an abandoned building.

Guides kept changing as they went from one village to another and the second night their opium was stolen. They walked through several small villages, with natives not of the Lolo tribe, and they were told that these villages often were raided by Lolos and their people taken into the mountains as slaves. They recalled seeing some of them near the chief's house who obviously were treated as slaves.

Once they arrived at walled villages, each of which had small standing armies of six to eight armed men, they felt more secure. The places were cleaner, and the food more to their liking. These people were familiar with Americans, and treated them well.

On July 4 they arrived at the home of a retired Chinese general. He welcomed them, saw that their clothes were cleaned, and they were given a magnificent banquet. For the first time, they felt they were back in civilization because they could communicate.

They arrived two days later at a trading post run by an Englishman. He fed them and put them on a river boat that took them to an American Air Force weather station. For the first time they were able to write letters home to tell of their experiences, and they went to Chengtu on the same plane that started their letters on their long journey to the States.

Their ordeal had lasted 28 days and, upon arrival in Chengtu, they were hospitalized two weeks to recover from the effects of their near-starvation diet. After a few days in bed, they were held for observation but were allowed to leave the hospital grounds. During this period the magistrate of Chengtu visited them, asking what he could do in the line of entertainment or otherwise. He offered to let them witness an execution. When they inquired if some criminal had to pay for his crimes, he said, "No," he'd just pick someone, saying they might enjoy such an unusual event. They declined hastily, trying not to show their revulsion.

The Imperial Iron and Steel Works at Yawata on the island of Kyushu had long had top priority among planners in Washington because it produced 24 percent of Japan's rolled steel. Although it was considered the most important target in Japan's steel industry, Chief of Staff Hansell thought the steel plant at Anshan, Manchuria, would be a better target because it was more vulnerable. He was overruled because the Joint Chiefs insisted on a mainland target that would coordinate with the invasion of Saipan.

Early in April the Joint Chiefs had adopted a target plan for early operations which included Japan's aircraft industry, its coke and steel plants, ships in harbors, and urban areas. At this stage, planners believed Superfortresses could best be used against coke and steel plants. They knew that the huge complex at Yawata was dependent upon its three coke plants, so the largest one was selected as the aiming point. As a compromise to those within the War and Navy departments who had been advocating plans for the destruction of petroleum refineries, such as the one at Palembang in Sumatra, the island of Ceylon was selected as the base for such an attack despite the enormous cost of preparing an airfield long enough for B-29 operations.

By imposing strict rationing of fuel in the forward area of China, and intensive efforts by B-29 tankers and cargo carriers, Wolfe committed his command to its first attack on the mainland of Japan.

His operations officers believed that B-29s could not fly to Yawata and back to China, a distance of some 3,200 statute miles, in formation, so with Arnold's concurrence, a night mission with planes bombing individually was scheduled, with each plane loaded with two tons of bombs. Wolfe realized that radar bombing was in its infancy so he ordered two pathfinder B-29s with special crews to take off a few minutes in advance of the other bombers to light up the target. Bombing altitudes were kept low despite the hundreds of guns around the target, hopefully to improve bombing accuracy. The first

Superforts would bomb from 8 to 10 thousand feet, he said, while the others were staggered at altitudes of 14,000 to 18,000 feet.

Wolfe asked Arnold's permission to lead the attack but his request was denied. Instead, Brigadier General LaVerne G. Saunders, 58th Wing Commander, and a veteran combat officer of the early days of fighting in the South Pacific, was the only general authorized to go of the eight who flew to China eagerly expecting to get the nod for this historic occasion and enhance their fitness file.

Superforts started leaving rear bases in India June 13 loaded with their first bombs for Japan, and their tanks were topped off in the cool of the early morning to get the last gallon of gasoline into them. The groups sent 92 B-29s on their way, but one plane and its crew was lost over the Hump. With those aborting and returning to their bases, only 79 reached China, and with the four already there, boosting the total to 83. The 40th Group's planes went to Hsinching, the 444th to Kwanghan, the 462nd to Kiunglai, and the 468th to Pengshan.

Late afternoon at 4:16 P.M. anxious eyes watched the pathfinders lumber down the long runways, bobbing up and down on the uneven surfaces, until they seemed almost to haul themselves reluctantly into the air at the end of the runways. Thundering after them at two-minute intervals, heavily laden bombers headed east until 75 had taken off. Such was the interest in the mission that eight war correspondents and three news photographers from major publications were on board to record the event. One bomber crashed on takeoff at Pengshan and seven others were unable to make it. Later, four B-29s turned back due to mechanical problems.

Bobby S. Roth, copilot of Major James W. Morris' 462nd plane "Hoodlum House," noticed there were few lights discernible as they droned through the night, and the countryside was just a blur below them. He still recalled the shock they had undergone as the map in the briefing room had slowly been unveiled with a string stretching out across the vast expanse of China, over the Yellow Sea, and to Japan. All he could think of was, "What the hell are we in for now?"

After leaving the China coast, Roth heard radar operator James G. Walmsley tell navigator Joseph Buchta that he could clearly see the demarcation line on his set marking the coastline. Later, with bombardier Burton L. "Woody" Wood joining the conversation, Walmsley said that Okina Island near Kyushu, their initial point of departure for a direct run at the target, was clearly visible on his scope. They were all relieved when the island was positively identified and a course correction was given by Buchta to Morris.

General Saunders' plane dropped its bombs at 11:38 P.M. Tokyo time, and his radio operator messaged the prearranged signal to command headquarters. In mocking imitation of the message the leader of the Japanese attack on Pearl Harbor sent to his carrier commanders, "Tora, Tora, Tora," Saunders used the words "Betty, Betty, Betty," indicating the target had been bombed. Betty, code name for the Yawata mission, was the first name of the wife of the command's intelligence chief, Colonel James Garcia.

With tension mounting, bombardier Burton L. Wood in Morris' plane peered down to spot fires the pathfinders should have set. He found Yawata blacked out with haze and smoke obscuring the city, so Woody let Walmsley release the bombs by radar.

With Japanese searchlights eerily probing the sky with long fingers of light, Morris dropped from their 8,000-foot altitude as antiaircraft guns found their range.

Sergeant Carrol D. Sigman searched the skies for enemy fighters. He had a ringside seat with his head thrust into the bubble at the central fire-control station, and he winced several times when impacts told all too clearly they had been hit.

Once away from Yawata, quiet returned and they were too exhausted to engage in much conversation.

On the ground, tail gunner Sergeant Ignacio Vaccaro was shocked to find two unexploded 20-mm shells lodged in his seat-pack parachute. If they had exploded, they might have torn the tail off the airplane.

Throughout the rest of Roth's combat tour in the CBI, and later in the Marianas where he served as an aircraft commander, Roth was almost unique among pilots because he never aborted a mission and his plane always hit the primary target.

Some crews over Yawata spotted explosions in the target area, or so they thought, and 15 planes tried to sight visually. Thirty-two crews had to rely upon radar, and 21 B-29s bombed other targets.

Sixteen Japanese fighters were reported but only three fired at the heavy bombers, scoring few hits.

The antiaircraft fire was heavy and, for those at the lower altitudes, the automatic weapons fire caused minor damage to six airplanes. The searchlights succeeded only in blurring the telescopes of the bombsights, and appeared to be of no help to Japanese gunners on the ground.

En route back, one entire crew was lost in a crash near Kiangyu. Two other Superfortresses were initially listed as missing, but it was learned later they had crashed, killing all on board, including *Newsweek* correspondent Robert Schenkel.

Only one B-29 was lost due to combat operations. Captain Robert Root had to make an emergency landing at a friendly Chinese airfield close to the battle lines. In the clear, he called for U.S. fighter cover while he and the Chinese tried to repair his B-29 to get it ready for flight. Unfortunately, the Japanese heard the call and sent their fighters and bombers to the scene where the B-29 was destroyed on the ground. Root's crew, with two injured, was rescued by a B-25 from Hsinching. Among those saved was Harry Zinder of *Time* magazine.

One of the B-29 photo-reconnaissance planes dispatched over the target after the mission was lost, bringing the total loss to seven planes and 55 airmen.

General Arnold was in London at a conference during the mission but received continuous reports. Despite the fact that damage to Yawata was insignificant, with only one hit on a power house 3,700 feet from the coke ovens, he was aware of the tremendous psychological impact on the Japanese people now that their home islands were no longer immune from attack. The war had been brought home to the Japanese for the first time, and there were beginnings of doubt among the more knowledgeable about Japan's invincibility.

The War Department issued a statement in Arnold's name saying, "This strike is the start of truly global aerial warfare." Also announced was the formation of the Twentieth Air Force, which had been kept secret until this propitious moment.

Despite the news from the Normandy beachhead, and the landings on Saipan the same day, headlines in Allied newspapers trumpeted the first bombing of Japan by the mighty Superfortresses. Officials of the Twentieth did their utmost to play down this first raid, knowing how little it had accomplished, but the news media used every adjective they could think of to play it up.

Wolfe's original estimate of 50 B-29s over Yawata came close to the actual 47 that bombed the primary target.

Chennault's Fourteenth Air Force had planned a diversionary raid against enemy airfields but it was canceled because of bad weather.

With B-29s clustered on their China bases, there was fear that Japanese bombers would retaliate. For some unexplained reason, they didn't take advantage of their vulnerability, which was fortunate because the 312th Fighter Wing's fuel supply had been cut drastically to get as many B-29s on the mission as possible. Now another 15,000 gallons of the fighter wing's limited supply had to be borrowed so the Superfortresses could return to their rear bases in India.

# CHAPTER 8

# An Incredible Journey

Arnold informed Wolfe two days after the Yawata mission that it was imperative to increase the pressure against Japan. In particular, he asked for a major daylight raid on an important steel plant at Anshan, Manchuria, several small raids against targets on the main Japanese islands, and a strike against the oil refinery at Palembang, Sumatra.

Wolfe's estimate of his command's mission capabilities in the near future was based on fuel stocks in the forward area, and he told Arnold they were very low and they couldn't possibly fly to Anshan until August. When Arnold protested, Wolfe said that if the Air Transport Command delivered 1,500 tons of fuel for the command in July he would schedule the Anshan mission for August 20. In regard to Arnold's call for a mission to Sumatra out of Ceylon, Wolfe had an easy out. Those fields wouldn't be completed for B-29 use until July 15 or later. Further, he said, if Arnold insisted on the Palembang mission, or the night raids to Japan, a large effort to Anshan would be impossible even in August.

Arnold was aware of the depleted fuel stocks in China but he didn't believe Wolfe and the bomber command were using the available C-46s and B-29 tankers to maximum advantage, and he insisted that Wolfe improve these operations.

Despite these shortcomings, Arnold directed Wolfe to prepare plans for bombing targets from one end of the Japanese empire to the other, with emphasis on the destruction of steel plants in Manchuria and Kyushu, and the major oil refinery at Palembang.

After Arnold returned from his trip to Europe, and saw by the reports from Kharagpur there were only 5,000 gallons of gasoline at the China bases, he used blunt language in demanding that Wolfe demonstrate immediate improvement of his operations. In a communication June 27 he ordered Wolfe to prepare for a series of missions, spelled out the number of B-29s he wanted sent on these missions, and gave him a choice of dates in July.

To add to Arnold's problems, he received word from General Chennault in China that he would no longer be responsible for defense of the Chengtu bases because fuel supplies for his fighter wing had been reduced below the safety minimum after they were diverted to the XX Bomber Command. General Stratemeyer was assigned to settle the problem. After some vitriolic exchanges, Arnold agreed to restore the monthly guarantee of 1,500 tons of fuel and supplies for the 312th Fighter Wing, and the XX Bomber Command relinquished its logistical responsibility for the fighters.

Arnold's problems with Wolfe were not so easily settled. When he ordered the command to send 15 B-29s to Japan in early July, and set up a major mission of 100 airplanes to Anshan between July 20 and 30, with another 50 Superfortresses to bomb the oil refinery at Palembang in August, Wolfe procrastinated, saying he would review the program and be back in touch.

In his own mind Wolfe was convinced that Arnold and the Washington staff of the Twentieth Air Force didn't understand the problems he faced in the Far East, particularly those of maintaining a new and untried airplane in the hot, humid climate of India. He wasn't proud of the in-commission rate, knowing it was far below the standards stateside, but he was aware that any comparison between the two was unrealistic, although he couldn't get this point across to Arnold.

Wolfe and his operations men reviewed Arnold's proposed missions and forwarded their own estimate of what would be needed to carry out these directives. He said he would need more B-29s and a guarantee that the Air Transport Command would commit itself to greater airlift of fuel and supplies. Arnold read these plans July 1 with growing impatience. When he saw that Wolfe would commit himself to only 50 or 60 airplanes for Anshan, instead of 100, even if all other requirements were met, Arnold decided he'd had enough. He sent orders removing Wolfe July 4, saying he had another important command assignment for him. Wolfe left two days later and

General Saunders, head of the 58th Wing, was named acting commander until a replacement could be made. In effect, it was a kick upstairs because Wolfe was given another star and named to head a reorganized Materiel Command where his excellent engineering background, and knowledge of the B-29 and its problems, would be put to better use.

Wolfe should never have been given the assignment to head the XX Bomber Command in the first place because he had no combat experience, but few of the old-timers that Arnold could draw upon had any either. Despite a thorough knowledge of the B-29, he seemed unable to use that background to make the B-29 the formidable operational weapon that it would soon become in more capable hands.

Months later, after Major General Curtis E. LeMay demonstrated what a potent weapon the airplane could be, Arnold told General Spaatz, "With all due respect to Wolfe he did his best, and he did a grand job, but LeMay's operations make Wolfe's seem very amateurish."

Through the use of 60 C-46 cargo planes, and B-29 tankers, sufficient fuel was airlifted to China for a mission July 7. Seventeen Superforts bombed a variety of targets, including the naval dockyards and an arsenal at Sasebo, the Akunoura Engine Works at Nagasaki, an aircraft factory at Omura, and steelworks at Yawata. About all that could be said for the mission was that it demonstrated that B-29s could attack at will anywhere over Kyushu. The damage at each of these places amounted to very little.

Back in Washington, the Joint Chiefs of Staff met July 11 to consider overall war plans for the defeat of Japan. It was their considered judgment that sea and air blockades of the home islands and massive air attacks would not in themselves guarantee an early surrender of Japan. They were in agreement that a sustained air attack, and the destruction of her naval and air forces, might conceivably force Japan to capitulate but at a much later date than was considered acceptable. Therefore, the Joint Chiefs approved an amphibious assault on Kyushu for October 1, 1945, with another attack on Honshu in the Tokyo area for late December. Again it was estimated that Japan could be defeated 18 months following the surrender of Germany. These plans were approved by Roosevelt, Churchill, and the Combined Chiefs at another Quebec conference in September 1944.

\* \* \*

Under Saunders, the command set a record in July for airlifting fuel and supplies to China, and for the first time approached the ideal of self-sufficiency that Wolfe had worked so hard to achieve. Arnold still wasn't satisfied, however, because the number of bombers dispatched on missions was only half the number he had expected.

Between May and the end of July gas consumption on a round trip was reduced appreciably, and the amount off-loaded from each plane in China rose from 495 to 1,326 gallons. Through precise scheduling, the command's statistical section helped crews to raise the amount of gasoline they could leave in the forward area to almost 2,500 gallons by the end of July. Some crews were more efficient in their cruise control than others and the worst ones burned 12 gallons for each one they delivered. Under the best of circumstances, the ratio was two for one.

During the early months, planes were sent along a northern or southern route according to weather predictions and the possibility of fighter attacks. When few fighters challenged the B-29s, with only seven contacts reported by crews by the end of July, a straighter and shorter route was flown up through the Assam Valley and over the Hump, bypassing Kunming. Although Japanese fighters were not a problem, the uncertain weather, primitive communications, and uncharted peaks that rose hundreds of feet above estimates on maps made flying hazardous so crews were given credit for combat time. They deserved it because they were flying under the most dangerous conditions of any place in the world. In the first four months of operations, 12 B-29s were lost over the Hump, mainly due to engine failure, plus six C-46s. Most crews were saved by Captain Frank Mullen and the men of the Air-Ground Aid Service, but there were harrowing tales by some crew members who were picked up by the Lolos and the fierce Naga warriors in the hills of Assam.

Despite Saunders' earlier misgivings about Arnold's insistence on a 100-plane mission to the Showa Steel Works at Anshan, Manchuria, he was able to schedule the mission for July 29. This time planes, not fuel, were the limiting factor because the command was down to 127 B-29s. To save the precious bombers for the mission, he eliminated all flights over the Hump to China for 10 days prior to D-Day. This was done for several reasons but mainly because of the increased danger of counterattacks against the exposed bombers on the

Chengtu-area strips. He had expected the Japanese to retaliate long before, and he still couldn't understand why they hadn't done so.

During the move to China, one B-29 crashed at Midnapore killing eight of its crew. With those out of commission at the rear bases, that left 107 in China available for the mission.

The Showa Steel Works at Anshan produced one third of the empire's metallurgical coke each year, so it was a vital target with top priority. With two tons of bombs in each airplane, Saunders believed they could destroy the battery of coke ovens that constituted the aiming point and cripple the entire operation for months.

The mission ran into difficulties at the start because the 444th at Kwanghan was unable to take off on time because a heavy rain the previous night had softened the surface of the runway. The other three groups got 72 out of 79 bombers off but one crashed shortly after takeoff and eight crewmen were killed.

En route, B-29s crossed the mountainous terrain of North China and crews marveled at the sight of the Great Wall sweeping serpentinely across hill and dale as far as the eye could see.

Mechanical troubles developed in 11 B-29s so they had to drop out of the four-plane formations before they reached the target in a valley surrounded by hills. Some, however, were able to bomb targets of opportunity.

At Anshan, the first formation hit a by-products plant near the aiming point and a thick pall of smoke spread over the plant, making it difficult for succeeding formations to synchronize on the aiming point. Fortunately, there was little fighter opposition and the flak, while heavy, was inaccurate.

Captain Robert T. Mill's crew was the exception to the general rule because flak knocked out his number two engine as he was pulling away from the target, and five Japanese fighters bore in on the straggler and shot another engine out. With the plane rapidly losing altitude, Mill gave the bailout order and eight of the crew did so but Mill failed to make it. Although the men parachuted into occupied China, with the aid of Chinese guerrillas they reached Chengtu a month later.

Another plane was forced to land at Ankang due to engine trouble and the plane stayed on the ground for five days while a new engine and spare parts were flown in. Chennault's fighters kept the Japanese away until the Superfort returned to Kiunglai August 3.

The 444th got off too late to take part in the Anshan mission so

16 planes went to Taku on Formosa and bombed without opposition.

The mission was beset with difficulties but it had its good points. Out of the 96 B-29s that took off, 80 bombed targets. The 60 that bombed the primary at Anshan caused substantial damage according to photos taken by reconnaissance aircraft. Arnold's confidence in the command was reaffirmed, believing that daylight, high-altitude missions against strategic targets could be made with acceptable losses.

Although only one Royal Air Force field was available for B-29 use at China Bay, Ceylon, Arnold pushed for an early date to bomb the refinery at Palembang and mine the Moesi River despite the fact that all groups would have to use the same field. Palembang had been approved as a top-priority target by the Combined Chiefs at the Cairo Conference. As a diversionary move, a small group of B-29s was scheduled to fire-bomb Nagasaki. Arnold believed that these targets, 3,000 miles apart, would demonstrate for the first time the versatility of Superfortresses.

At first, Arnold insisted on a daylight mission with 112 B-29s. Saunders argued against it because staging out of one field with that number of airplanes would be impossible. Arnold agreed reluctantly to Saunders' proposal of a dawn or dusk attack by at least 50 airplanes.

After details were worked out it was decided to make the mission against the Pladjoe Refinery a night-radar attack, while other B-29s mined the Moesi River, which was used to transport the refinery's products. The British not only agreed to turn the Ceylon base over to the Americans, including the whiskey rations, but to provide the fuel for the mission.

Twentieth Air Force planners in Washington knew that the refinery was of great strategic value, producing 22 percent of Japan's fuel oil and 78 percent of its aviation gasoline, but many planners were against the mission because Japan had lost so many of its tankers that the strategic importance of the target was lessened. Aviation gasoline, in particular, no longer could be transported in quantity to Japan because of the shortage of tankers. By now, United States Navy submarines dominated the sea-lanes in the South Pacific, and the chances of a tanker sneaking through a net of American subs was slim.

Superfortresses started arriving at China Bay August 9. Each of the 56 was parked in the order it would use on takeoff because the 7,200-foot runway was too crowded for maneuvering later.

Late that afternoon, Major Thomas R. Vaucher of the 462nd Group joined aircraft commanders in a special briefing. Such a briefing was unusual, and he soon learned why. When the crews departed India they were not told where they were going other than they would be based temporarily at China Bay, Ceylon. Vaucher listened carefully as the group's operations officer, Lieutenant Colonel Donald A. Roush, explained the importance of the mission to the total war effort in the Pacific, and how it was the start of a large B-29 mine-laying campaign. He jerked to attention when Roush said, "General Arnold is prepared to sacrifice every B-29 on the mission to achieve success."

Almost in disbelief, he heard Roush explain that the round trip of almost 4,000 miles was expected to be beyond the capabilities of the B-29 so the British had positioned destroyers and a cruiser 600 miles from Ceylon along their return route. "When you reach them," Roush said, "you should know whether you have fuel enough to make it all the way. If not, ditch near the ships and you'll be picked up."

In conclusion, they were told that it was vital to make sure that each crew member had his papers in order such as last will and testament, insurance, etc. The gravity of the mission was brought home by these words more than anything else.

The 462nd Group was assigned the job of mining the Moesi River. Its bombardiers were briefed long before they left Piardoba because they were unfamiliar with the 1,000-pound aerial mines they would drop. Lieutenant Commander Kenneth L. Veth of the United States Navy patiently explained the inner workings of the mines, how they were to be set, and that mines had to be dropped at least 400 feet apart so detonation of one wouldn't set off another. He described in detail how the mines were to be dropped by drag chute from altitudes below 1,000 feet.

That night all crew members were briefed, although they were not told that the mission might be a one-way affair. Still the briefers didn't minimize the risks and there were sober glances and a hush throughout the briefing room. They were told that while the 462nd mined the Moesi River, the other groups would attack the Pladjoe Refinery. This attack, they were advised, was to draw attention away from the mine laying. Such an attack, it was hoped, would distract the Japanese so they wouldn't know the river was being mined, and not learn about it until ships were blown up.

For the strike against the refinery, 42 aircraft were assigned to attack it from high altitude, while 14 B-29s from the 462nd Group came in low, following the contours of the river, and dropped two mines from each aircraft. Bombardier-navigators were told that the bombsight wouldn't be required at that low altitude and the mines would be positioned by the navigator using radar, or dropped by the bombardier visually. Each aircraft was assigned specific points on the river to place their two mines.

The flight plan called for the longest mission ever flown by the B-29s. As it turned out, it was even longer for the mine-laying Superfortresses because they had to climb to over 12,000 feet to get over the mountains, descend to the target at sea level, and then climb back up to their original altitude to get back.

The following day the crews were given a final briefing. A Dutch ship captain, who had piloted the Moesi hundreds of times prior to the war, was flown in to offer assistance. He described the river's navigation lights, where they were placed, and what their positions meant. In remarkable detail, he described every bend in the river, explaining that the coded lights were placed so one could determine his precise position on the river. In other words, he said the lights were coded so that a person could determine whether he was three miles, five miles, or any specific distance up the river from the mouth. When he was asked if he thought the Japanese might have changed the system of lights, he was frank in saying he didn't know. He did pick out specific bends in the river that, if a ship were sunk there, would cause the greatest disruption of traffic. He was so precise in his description of the lights that he advised Vaucher's crew to fly to light 10 and then count three more lights, and they would find a bend in the river. Then, he said, "Fly one more light and drop your first mine."

At first, while Vaucher made notes, he thought the captain's description rather farfetched but he had to admit the captain seemed to know the river's every turn. It had been over three years, however, since the Japanese had taken over and Vaucher found it difficult to believe that the Japanese hadn't changed the lights, or at least altered the code.

At 4:45 that afternoon Colonel Richard Carmichael, group commander of the 462nd, took the first B-29 off. With him were the plane's regular pilot, Major Conrad Kollander, who sat in the copilot's seat; Major Edward A. Perry, group navigator; Lieutenant James Bell, bombardier; and Commander Veth as observer.*

Despite the crowded runway, all 54 B-29s were off in 84 minutes although two soon aborted. One fixed a leaky engine and took off again.

Vaucher's airplane didn't seem to have any lift as it roared down the runway, and when he pulled back on the yoke the airplane refused to leave the ground. He couldn't understand the problem although he knew this was the heaviest weight they had ever attempted to lift in a B-29. He was now beyond the point of no return and he had to keep going. A quick glance out the window brought instant recognition of the problem. The small runway flags were all flying with him, instead of against the airplane. The wind had changed so now there was no helpful lift from a normal head wind. He was quickly running out of runway and when he got to the end he pulled back on the wheel. Still the plane hugged the ground and he used up the remaining surface beyond the runway until he was over the ocean. He couldn't believe it! The airplane was flying just when he had expected it to plow into the ocean. He was just skimming the surface, and when he tried to climb, the airplane refused to go up another foot. He used every bit of wisdom and skill he had gained in hundreds of hours of flying four-engine bombers just to keep the airplane in the air. For three miles he held the plane just off the water, struggling to gain just a few feet to give them a slight margin of safety, but the airplane refused to cooperate.

The navigator, Lieutenant Michael P. Egan, stood between Vaucher and his copilot, Ralph Todd. Right in the worst of Vaucher's struggle to keep the airplane flying, he felt a hand rest lightly on his shoulder and heard the words, "God be with you." Vaucher was so tense that he almost jumped out of his seat. For a second, he actually thought it was God speaking. For "Mike" Egan, a slim, blue-eyed Irishman and former divinity student, the words came naturally in this moment of peril.

One of the side gunners called Vaucher. "Skipper, can't you pull up just a little bit? There's spray coming in back here from the props."

* A painting in honor of Carmichael's flight hangs in the Pacific War Museum of the Admiral Nimitz Center at Fredericksburg, Texas.

Vaucher didn't reply. He only wished he could gain just a few feet. Then, dead ahead, a tiny island appeared. He didn't dare bank around it, flying as they were just above the wave tops. He sat helplessly as they bore down on this spit of land out in the Indian Ocean. As they got close to land the airplane rose all by itself, flew up and over the island, gaining altitude all the time as Vaucher gaped in astonishment. Years later, he learned it was a condition called ground effect, about which they knew nothing in those days. The compression of air between the land and the airplane's wing helped to lift the bomber higher into the air.

Vaucher's problems were still not over because he had to fly the next 500 miles manually at an average altitude of 1,000 feet. The tension of the last few hours brought on a splitting headache and he was in agony.

Two hours from Sumatra, Flight Engineer William M. Boyer informed Vaucher that his calculations showed they not only didn't have enough gasoline to get back to Ceylon, but they wouldn't even have enough to get back to the British ships!

Vaucher stared at him in disbelief, his head throbbing worse than ever. Their calculations couldn't be that far off! Boyer solemnly assured him that he had checked the figures carefully and there could be no mistake. Vaucher felt so miserable that he couldn't concentrate on the figures. He had to make a decision whether to abort the mission or go on for what truly might be a suicide mission for all of them. "If I could only think clearly," he thought, but his splitting headache made that impossible. He decided to take a short nap and turned the controls over to copilot Todd.

After 30 minutes, he woke up refreshed, and mercifully the headache was gone. He went over Boyer's cruise-control figures and found that his flight engineer had made a mathematical error. He was sure now they could go on to the target and at least get back to the ships. He elected to go on and so informed the crew.

Boyer felt miserable. Vaucher said nothing in rebuke, knowing the young and inexperienced flight engineer had suffered enough, even though he had scared him half out of his wits.

Judging their route by radar vectors off the Sumatran mountain peaks, Vaucher climbed to 12,000 feet until they passed over the mountains and, knowing they would be short on gas, he went through a pass despite the cloudiness. Then he let down on the other side over the ocean and broke out of cloud cover at 1,500 feet just as a full moon rose in the east. And there before them was the mouth of the river just as the Dutch ship captain had described it. It seemed a miracle but Vaucher knew it was due to Egan's superb navigation that they had broken out of the clouds just where they were supposed to be. From then on, everything unfolded just as the captain said it would. The lights were on along the sprawling, 500-foot-wide tropical river surrounded by dense jungles. They found light 10, and as Vaucher maneuvered the B-29 up the river at 500 feet, Ray Stone and Mike Egan counted three more lights, and sure enough there was the bend in the river. Vaucher saw one ship but he swerved around it. Up until now they had been unopposed. Now orange tracers sparkled eerily as they streamed from the river's bank as a machine gun opened fire. Then there was the next light and bombardier Stone dropped his first mine. Later, in precisely the spot where it was supposed to be, the second mine was hurtled riverward with its drag chute trailing behind.

It was time to get out and Vaucher climbed rapidly away from the river, on up and over Sumatra's spine, and they were on their way. It had all been so easy, or perhaps it seemed so after the harrowing experiences they had undergone on their way to the target area.

After the attack on the refinery, Japanese defenses were fully alerted and fighters were dispatched. With other B-29s in the area, Vaucher cautioned the crew to make certain before they fired. The gunners were edgy, ready to shoot at anything as they flew in and out of the clouds. Once or twice Vaucher had to admonish them because he was sure they were shooting at B-29s in their fear of that dark void outside their windows.

Finally, they were miles away from the island and headed for the British ships along their route back to Ceylon. Vaucher called one of the gunners amidships but they were all asleep. This often happened on a long flight, and Vaucher thought the plane could blow up and most of the crew wouldn't know what happened to them.

Vaucher was jolted to attention when Boyer yelled, "Fire in number three!"

The propeller was quickly feathered, and fortunately the fire went out. Vaucher studied the cruise-control curves. According to them a B-29 should use more fuel on three engines than on four. "If that's true," he thought, "we have little chance of making it to Ceylon." He lowered mixture levels thoughtfully as they headed west.

Later, they spotted the British cruiser. Now Vaucher had to reach a decision. Unbelievably, the fuel gauges indicated they had enough gasoline to make it back to Ceylon. He decided that if they ran out of fuel, he'd have to ditch near Ceylon, and that seemed preferable to ditching in the middle of the Indian Ocean. Without signaling the cruiser, he decided to go on.

Just as he was hopeful they could make it all the way, an engine sputtered 10 miles from Ceylon, and Boyer quickly transferred gas to it. Vaucher watched anxiously as Boyer methodically played his switchboard like a piano, transferring fuel from one tank to another each time an engine faltered for lack of gas. With tanks down to their last gallons, Vaucher greased the Superfortress into the field and their incredible journey of 4,030 miles in almost 19 hours was over.

The mission taught Vaucher several important lessons. He realized how primitive their cruise-control techniques were, and that the B-29 if properly flown could fly farther than anyone imagined. Also, he was convinced that the Superfort actually could fly farther on three engines than four once its bomb load was released to reduce the gross weight.

After Vaucher surveyed the burned engine, which was full of white powder because the magnesium accessory housing had burned, he believed it was just dumb luck that the airplane hadn't been destroyed, and the crew with it.

When a new engine was delivered, Vaucher and his crew changed the burned-out engine amid snide remarks by British officers about American officers working as grease monkeys. Vaucher was amused, realizing such work was unthinkable for officers of the Royal Air Force.

Only eight planes dropped mines but none was lost. Twelve B-29s failed to find any target but 39 others did. Colonel Carmichael's plane was one of those that dropped its mines. It was the first to take off and last to get back, flying 18 hours and 54 minutes.

There were 37 fighter attacks, and some Japanese followed the bombers 350 miles out to sea. Only one B-29 was forced to ditch, and the crew, minus a gunner who was killed in the ditching, was picked up 90 miles from China Bay.

Arnold declared the mission an operational success, although at the time it was reported that only one small building in the refinery was destroyed. After the war, it was learned that three ships were sunk in the Moesi River, and four damaged by the 16 mines laid by the 462nd Group. Most importantly, oil shipments were delayed a month before the channel could be cleared of mines. Although there were many long B-29 missions before the war ended, the journey to Palembang turned out to be the longest nonstop bombing or mining mission ever attempted by the Twentieth Air Force.

Three thousand miles away, a small number of B-29s raided Nagasaki with fire bombs. Saunders picked shipyards and military installations as targets because they were close together. He also selected the docks at Hankow in occupied China as a last-resort target because Chennault had been pressuring him to hit key points in the Japanese supply network.

The 24 B-29s that bombed Nagasaki did little damage. Technical Sergeant H. C. Edwards got the command's first official kill when he shot down a Japanese fighter with his tail guns.

Stanley Brown's crew had a hair-raising time when their plane got lost and, almost out of gas, landed close to the front lines in China. When the plane bogged down in mud at the end of a field, Japanese fighters poured shells into it and knocked out two engines. After the 312th Fighter Wing was alerted, air cover was provided while parts and mechanics were flown in and American fighters shot down three enemy fighters.

Once the B-29 was repaired, it was stripped of all unnecessary equipment, jacked up out of the mud, and moved slowly across a makeshift runway created by sinking 4,500 railroad ties in soft spots. With a minimum of four crewmen, the airplane flew out August 23 to its base at Kiunglai.

# CHAPTER 9

# LeMay Takes Over

The deteriorating tactical situation in South China, as the Japanese forced back Stilwell's Chinese divisions, caused Arnold increasing concern. When Chennault insisted upon heavy assaults against Hankow and Wuchang, Arnold faced a difficult decision. Saunders had bucked the problem to him because he didn't feel he should pass judgment on Chennault's request. He told his boss that such an expenditure of gasoline and bombs to assist a purely local situation would prevent his command from carrying out its express orders for the strategic bombing of Japan. Chennault's request was denied.

On August 10, the day B-29s were sent to Palembang, Chennault pressed his case, demanding that B-29s be used in China or be withdrawn to another theater. Arnold, ever suspicious of Chennault's motives, sent Stratemeyer to Fourteenth Air Force Headquarters. As Stratemeyer told Arnold later, Chennault was trying to save his own supplies while attempting to force the XX Bomber Command to use up its supplies for tactical-support missions. Again, Chennault's requests were denied because such a diversion of B-29 operations would disrupt more vital missions, and he was reminded that he had his own bombers to use for such missions.

Chiang Kai-shek had insisted from the start that the China bases be operated by Chennault, so about 14 Fourteenth Air Force personnel were placed on each base ostensibly to run them. LeMay put his own men on the bases to supervise them and gave them specific orders that Chennault's people were not to get in their hair. In effect, LeMay ignored Chennault and told his officers, "Don't pay a damn bit of attention to Chennault and his people." He conceded later that Chennault's men did make a contribution, particularly in smoothing relations with the Chinese, who really ran the bases.

Chennault's basic fault was his limited ability to organize large operations, and this led to his removal before the war ended. Arnold had long been considering a change in China and he wrote to Wedemeyer June 17, 1945, saying that what was needed in China was a "senior, experienced air officer in whom both you and I have confidence. General Chennault has been in China for a long period of time fighting a defensive air war with minimum resources. The meagerness of supplies and the resulting guerrilla type of warfare must change to a modern type of striking, offensive air power. I firmly believe that the quickest and most effective way to change air warfare in your Theater, employing modern offensive thought, tactics and techniques is to change commanders. I would appreciate your concurrence in General Chennault's early withdrawal from the China Theater. He should take advantage of the retirement privileges now available to physically disqualified officers that make their pay not subject to Income Tax. Otherwise he may be reduced and put back on the retired list at his permanent rank."

General Marshall had assumed for weeks that Stratemeyer had taken command because he had been promoted with that in mind. He also asked Wedemeyer to be brought up to date. Wedemeyer wrote Marshall three days later that he agreed with Arnold's recommendation for reorganization of his air forces, and that Stratemeyer would command the China Theater Air Forces.

Chennault objected strongly and delayed his request for retirement status until July 6. He was replaced as head of the Fourteenth Air Force by Major General Charles B. Stone.

LeMay met Chennault only once, and considered him a fine air officer who did a remarkable job with what he had to work with in China. He told intimates, "The good Lord himself couldn't have done a very good job over there."

Meanwhile, in August of 1944, Saunders argued with Twentieth headquarters in Washington about future missions. Arnold's staff now wanted to attack aircraft plants, and to cease further attacks on steel plants. Saunders objected, not because he didn't understand the strategic importance of aircraft plants, but because he wanted to finish off the steel plants at Anshan and Yawata before taking on another assignment. Arnold backed him up.

Just when Saunders felt he had resolved his problems with Arnold's staff in Washington, he was asked to consider use of the B-29 as a night bomber exclusively. There were times like these when he wished some of the headquarters staff would get out into the field and learn the real world of B-29 operations. As justification, they told him, crews hadn't been able to make effective attacks at long range while flying in formation on daylight missions. And, they reasoned, heavier bomb loads dropped at night by radar would be far more effective than lighter loads from high altitudes during daylight operations. Saunders was aware, and tried to get the point across, that radar bombing was in its infancy, and to date had not been satisfactory.

There were other arguments that Saunders should increase the number of converted B-29s as full tankers so he could send a greater number of aircraft on a mission. All well and good, he argued, but you're not sending me an adequate number of replacement airplanes as it is.

After a report was released in Washington, along with reconnaissance photographs of the July raid on Anshan, Saunders' case was strengthened because they showed more damage than had been expected.

The first of many changes occurred in the first week of August as Colonel Engler, commander of the 468th Group, was transferred to bomber command as deputy chief of operations. To replace him, Saunders put Colonel Ted S. Faulkner in command of the group with Lieutenant Colonel James V. Edmundson as deputy. The two complemented one another. Faulkner was a rugged personality—a no-nonsense officer—and Edmundson was a quietly efficient, always smiling, popular officer. Colonel William H. Blanchard took command of the 40th Group August 4, replacing Colonel Leonard F. Harman, who was promoted to another job.

Saunders' permission to make the first daylight attack on the Imperial Iron and Steel Works at Yawata was approved in Washington. He proposed a high-altitude attack and, because of the distance, and the fact they were still experimenting with cruise control, he set a one-ton bombload minimum with the more efficient crews permitted to carry more.

There were 98 B-29s in China ready to take off August 20, after one Superfort was lost en route from India. For three groups the takeoff for Yawata was routine, but the eighth plane at Kiunglai crashed, effectively blocking the end of the runway. For the time being, the rest of the 462nd's planes were grounded. By afternoon, eight more planes managed to get off the ground after gross weights were reduced, and they joined five other early returns from other groups and went to Yawata at night.

The daylight groups ran into intense flak, and persistent fighter attacks. Three Superforts were destroyed, two by the first case of ramming reported in the command, and one by a combination of aerial bombing and gunfire. In the ramming incident, a Nick fighter came in level from 12 o'clock, banked sharply toward them, and drove its wing vertically into the outboard wing of a B-29. This Fort was flying outboard in a four-plane diamond formation and, when the fighter and the bomber disintegrated, the fourth bomber was showered with debris and sent spinning to earth. Intensity of the attacks could be gauged by the reported claims of 17 destroyed, 13 probables, and 12 Japanese fighters damaged—claims that were not supported by postwar interrogation.

The plane flown by Colonel Richard H. Carmichael, group commander of the 462nd, was shot down after it dropped its bombs, and crash-landed on Iki Island. The crew included Group Navigator Major Edward A. Perry, Wing Bombardier Major Harold J. Mann, and Group Gunnery Officer Captain Chester E. Tims. Tims was wounded by shrapnel before he bailed out and his parachute failed to open. Copilot Lieutenant Carl A. Skedsvold was strafed by Japanese fighters as he floated to earth and his body was riddled. He and Tims were buried on Iki Island. Radio Operator Sergeant Remick Wallace evidently stayed at his set too long trying to contact an American submarine and failed to leave the airplane.

Carmichael and the others ended up as prisoners of war, emerging at the end so emaciated and ill that it was a miracle they survived. Carmichael, along with other officers, was held in solitary confinement for six months. They were kept in small cages where they couldn't sit up or stretch out. Some officers lost their minds because of the horrible treatment in which they were beaten almost to death. With indomitable courage, Carmichael refused to let his tormenters destroy him. After the fire raids on Tokyo, Carmichael was one of those who was forced to carry the "honey" buckets containing human waste through the streets of the capital. Before he was shot down, he was a 220-pound, raw-boned Texan without an ounce of fat. After release, his weight was down to 140 pounds. He hadn't lost his sense of humor. He said he was proud that during his "honey" bucket period he never spilled a drop.

Carmichael was replaced by his deputy, Colonel Alfred F. Kalberer, a veteran of 40 missions in the Near East who had volunteered to return to a combat theater. He was one of the truly outstanding pilots of the early years of aviation with over 18,000 flying hours.

Ten B-29s bombed Yawata that night, reporting hits on two coke ovens. Actually, little damage was caused, and the command's losses were severe. In addition to the three B-29s that were shot down over Yawata, 10 others were lost to a variety of causes and 95 airmen were either dead or missing. One crew bailed out near Khabarovsk, Russia. This was the second instance of a damaged Superfort seeking the sanctuary of a so-called friendly nation because an earlier plane had been forced down by Soviet fighters near Vladivostok. Before the year ended, two more B-29s ended up at Russian bases, the planes were impounded, and the crews interned. Later, after the U.S. Embassy in Moscow protested, the crews were allowed to escape via Tehran. The B-29s were kept, however, and after the war served as models for a Red Air Force bomber known as the TU-70. In many respects, it was faithfully reproduced, including all the B-29 defects of that period, much to the amusement of Air Force officials after the war.

Following the Yawata mission, which gave crews a foretaste of rougher opposition in the months ahead, there were more than the usual furtive departures to the rice paddies around the perimeter of the bases. There, while young "Rice Paddie Hatties" relieved some of the tension of eager airmen, their mothers picked GI pockets while they were otherwise engaged. As the venereal disease rate rose, some base commanders made plans to import young girls, place them in secluded houses where they would have contact only with Americans, and be checked regularly by doctors. The command chaplain, a strict Catholic, put a stop to such plans and became, for many airmen, the most unpopular officer in China.

One enterprising Chinese businessman, brother-in-law of the local commander, set up wine shops near each base. Each was located between the hostel or quarters area and the airfield, but outside the base itself, so the determined efforts of the base commanders to stop the practice of a few snorts or more of orange whiskey or rice wine en route to the flight lines came to naught.

The next scheduled flight to Anshan was postponed twice. Once because of Chennault's fear that the Japanese would attack the Chengtu fields, and the second time because of bad weather. Saunders finally set the date for September 8, the day that Major General Curtis E. LeMay was scheduled to take over the command. The dark, heavyset LeMay had left England three weeks after D-Day and spent a few days in Washington before going on a short leave. He was told that he would replace Wolfe as head of the XX Bomber Command. Arnold gave him no special instructions, merely saying, "Get out there and get to work."

Later, he went to Grand Island, Nebraska, to check out in the B-29. He didn't particularly like the airplane after he flew it the first time because it was heavier and clumsier than other bombers he had flown. He thought it handled more like a truck than an automobile and, like many another pilot before him, initially he had trouble getting lined up to land sighting through the "bird cage" as he called the cockpit enclosure. After he got used to the airplane, he found it was a pretty good flying machine. What he appreciated most was its range and its large payload.

After about a month or so in the States, he went to India. He had argued with officials in Washington about flying missions with his new command, but Arnold was adamant. He could fly one mission, and that was all. Personally, he thought such a restriction was kind of silly, but he'd fought that battle in England. After he had flown eight missions against Germany, he was told that group commanders could no longer fly combat. He learned the reason later. Somebody had found out that the British had lost a lot of their commanders early in the war, and Arnold didn't want that to happen to the U.S. Air Forces because there were so few qualified commanders to begin with. LeMay protested that such a restriction was no good, saying, "You can't have a fighting organization in which the commander doesn't fly combat missions." He made it clear that he didn't believe the commander should fly every mission with his unit, but that he should fly enough to know what's going on and, particularly, that the commander should lead some of the tough ones so he would know what he was talking about.

Now that he was restricted to one mission, he picked the one to

Anshan because Intelligence told him the best fighter outfit in the whole area was at Anshan and he was particularly anxious to see firsthand how efficient the Japanese fighters were against the Superfortresses.

One of Saunders' last official acts was to award the 468th Group the General "Billy" Mitchell Flag in recognition that this group, on three occasions, had proved its superiority over all other groups in combat and cargo operations.

The day LeMay was assigned as commanding general of the XX Bomber Command, General Hansell was appointed to head the new XXI Bomber Command at Salina, Kansas. It wasn't until October 12, 1944, that "Joltin' Josie, the Pacific Pioneer" led the vanguard of 73rd Wing B-29s to Saipan in the Marianas. Meanwhile, the 58th Wing in India and China carried on the only operations of the Twentieth Air Force.

Arnold had been pressing Saunders to get more B-29s over targets for weeks, so for Anshan Saunders told him that he would dispatch every B-29 in commission. When they took off September 8, 108 got away, leaving seven on the ground, and 95 reached the target at Anshan. For a change, the weather was perfect and 200 tons of bombs were dropped by 90 Superfortresses. Crews welcomed the ineffective antiaircraft fire, and the fact the fighters didn't bore in with their customary aggressiveness. For such an effort, there were losses of four planes.

LeMay studied the tactics of Japanese fighters over Anshan with keen interest because his evaluation of their relative effectiveness would be crucial to a number of changes in combat strategy he planned for the future. He thought the flak was accurate over the target, and his B-29 was chewed up a bit although no airplanes were lost.

Back at base, he told Saunders that the efforts of Japanese fighters were "stinkin'. They were up there, in position to make a beautiful attack on us, and then turned the wrong way! Only one guy got a fleeting shot but the rest of them never could catch up."

He told Saunders, "My first impression about Japanese fighters is that they won't be as tough as the Germans."

LeMay and Saunders viewed the strike photographs with interest. They listened as target specialists said they believed that three of the 16 coke ovens would be out of service for a year, and another three for at least six months. Some of the other ovens sustained damage and a by-products plant was destroyed. The generals were told that the two attacks probably had cost the Showa plant 35 percent of its coking output. When LeMay asked what such a loss would mean to Japan's rolled-steel production, he was told that it probably would be reduced by over 9 percent.

Tired crews at Hsinching were rousted out of bed shortly before midnight by Japanese bombers. Chennault's fighters were helpless because they couldn't fly at night, and there were no night fighters at this time. Damage was slight, with one Superfortress and a C-46 sustaining minor damage.

LeMay was not impressed by the way the mission to Anshan was run, calling it amateurish and ineffectual. He told group commanders that he was grounding the command until crews were completely retrained.

In regard to the Bomber Command staff, he wasn't critical but he made it clear that he wasn't at all satisfied with what they'd accomplished. He knew there were many good people on the staff, but it was obvious to him that changes were needed. He told them, "You're just getting your feet wet over here. I've had my feet wet, and this is what we learned by seeing a lot of people get killed. Now, here's what we're going to do."

There was some grumbling but he quickly stamped that out and insisted they run operations the way he had learned in Europe was the way to fight. Although he was stern when it came to opposition, he told them, "None of us knew what we were doing at the start of this war, and we've had to learn as we went along. I'm going to tell you some things that you'd learn the hard way by yourselves over a long period of time.

"When we went to war the Army Air Corps was a complete rabble of inexperienced people. In 1942, I was given command of the 305th Group which wasn't a combat outfit but just a bunch of individuals. We didn't even have a cadre of experienced people to train the rest of the outfit. My group adjutant was a former master sergeant who had been promoted to major. The engineering officer had been a tech sergeant on a B-17 line. My ordnance officer had been a Marine corporal who knew something about machine guns and that was all.

"The pilots came right out of single-engine school. Only three of us in the group had flown a B-17 and we checked out all the pilots.

At that time, there were only three airplanes in the group for 35 crews.

"Of course, crew members straggled in over months. I got the navigators two weeks before we went overseas. Most of them saw an ocean the first time they navigated across it. The bombardiers had never dropped any bombs. Oh, they'd dropped some practice bombs on a circle out in the desert they could see for miles, but they'd never dropped a real bomb, and they'd never had any practice against real targets. The gunners supposedly had been to gunnery school but they didn't have anything to fly so guns were mounted on a truck and they'd shoot from that. I gave them a ride in a B-17 before we went overseas so they could shoot at a target as we flew across the desert at a hundred feet.

"That was it. That's what we went to war with. They were not only a rabble but I didn't have any confidence in their commander— me! I had never commanded anything. I did command a squadron for two months that had no airplanes and only half its people.

"The first day in England I got a formation up. It was a complete debacle because we'd never had bombers to practice with.

"The next day, I flew in the top turret of the lead bomber and tried to get them to fly as close as they could for protection over a target.

"The third time we flew we headed across the channel on our first bombing mission. This is the type of unit I went into combat with."

The staff listened with amazement as he candidly told of his experiences. They had never heard a general speak with such frankness, and found it refreshing.

LeMay warmed to his subject once he had their attention. "I know what you're going through. You've had to learn the business as you went along, and get the airplanes combat ready despite all kinds of mechanical problems. It will be a tremendous job to get a few bombs on targets in Japan from here and the main burden will fall not on the fliers, but on the maintenance crews on the ground.

"Your pilots have more flying time possibly than most pilots sent to combat but most of them came right out of the training command and all they've done is teach others to fly. Until they are combat trained, they'll be about as useful here as Boy Scouts.

"Even K. B. Wolfe hadn't been in combat before. As an engineering officer he was a good one but he spent most of his Army career at Wright Field supervising the building of airplanes. He really knew his stuff and did a remarkable job of getting that airplane into combat as soon as he did. Of course, it wasn't ready but just to get it that far was an achievement, but as a combat commander he knew nothing.

"He was in the same position as when I went out. I knew nothing, either. So, you don't have a fighting outfit over here. I know that. From now on, we're going to bomb in formation and drop on a leader. I learned in England that you pick some level-headed guy who knows what he's doing, and is able to find the right target, and put the bombload down where it's supposed to be. I was most successful over there because I picked people who were more capable of doing the job and gave them extra training as lead crews."

Later, in a meeting with group commanders, he told them he had brought specialists from the Eighth Air Force who would conduct a school for lead crews. He told each group commander to select six of his best crews, a number that later was increased to eight, and send them to Dudhkundi for an 11-day course in bombing techniques and formation flying.

When he told them he was abandoning the previous four-plane diamond formation for a 12-plane formation like those used in the European theater, a few of the braver colonels voiced objections. They claimed that the B-29 couldn't be flown like the B-17 in large formations at the distances necessary in the Far East. LeMay didn't mince words, telling them that they were going to do things his way.

His proposed straight-in bomb run at first caused consternation. He had initiated it in England and found that it increased the number of hits on a target and actually reduced aircraft losses. As he explained, "By using a straight-in approach, in most cases the target is knocked out the first time instead of going back again and again." He refused to listen to arguments because he had proved the technique in Europe. For the doubters, he patiently explained that evasive action on the bomb run only increased the time over target, and often made it impossible to hit the target.

When the commanders briefed their own group staffs, emotions ran high, and there were many bitter words about this "hotshot" from the Eighth Air Force and how he would learn, as they had, everything the hard way.

LeMay was emphatic when he said the long-range B-29 gives the Air Force a chance to open a new field in the strategic employment of airpower. "Our major problem," he conceded, "is supporting operations from India and China, thousands of miles from sources of supply in the United States."

Despite their protests about 12-plane formations, he made it clear that he would use the B-29 much as the B-17s had been used in England.

For the most part, group commanders let the tide of emotion run its course. When it subsided, in each case group staffs were told that LeMay meant what he said and they damn well better get used to doing things his way.

For the crews who went to lead-crew school at Dudhkundi, after the extensive ground training, the bombing runs over Halliday Island, and the simulated missions against a Bengal steel plant, there was a growing awareness that LeMay was a true professional. In reality, they knew their operations had been the work of amateurs, and they were because for most it was their first experience in combat. Few top men had had previous combat experience so little of value was passed down to the crews who flew the missions. As the crews gained competence, they gained something vastly more important and that was confidence in themselves, a knowledge that at last they understood what they were doing, and their feelings toward their tough-minded new boss, whom they now privately called "Old Smiley," gradually changed from bitterness to a grudging respect that later became outright admiration.

The technique for approving the bombing had been developed in England whereby all planes dropped on signal from the lead crew. The lead bombardier and radar operator worked together on the bomb run, each supplying information and data right up to the moment of release. There was nothing complicated about the procedure, and many bombardiers wondered why it had taken so long for them to be taught it.

One of LeMay's first moves was to eliminate two crews per aircraft. This step was the first of many that involved a complete reorganization of the command. At first, double crews were considered mandatory because so many missions would be flown. As it turned out, the airplane itself was the limiting factor, and not the crews, because it couldn't be kept in commission that often. LeMay had thoughts about that problem, too, and he told the group commanders to fly hell out of the airplanes. "They get out of commission quicker sitting on the ground than they do flying," he said. Although there were many who doubted, LeMay had given them a shot in the arm with his knowledgeable approach to operations that started to pay off. The staff soon learned that he spoke the truth. And lastly, with two crews per airplane, it was difficult for both crews to keep their proficiency.

When some staff members complained about tight control of their operations by Washington, LeMay replied, "I don't have the slightest feeling that I am being controlled by General Arnold or the Pentagon. True, we get the target lists, but how I handle missions is my business. There certainly isn't the interference here we had in England.

"I understand the situation here, and what I was sent out to do. I know what Arnold expects, and he has never given me any verbal instructions or anything of the sort. I fully understand what my job is, and why I was sent out here.

"First of all, you must realize that General Arnold has done a remarkable job in getting the resources allocated to build the B-29. Remember, the B-17 was dead as a dodo a year or so before war broke out. To get it, the B-24, and another bomber built really was a remarkable achievement under the conditions he had to work with at the time."

Some staff members were not convinced, and continued to grumble.

LeMay took pains to make them understand how Arnold had fought to gain the semiautonomy they now had. "Just getting the B-29s out from under the theater commander and under the Joint Chiefs was a major miracle," he said. "The airplanes are here in a combat theater which is another miracle. True the damn things don't fly very well, and they've got plenty of problems, but they are here and they're not pulling their weight so Arnold is upset. I was sent here to see if I couldn't do something about it. Arnold didn't tell me so in so many words, but I understand his reasoning.

"Sure the supply situation is bad. It quickly became apparent to me that no one is going to make a big mark with these B-29s from India and China against Japan. You just can't get the resources to do it. That's what I repeatedly tell Washington."

LeMay was baffled by the command organization in the China-Burma-India theater. He realized there were two theaters really—Mountbatten's and Stilwell's. Then the XX Bomber Command had been forced upon them for administration and supply while its operations remained under the Joint Chiefs of Staff. He considered the situation a sorry arrangement because the theater commander was supplying his life's blood in the way of resources for which he got no credit for the command's successes, or censure for its failures. Such a situation, he knew from personal experience, got you little attention.

Shortly after he arrived, LeMay went up to New Delhi to call on Stilwell. He was out in the jungle so he said hello to the chief of staff, tossed a couple of calling cards on Stilwell's desk, and went home.

A short time later he thought he'd better go down and see Mountbatten in Ceylon, although he wasn't sure just how he fitted into the picture because he wasn't supplying him with anything now that the bases were built. He got up at 4 A.M. and flew down, hoping to see the admiral and return the same day. He arrived there at 10:30 and learned that he couldn't see him until the following day. He almost went back to the airfield and returned to India. "But," he thought, "while I'm here I might as well stay over and see him." He walked around Kandy and looked at Buddhist temples the rest of the afternoon.

Next day he went up to the top of the mountain where Mountbatten resided in royal splendor and joined him for lunch. It was a very formal lunch with natives pulling a rope back and forth with a carpet attached to keep a cooling breeze flowing for the diners.

After cigars they went over to the daily briefing. During the first 20 minutes, they were briefed on events throughout the world. Then a major general took 40 minutes to discuss an action by Mountbatten's men in Burma in which a British squad tried to take a Japanese machine-gun nest, lost two men, but failed to knock out the machine gun. LeMay was restless with all this trivia and longing to escape back to his own command.

Mountbatten turned to him. "I'm going to invade Akyab Island on the Burma coast and I want you to saturate the place before I go in."

LeMay tried not to let his emotions appear on his face. He wasn't about to commit his command to such an operation because that would have been just the start of more demands for assistance.

"I'm doing some practice bombing down that way. If one of these practice missions would be of help, I'll see what I can do. I'd rather bomb Japs than just a target." He thought quickly how he could avoid trapping himself into an unnecessary operation because he had just seen reconnaissance photographs of Akyab and it was apparent there wasn't a single Japanese on the island. Diplomacy was not one of his strong points and he found himself saying, "Admiral, I've seen recent photographs. There isn't a Jap on it. If you want Akyab send a rowboat down there with some troops and take it."

"Oh, no," Mountbatten said. "There are Japs on it."

"Not according to my pictures," LeMay said stubbornly.

In polite words, LeMay told Mountbatten that he wasn't about to waste time on Akyab. That was the last time he saw the admiral during the war but years later he got to know him well and admire him.

Once the lead-crew school closed down at Dudhkundi, now the home of the 444th, LeMay talked with Twentieth Headquarters in Washington about the next target. Staffers again insisted on attacks against mainland aircraft factories but LeMay's own target specialists recommended another attack on Anshan. LeMay agreed with them, and forwarded his reasons back to Washington, explaining that a third attack should cripple the plant and that it would make an ideal target to try out their new bombing techniques.

LeMay promised Arnold that he would have 100 B-29s over the target at Anshan September 26. At first, it seemed as if he would make good on his promise because 117 B-29s, plus a photo-reconnaissance airplane, were ready to go on the morning of the attack. Despite weather forecasts that predicted four-tenths cloud cover at the target, a cold front moved in and all Superforts had to bomb by radar, and only 73 made it all the way. The strike caused no new damage but not a single airplane was lost.

The Japanese now were aroused and bombers swept the Chengtu bases and five Superfortresses were damaged, two of them seriously. Only one of Chennault's P-47 fighters took off and the pilot failed to find the bombers.

Chennault had transferred many of the fighter wing's airplanes to assist in trying to halt the Japanese drive into South China. He believed it was uneconomical of planes and pilots to tie them down in the rear on the off chance the Japanese might attack the bases. LeMay agreed but he also insisted that night fighters be dispatched to China, which should have been done in the first place instead of sending only day-fighting P-47s. The first P-61s of the 426th Night-Fighter Squadron arrived at Chengtu October 6, but another five weeks went by before an integrated defense between ground and air could be established with the arrival of the 843rd Anti-aircraft Battalion. Fortunately, the Japanese never pressed their early advantage when the almost defenseless bases were vulnerable. If they had done so serious disruption of B-29 operations would have resulted. A total of 10 raids on the bases were made before B-29s were withdrawn to India in December. Never at any time were these raids a problem despite Chennault's dire predictions. They were more of an annoyance than anything else.

LeMay wasn't impressed with the work of the night fighters. He kidded their commanding officer, "Russ" Randall, for weeks that the only time the night fighters did any good was when the Japanese bombed one of his fighter bases by mistake instead of the B-29 fields. Then, he said, "Your men flew into a rage and shot the Japanese bomber down."

Originally, the XX Bomber Command was conceived as an independent force that would be self-contained so it could operate far removed from normal sources of supply and maintenance. It had been visualized as a prototype for follow-on organizations. To maintain its independence from other theater commands, each flight crewman was trained for combat in the air and for maintenance on the ground. Each group also had a service group to provide base services, and maintenance and support personnel were not under the same command as the flight crews. It was a weird pattern of command responsibility totally unlike any other Air Force organization. The fact that it worked at all, although not very well, was remarkable because there was no straight line of command from top to bottom in each group. Many of Wolfe's problems were due to inadequate maintenance of aircraft that was directly traceable to the manner in which the groups were organized, so his combat operations suffered.

LeMay constantly had to battle with the headquarters staff in Washington, and the reorganization was delayed until October. When his plan was approved, 16 maintenance squadrons were disbanded and the personnel assigned to bombardment squadrons. In a further attempt to streamline his command, a bombardment squadron was eliminated in each group, leaving three squadrons with 10 planes each and one crew for each airplane. Originally, double crews were considered necessary because they were trained to maintain the aircraft as well as fly it. The concept wasn't all that bad for a primitive theater like China-Burma-India, and proved its worth at Palembang and in many of the forced landings in China. LeMay considered the practice too costly, and Arnold agreed with him.

Earlier, the 58th Wing Headquarters was dropped as an unnecessary appendage when Saunders replaced Wolfe. When the headquarters was first established in Kansas, it was one of two that was assigned to the XX Bomber Command, but later the 73rd Wing was removed so there was no need for another headquarters between the four groups and the bomber command.

During August, there was a constant flow of new officers hand-picked by LeMay to take over from those initially selected by Wolfe. Many careers were halted in mid-stride even though those returning to the States presumably were transferred to form the nucleus of other B-29 commands. Arnold and LeMay were as one in regard to incompetent officers, and they were without mercy on those whom they considered inadequate to command.

Saunders stayed on for several weeks but LeMay considered him surplus to the command's needs. Before he could be routinely trans-ferred to the States, he was seriously injured in the crash of a B-25 at Piardoba in which several others were killed. He lay out in the jungle for hours critically injured before it was learned that his plane had crashed. He was evacuated to the States and was crippled for the rest of his life.

In Washington, there were high-level changes going on simulta-neously as Hansell left to take over the XXI Bomber Command that was soon to be deployed to Saipan. Brigadier General Lauris Nor-stad replaced him as the Twentieth's chief of staff.

In the field, LeMay reported November 2 that his reorganization was almost complete, reporting a surplus of 75 officers and 484 enlisted men who were eligible for reassignment. He told Arnold that he needed 900 men for air-transport flying of the Hump so he could increase operations out of China once more fuel was available. He offered to trade his surplus B-29 crews for such men. LeMay tended to agree with Wolfe that one reason for the failure of the original plan was transfer of the 73rd Wing to another command, which left him with insufficient bombers for a self-supporting role. LeMay ex-plained to Arnold that increased operations out of the forward bases were possible only if three C-46 air-transport squadrons were made available.

After the third Anshan mission, target priorities were changed, and Arnold insisted on closer coordination of the command's activi-ties with operations in the Pacific. He pointed out that coke and steel targets should have been destroyed by now, but that only two mis-sions such as the first and second Anshan could be classed as successful even though it appeared they had little impact on total Japanese production of steel. Arnold was emphatic when he told LeMay that he would consider moving the Superfortresses to another theater unless operations improved.

Now that LeMay was on the firing line, he began to sympathize with Wolfe and the problems he had faced, many of them not under his control. Wolfe had told him of a meeting that he had had with Arnold in Washington when he told his boss there was only one way to increase the number or weight of attacks from China and that was to increase the number of B-29s to 180, which would give him 128 for combat operations and 52 for tankers. One of his major problems, Wolfe said at the time, was how to get 2,000 tons of fuel and supplies from the Air Transport Command without depriving other organizations. He reminded Arnold that Stilwell allocated Hump tonnage, and the Joint Chiefs had refused to interfere with his authority by directly allocating tonnage to the XX Bomber Command. At the time, Arnold tried to get Wolfe to use excess B-29 crews to operate additional tankers but Wolfe refused because he thought it was a terrible waste of highly trained B-29 crews, and he was right.

Now the problem was in LeMay's hands. Arnold did recommend to the Joint Chiefs that increased ATC tonnage be authorized so that 225 sorties could be flown each month. He said that with the command's own transport efforts, operations out of China could be stepped up. His suggestions were sent to appropriate agencies for further study.

LeMay decided to assign 72 B-29 crews to fly C-109s, or converted B-24 bombers. Each crew would have five men, plus a ground crew of eight at their base in Kalaikundi, and they would be rotated every 60 days.

August delivery of fuel was less than July but got better in September as B-29 tankers started flying again. For October, LeMay's estimate of 10,685 tons was exceeded. In November, however, Arnold insisted that all B-29 tankers be removed from fuel hauling because such intensive flying was wearing out the expensive bombers. He assigned the India-China Division of the Air Transport Command to handle all freight operations over the Hump with exception of bombs, which B-29s still transported. The original idea of a self-supporting command had been unrealistic and poorly thought out, and its demise was long overdue.

With more fuel in China, LeMay stepped up plans for utilization of the Superfortresses. Although he didn't fully realize it at the time, the worst was behind him. There hadn't been a mission since September 26, and when a strike at Formosa was scheduled for the middle of October, it ended the longest hiatus between missions the command would ever know again. It wouldn't happen because there'd been a strategic shift in targets, and the command would closely integrate with the large-scale operations now getting underway in the Pacific to reconquer the Philippines.

# CHAPTER 10

# The Turning Point

The Committee of Operations Analysts in Washington had drawn up a series of target systems for the Twentieth Air Force on November 11, 1943, but now almost a year later the tides of war had changed drastically in the Pacific so Arnold called for a new look, particularly since the XXI Bomber Command would soon be operating out of the Marianas.

MacArthur's forces were bypassing islands once thought crucial in a step-by-step approach to the main islands of Japan. By leapfrogging over great distances, huge enemy-held areas were left to stagnate in the backwash of a rapidly changing war.

Nimitz' Central Pacific forces were also forging ahead on the seaways to Japan, while remnants of the Japanese fleet scuttled to the doubtful security of home ports.

Arnold issued the order September 8, 1944, and he grew impatient when it wasn't forthcoming quickly enough. LeMay, too, was anxious to hear what the new targets would be because his own plans couldn't wait. He had to know, and know soon, because Arnold had told him that he was considering transfer of the XX Bomber Command because the ground war in China was deteriorating so rapidly as the Japanese drove into South China. Arnold's staff did give LeMay the benefit of their thoughts that priority should be given to aircraft plants at Omura, Mukden, Watanabe, and Okayama. They weren't the most important aircraft plants in Japan, but they were the only ones within reach of China-based B-29s. LeMay decided, therefore, to attack the air depot at Okayama, Formosa, on his next mission. The target itself was a strategic one, but most important, destruction of its facilities would provide direct aid to MacArthur's forces, which were preparing to land at Leyte in the first step to recapture the Philippines.

While preparations were under way, the Committee of Operations Analysts submitted its findings to General Arnold. He had asked that they prepare the report in two parts with alternative assumptions. The first was that Japan could be defeated by sea and air blockade. The second, that these means would be used but supplemented by an invasion of the Japanese homeland. COA officials recommended that B-29s should start a campaign against shipping, including extensive mine laying, press attacks on Japan's aircraft industry, and use saturation bombing of six urban industrial areas. Their plan called for simultaneous mining operations and attacks on aircraft factories, but strongly recommended that attacks on urban areas await larger B-29 forces. The plan called for continuing reviews to determine other suitable targets. Arnold was advised that if plans to invade the home islands were contemplated that attacks on the aircraft industry and urban industrial areas should be given top priority, along with intensification of the mining campaign. For Arnold and his staff's perusal there were detailed reports to guide future operations.

COA predicated most of its findings on future operations because the committee believed that operations out of the Marianas, and possibly other areas yet to be captured, would far outweigh the importance of the lone wing of 120 B-29s in India and China. Prospects of mining the strategic Shimonoseki Strait weighed heavily in their analysis of important targets but a thorough mining of the strait would have to await B-29s in the Marianas.

When the COA issued its earlier report in 1943, the emphasis was on expanding Japanese industries that, they believed, could be crippled by attacks on coke ovens in steel plants. That was the reason for the emphasis on attacks on coking plants in Manchuria and Kyushu. Since that report was filed, however, Japanese shipping losses had been huge. Thus steel production suffered far more from attacks against shipping by aircraft and submarines of the United States Navy than they did from B-29 attacks against coke ovens. After the war, however, it was learned that these Superfortress raids had done far more damage than was known at the time. It was learned that iron ore from the Philippines, Hainan, and the Asiatic mainland was not getting to processing plants in Japan due to a shipping shortage.

Therefore, coke wasn't the limiting factor. It was iron ore. Thus, it was reasoned, with Arnold's concurrence, B-29s could be put to more profitable use by attacking such targets as the aircraft repair and modification center at Okayama. Admiral Halsey's carriers struck such plants October 12 in his sweep of the area in support of MacArthur's upcoming landings at Leyte. Although the Japanese after the war denied such attacks had any appreciable effect on Leyte operations, Okayama was a principal staging center for Japanese aircraft en route to and from the South or Central Pacific, and there's no doubt but that the combined sea and air attacks were helpful to the general situation in the Philippines.

The Joint Chiefs at this stage of the war believed that control of most of the Luzon-Formosa-China coast was a necessary prerequisite to invasion of the home islands. Outside of Arnold and King, other members had little faith that sea and air attacks, coupled with a blockade, would bring Japan to her knees. Arnold didn't press the issue because B-29 attacks had not yet given any indication of the impact they would later have on the course of events.

Although the strategy for the defeat of Japan had undergone long discussions between Nimitz and MacArthur, each of whom had strong theories on how to proceed, the Joint Chiefs settled the issue March 12, 1944, by calling for separate approaches.* Nimitz was instructed to move toward the home islands on routes that led through the Marianas, the Carolines, and the Palaus island groups. While these stepping-stones were acquired, MacArthur was ordered to advance his forces from New Guinea to Mindanao in the Philippines November 15, and to make an attack on Formosa February 15, 1945. The Joint Chiefs gave him the option of taking Luzon if he believed it necessary, and to make his assault there in February instead of Formosa.

Chennault and Stilwell were unhappy about such a strategy because it left the China-Burma-India theater in the role only of supporting Pacific operations. In effect, the CBI's status was downgraded to a holding operation for the rest of the war, except for aid by Chennault's Fourteenth Air Force and LeMay's XX Bomber Command to

---

* Earlier in the war, President Roosevelt supported MacArthur's views and tried to force them on Nimitz because MacArthur was a possible Republican presidential candidate in 1944. The King/Arnold position to use the Marianas in an attempt to bomb Japan into submission won out in the end.

MacArthur's forces in their attacks on Formosa and the Philippines.

Arnold, acting on behalf of the Joint Chiefs, directed Stilwell May 2 to commit his air forces to these operations. Further, he was told to prepare for such aid despite the Japanese invasion of South China, which was draining Chennault's supplies to support the Chinese Army, and the necessity of using a certain amount of Air Transport Command tonnage over the Hump for B-29 operations. Stilwell's dilemma was not fully understood in Washington but it did play an important part in getting more airplanes and crews to augment ATC operations.

Admiral Halsey's Task Force 38 started September 12 to sweep enemy sea and air forces from the Philippine area. Much to his surprise, his carrier planes encountered little opposition, particularly at Leyte. In a communication to Nimitz, he recommended a change in overall tactics and that Central Pacific forces should bypass the Talaud's, Yap, and the Palaus Island groups, and that MacArthur's forces should skip Mindanao and go directly to Leyte, which wasn't scheduled for invasion until December 20. Nimitz agreed with Halsey's evaluation of the situation, although the attack on Palau was too far along to be stopped. Nimitz sent a memorandum to Admiral King, who was meeting with the Combined Chiefs of Staff at Quebec, recommending the changes proposed by Halsey. King agreed and, in one of the most remarkably quick agreements of the war, got MacArthur's concurrence to set the Leyte operation for October 20.

While these broad changes in Pacific strategy were under way, LeMay was getting his command trained to a fitness it had never known before. He had committed his command to provide 225 sorties toward the original Matterhorn plan, plus 125 more to aid Pacific operations. With the fuel situation in China improving rapidly, he hoped to send a total of 425 B-29s on missions in January. He also found Stilwell more amenable than his predecessors when he agreed to guarantee sufficient Hump tonnage to support 350 sorties in October.

LeMay received the plan for support of the Leyte operation September 22. It called for two missions against Formosa to help protect MacArthur's north flank, plus use of a few B-29s for long-range reconnaissance if MacArthur should request it.

MacArthur asked that B-29s attack airfields on Luzon, but Nimitz approved the Joint Chiefs' plan that would coordinate B-29 raids with strikes by Mitscher's fast carriers. These strikes were designed to minimize aerial reinforcement of the Philippines by attacking airfields on Okinawa October 10 and Formosa on the 12th and 13th. Arnold told LeMay to change his original date and attack on the 11th and 14th but bad weather precluded attacks before the 14th and 16th.

Halsey's Task Force 38 roamed the seas from the Ryukyus to Formosa on a sweep that included attacks on Luzon on the 11th before a two-day attack on Formosa. Despite determined opposition, Halsey's fast carriers were highly successful, claiming the destruction of 520 enemy planes, 36 ships sunk, and probably 74 more sent to the bottom. The attacks by Mitscher's pilots caused damage to Okayama but it wasn't critical. A greater weight of bombs was needed, far more than carrier aircraft could carry to destroy the large aircraft repair and assembly plant at Okayama and its adjoining air base.

Stilwell appeared at a base in China while LeMay was trying to get a mission out, seeking a full briefing on the XX Bomber Command.

"Follow me around, and let me get the work done," LeMay told him, "and once the mission is off I'll have time to give you a good briefing about what we're doing here. And, this way you'll pick up a little something of what we're doing."

Stilwell agreed. Once the bombers were on their way to Formosa, LeMay invited his guest for dinner and later spent most of the night telling him what they were doing. LeMay, exhausted from a day and a night on his feet and without sleep, felt frustrated because he could see he wasn't making any headway in getting the general to understand the finer points of strategic bombing. He admired Stilwell, knowing he was a fine field commander, perhaps somewhat old-fashioned in his views of warfare, but still doing a difficult job under very trying conditions. When he said good-bye to him, LeMay felt that he had failed completely to instill in Stilwell how important strategic bombing was toward shortening the war and making an invasion of the Japanese homeland unnecessary.

When B-29s went out October 14, carrier attacks had blunted the resistance and they didn't meet extensive fighter attacks. One hundred and four B-29s loosed bombs on Okayama causing severe damage throughout the complex. Although 12 Superforts had to make emergency landings in China, only one crashed and all but one of its crew was saved.

After viewing the strike photos, LeMay saw no reason for another maximum effort so he sent only two groups back to Okayama, while others were assigned targets in various parts of Formosa. Incredibly, one 11-plane formation from the 444th flew right by Okayama and the lead bombardier dropped the formation's bombs on Heito. LeMay had some caustic words to express his disgust for such incompetence when he met with the group's commander.

For once, photo reconnaissance confirmed the crew reports of extensive damage. Target analysts said it would take four to six months before the Okayama base could be back in full operation. Actually, they underestimated the damage. The air depot was so destroyed that it was never rebuilt.

On October 11, Arnold officially notified LeMay what he had known for weeks, that the Japanese aircraft industry had first priority. For the XX Bomber Command, this meant the Omura Aircraft Factory on Kyushu because it was the largest within B-29 range.

Operations against Formosa had exceeded the command's quota of fuel so LeMay was unable to get the maximum number of Superforts over Omura October 25. The 59 that did bomb caused considerable damage to the plant's fabrication facilities, but 19 others bombed targets of opportunity.

In November, a shortage of fuel limited the number of missions out of China, but two were set up to be flown from rear bases where fuel was not a problem. An attack November 3 on the marshaling yards at Rangoon demonstrated the effectiveness of the B-29 when it could drop a full load of bombs visually on a target. The British had been trying for three years to knock out these yards but a small force of B-29s completely destroyed them in one of the finest examples of precision bombing shown to date. The Japanese rail system had always been critically short of locomotives so their loss during this raid was felt acutely.

Two days later, B-29s were loaded with 1,000-pound bombs for an unusual mission to Singapore. The target was only 10 feet wide and 200 feet long, and bombardiers were told that only precision bombing at its best could knock it out. The aiming point was the sliding gate of the main dry dock, a dock the Japanese inherited from the British and which was now used to repair Japanese warships.

Crews gasped when they heard the distance of 3,800 miles for the round trip, which would keep them in the air for over 18 hours.

With bomb-bay tanks filled to the brim, leaving room for only three 1,000-pound bombs, B-29s took off after midnight.

The Bay of Bengal spread out before them as Captain Charles "Doc" Joyce's crew from the 468th headed out toward the Andaman Islands. They were dimly visible below as they passed, giving assurance they were on course. It was a dreary experience flying through the long night, feeling so alone in the vast sky, even though Doc knew there were B-29s all around them. Once the sun rose in the east, they spotted them all headed in the same direction, passing over a ship here and there plodding along for some destination unknown to those above them.

With the sun came haze but they could dimly see the Malay Peninsula on their left and Sumatra on their right as they rode down the middle of the Malacca Straits. The target was located on the peninsula side of the island of Singapore, which was connected to the mainland by a narrow causeway across the Johore Strait.

As Doc joined a formation at the assembly point, he had a quick glance at the countryside below them. An impression of incredible greenness was all he got but he could imagine those steaming jungles and what they were like. He shuddered at the thought of a bailout.

Once they turned on the initial point, he could see the Strait of Johore, and his bombardier, Lieutenant E. D. "Ham" Faulknham, called that the target was clear. The formation ahead was catching hell, and he caught his breath as flak surrounded them. Then it was their turn, and he could see wicked red flashes all around them as they steadily droned toward the release point. Loud bangs let him know that some of the heavy guns had found their range and he wondered how they could fly through that wall of flak that separated them from the target. The bombardier added to the excitement by announcing that there were several warships in the strait and they were firing with everything they had. Their B-29 was taking punishment such as he had never known before, and Doc began to wonder if they would live through it.

Then he felt the plane lighten as the bombs fell away and he watched the formation leader and followed him as they turned left from the target while Japanese fighters moved in for the kill. Once, a huge mushroom cloud exploded near them as a fighter dropped a phosphorus bomb. Just a few pieces of flaming phosphorus in a hot engine nacelle would end their combat careers, he knew, as he busied himself to keep in formation.

Miraculously they were away from those murderous guns, and heading across the lower end of the peninsula to get back to sea.

Most of the way back was uneventful, but an hour from base flight engineer Charles Passieu told Doc they were running short on fuel. Joyce had been worrying about it for some time, but until now he thought they could make it.

He called to Lieutenant Howard H. Fauth and asked the navigator, "What's your maximum ETA?"

"About twenty minutes to base."

Joyce turned to his flight engineer. "What do you think, Pass? Can we make it?"

"I think it will be a tie."

They flew for another 10 minutes and now they were over land. One engine sputtered, caught, and then ran smoothly again as Passieu transferred fuel to it. That was only momentary because the engine started to cut out again. Frantically, Passieu switched fuel from one tank to another, trying to keep all engines going. Now they were all sputtering as they used up the last fuel in the tanks. They were flying at 13,000 feet and Lieutenant Faulknham spotted the runways of the 468th base ahead, drawing Doc's attention to it.

"Gear down!" Joyce called, and his copilot, Lieutenant William Greenwald, lowered the wheels.

"Flaps," he said, and "Greenie" ran them down.

Passieu called, "Number three is out." There was a pause as Joyce tried to steady his emotions. "There goes number four!"

Joyce struggled to hold the plane level as its right wing dropped, calling on his copilot to assist him.

"Number two is out," Passieu yelled. "Number one's about gone."

At 7,600 feet, Joyce shouted, "Bail out!"

Fauth came forward and looked at Doc. The latter repeated the bailout order so Fauth faced the rear and dropped through the nosewheel well. Once his body hit the air his feet flew up and his head went down. He waited until he cleared the tail before he pulled the rip cord. He could see three chutes below while the plane above seemed to be flying level and under control, and he watched with growing concern for more parachutes but they didn't appear. He landed in brush and soon heard two pistol shots so he went in that direction where he joined Faulknham, Greenwald, and Sergeant Vernon Egertson. They walked for an hour before they were picked up.

In the nose of the airplane only Joyce and Passieu remained and they elected to ride it down thinking that all others had obeyed the bailout order. Doc feathered all four engines to stop windmilling of propellers of the dead engines. He was coming in much too fast but he flared and the airplane hit the ground short of the runway and bounced onto it as Joyce almost sobbed with relief. Once they were stopped, the rest of the crew came out of the rear of the airplane, much to Joyce's astonishment. He thought they had all bailed out.

After performing the impossible, Joyce was shocked to learn later that their group commander, Colonel Faulkner, Major Arnoldus, group navigator, and group bombardier Major Harvey Johnson were lost on the mission.

It was a spectacular success because the gate was knocked out, and the stern of a ship in the dry dock was seriously damaged. It was an example of the kind of precision bombing that was expected but seldom achieved.

The top priority given the Omura Aircraft Factory made it mandatory to schedule the next two missions in November out of China in another attempt to knock it out. The November 11 mission was a fiasco because only half the B-29s headed there heard the signal to cancel the strike at Omura and bomb the last-resort target at Nanking. Those who went on to the target were buffeted by hurricane winds of 150 to 175 miles an hour, and bombs were strewn everywhere but on target. To make matters worse, five B-29s were lost but not because of Japanese defenses. The attacks on Nanking were also futile with no damage of military significance.

Captain Weston H. Price headed away from the target at Omura in the "Gen. H. H. Arnold Special." This was the airplane that Arnold had personally selected off the factory lines in Kansas for earlier delivery than scheduled. It was soon apparent to Price that he wouldn't have fuel enough to fly back to the Chengtu area. He discussed the problem with his copilot, Lieutenant John E. Flanagan, and decided he preferred landing at the Russian base at Vladivostok in preference to crashing in Japanese-held China.

Once they were over Russian territory, they were escorted by 10 fighters and led to a naval air station. On the ground, they were ordered peremptorily out of the plane and taken to naval headquarters, and they never saw their B-29 again. They were treated almost like enemy airmen, and they were bewildered and resentful.

After the U.S. State Department protested about their treatment, they were allowed to leave by being brought to the Allied Lines in Iran February 2, 1945.

Arnold was particularly bitter because he considered the Russian actions inexcusable, and hardly what one should expect from an ally. As he told his staff, it was the easiest way he knew for the Russians to acquire one of the world's most advanced bombers without cost. Privately, he believed the State Department had not tried hard enough to get the airplane back.

Arnold advised LeMay that he wanted another attack on Omura November 14 to coordinate with a Navy carrier sweep of Honshu, and the XXI Bomber Command's first strike at Tokyo. When the Tokyo strike was delayed for 10 days because of a typhoon, LeMay promised he would send 110 B-29s to Omura on the 21st, or three days before Hansell's new command on Saipan was scheduled to hit Tokyo. Although 109 airplanes got off the ground, with one crashing after takeoff with the loss of all but one crewman, bad weather met them over the target. Sixty-one airplanes bombed by radar, but it was a chaotic release as two formations broke up when lead planes switched on the bomb run. Antiaircraft fire was minimal but Japanese fighters showed their greatest aggressiveness yet as "Frank" and "Jack II" fighters made their first appearances, with one of them shooting down a B-29. So determined were the Japanese fighters that they closed to 100 yards, and as a result five bombers were lost. Twenty-three other B-29s bombed targets at Shanghai and other cities with some success. On the whole, it was a costly mission in losses for the limited damage done to the targets.

Before November closed, the command sent bombers to targets at Bangkok, more or less as a training mission.

LeMay was told to continue his attacks against Omura but the weather was bad December 7 so he wired Arnold for permission to bomb the Manchuria Airplane Manufacturing Company plant at Mukden. With 108 crews standing by in China, where it had turned bitterly cold, LeMay and his staff waited impatiently for word to go ahead. The target was not a large complex but a plant for assembly of advanced trainers. The word from Arnold came only hours before they were scheduled to take off.

Formations assembled over the Shantung Peninsula. As they moved toward Manchuria, the temperature at their altitudes dropped to 52 below centigrade. Bombardiers noticed the bay around Dairen was frozen. It was a sheet of ice that reflected the glare of the bright sun. Once over land, the countryside was covered with snow, with houses standing out prominently in an expanse of whiteness.

As they neared the target, crews got a glimpse of Mukden, with its walled inner city on the left, and up ahead the arsenal spread to the right of the city. Bombardiers searched for the aircraft plant to the arsenal's right but it was difficult to see because of a smoke screen. While lead bombardiers carefully adjusted their sights, Japanese fighters made graceful vapor trails as they streamed in to attack, while retreating B-29 formations, which had already dropped their bombs, made beautiful white patterns against the deep blue of the sky.

The intense cold frosted windows and bombardiers and pilots frantically scraped holes so they could see. Each 12-plane formation headed straight to the target while guns roared as Japanese fighters swept dangerously close.

One formation dropped too soon, hitting a rail yard nine miles short of the target. Others made excellent runs, causing some damage to the airplane factory, but more to the adjoining arsenal. Bombardiers found it difficult to spot the aiming point because the Japanese had set smudge pots to conceal the plant.

Fighter attacks were the most aggressive since Omura, and crews reported a total of 247 separate attacks. There were three air-to-air collisions, although two undoubtedly were unintentional as one Japanese fighter was destroyed while only a propeller was bent on a B-29, while another collision destroyed both planes. The one possibly intentional attack was caused by a damaged fighter that appeared to ram the Fort.

Air-to-air bombing from Japanese fighters dropping phosphorus bombs, which had become a more frequent tactic in the desperate Japanese attempts to destroy the huge bombers, brought one crew a nightmarish encounter with near disaster. A phosphorus bomb landed on the wing, and, while the crew stared at it in horrified fascination for hours, it burned all the way back to base without causing serious damage.

For months Chennault had been demanding that the command hit Hankow because it was the major supply base for the Japanese in their drive southward toward Kweiyang with Kunming, terminus for Hump aircraft, the ultimate goal so aerial supply of China could be cut off. Arnold had stubbornly resisted such requests, although Hankow had been bombed as a last-resort target with minor damage.

He pointed out to Chennault that Hankow was within range of his Fourteenth Air Force bombers, and that diversion of B-29s to such a target would interfere with their primary mission of attacking strategic targets.

# CHAPTER 11

# A Conflict of Personalities

LeMay's position in the political controversy boiling around him was difficult because he took orders only from Arnold and the Joint Chiefs. He kept out of it as much as possible by forwarding all requests for B-29 attacks of strictly China targets to Washington.

The situation in China was complicated by Stilwell's blunt assertions of corruption and what he termed false pride, apathy, and military ineptness on the part of Chiang's military staff. His personal relationship with Chiang had always been frigid, and it had become more so since the spring of 1944. Stilwell's tight control of lend-lease materials caused some of the antagonism because Chiang considered such control a personal affront, and he wrote Roosevelt to complain about it. The President, however, wasn't about to turn over control to the Generalissimo and, in this respect, supported Stilwell.

Roosevelt grew more and more concerned about the personal conflicts between Stilwell and Chiang so he sent Vice President Henry A. Wallace to Chungking June 20, 1944, to report personally about the true status of the deteriorating relationship between the Chiang government and the United States. Wallace was upset by what he found in China, intimating to Roosevelt that the situation was explosive.

After a meeting with Chiang, he learned that the Generalissimo wanted a personal representative appointed to act as liaison between him and the President. Wallace advised Roosevelt that Chiang told him Stilwell no longer had his confidence because he didn't understand the political considerations involved between the two countries.

Wallace was frank in telling the President that he didn't believe any military officer in China would be suitable for such an appointment. Chennault, he said, had Chiang's confidence but he didn't believe he was the man for the job, and that he should remain where he was. The Vice President recommended that whoever was selected should be a man who could not only win Chiang's confidence, but be able to influence political as well as military decisions. Of greatest importance, he emphasized, the man who commanded American forces in China should also understand the necessity of closely coordinating American and Chinese military efforts. In effect, Wallace was recommending two courses of action. One, that Stilwell retain his responsibilities in Burma, but that another commander should be selected for China, possibly as Stilwell's deputy, but be given broad responsibilities for acting independently in China, and the right to deal directly with Washington on the political level. Second, he said that China might be treated as a separate command without reporting to Stilwell. For the second alternative, Lieutenant General Albert C. Wedemeyer had been recommended to him for such a command.

It was unfortunate that Wallace never had a chance to talk to Stilwell and get his side of the story but time didn't permit, and he expressed that regret to the President. He made it clear to Roosevelt that loss of eastern China could cause a violent economic and political upheaval that was sure to rock the Chiang government. He urged Roosevelt to give immediate attention to the problem, and try to persuade Chiang to reform his regime because only a united front by all Chinese, including the Communists, could restore sagging morale and assure eventual victory.

When the Joint Chiefs met in Washington July 4, 1944, Stilwell received their strong backing. They urged that he be promoted to four-star rank, and that Roosevelt use his influence with Chiang to place all Chinese forces under Stilwell. Along with their endorsement, they said they recognized the differences between Chiang Kai-shek and Stilwell but felt that the latter's war record, despite negative British and Chinese attitudes, should be the overriding factor instead of political considerations. They pointed out to the President that if Stilwell's earlier advice had been taken, the Japanese would have been defeated in northeast Burma before the monsoon season, and more effective actions would have been possible against the Japanese drive into southeast China.

Roosevelt took the advice of his Joint Chiefs and, two days later, told Chiang that he was promoting Stilwell to full general and that he hoped the Generalissimo would place him in charge of all Chinese and American forces.

Marshall notified Stilwell of these actions, but chastised him for failure to work harmoniously with Chiang. He told Stilwell that many of his words and actions had offended the President as well as Chiang. In conclusion, Marshall said, "I hope you will make a continuous effort to avoid wrecking your and our plans because of inconsequential matters or disregard of conventional courtesies."

Stilwell was moved by Marshall's letter and in a reply July 9 he promised to justify Marshall's confidence, even though "the load promised to be heavy for a country boy."

Chiang agreed to go along with the President's suggestions the same day although he hedged by saying that political considerations might delay action.

The President, feeling that at last they were making some headway in the frustrating, oftentimes tortuous approach to fairly simple problems, expressed his appreciation in reply. He also urged immediate action because of the military situation, saying he hoped that political considerations wouldn't delay implementation of such necessary actions.

Stilwell was an outstanding leader of ground troops, but he had a stubborn, often willful streak that made him difficult to work with at the highest level. When it came to Chiang Kai-shek, there was never any possibility of them getting along. If Roosevelt thought he had resolved the China situation, it was wishful thinking. He had just postponed the inevitable. When Stilwell refused to accept additional assistance for the Chinese during the fight for Hengyang, his relations with the Generalissimo broke down completely.

Roosevelt, meanwhile, acted upon Wallace's recommendation that he send a personal representative to China. Brigadier General Patrick Hurley was selected. On September 6, Hurley got Chiang to agree that Stilwell would command all forces. It had taken two months to get this agreement, and meanwhile the military situation in China had become desperate.

Without Hurley's knowledge, Chiang had summoned Stilwell and told him to withdraw the Yunnan divisions to the east bank of the Salween River unless Stilwell advanced his forces from below Myitkyina toward Bhama within a week.

Stilwell was irate and all his old suspicions of Chiang's basic motives came to the fore. He sent a wire to Marshall that his troops weren't ready for the offensive. He said Chiang's threat to withdraw the Chinese divisions was another attempt by the Generalissimo to sabotage the Burma campaign. Stilwell told Marshall that Chiang wouldn't listen to reason. Whether deliberately or not, Stilwell didn't send copies of this wire to either Chiang or Hurley, but it was another step leading toward his eventual dismissal.

Marshall composed a letter for Roosevelt's signature to Chiang that was mailed September 16. Roosevelt was more frank than he had ever been with the Chinese President. He said the Generalissimo's cooperation was needed so that a land route to China could be opened early in 1945, and that Chiang must help to press the Salween offensive by placing Stilwell in complete command of all forces. The President said such action would strengthen the British and American decision to open such a land route, and that withdrawal of the Salween forces would also jeopardize the air route to China and that, if this occurred, he must be prepared to accept the consequences of his actions, and accept personal responsibility.

It was an ultimatum from one head of state to another. And, it was delivered, to make matters worse, by Stilwell personally to the Generalissimo. Three days went by after Chiang received the communication and no word came from him.

Stilwell decided that he'd better mend his fences with Hurley so he sent him a memorandum. In it he said his basic problem with Chiang was over the handling of lend-lease materials, over which he personally exercised tight control, and he believed that the Generalissimo resented the fact that Stalin and Churchill controlled their lend-lease whereas he was not permitted to do so. Stilwell suggested that he visit Mao Tze-tung and seek Communist acceptance of Chiang Kai-shek as China's sole head of government, and he would help equip five Communist divisions to fight under American leadership. Further, Stilwell offered to give Chiang control of lend lease if his forces in Burma along the Ledo Road and the Salween were given first priority for its use.

Hurley told Stilwell that his suggestions might be helpful and he wanted the two of them to meet with Chiang and discuss the matter.

Before such a meeting could be arranged, Chiang sent a note September 25 to Hurley formally requesting Stilwell's recall because, he said, Stilwell refused to cooperate with him. He did agree to all other conditions that Roosevelt had spelled out in his ultimatum.

Hurley referred the matter to the President, who tried to get Chiang to change his mind in a letter October 5 but, in reply, the Generalissimo charged that Stilwell had deliberately sacrificed eastern China for the sake of the Burma campaign.

Hurley now realized that Stilwell had to go. Tempers had gotten to the point that there was no way that Chiang and Stilwell could ever cooperate with one another. Hurley said as much to Roosevelt when he wrote October 13, saying that any attempt to retain Stilwell would result in Chiang's loss to the Allied cause, and possibly China, too.

Roosevelt was convinced that he had no other choice but to seek Chiang's recommendations for Stilwell's replacement. In response, Chiang said his first choice was Dwight D. Eisenhower, but Generals Alexander Patch, Albert C. Wedemeyer, or Walter Krueger would be acceptable with Wedemeyer the most acceptable of the latter group.

The conflict of personalities brought near chaos to the China theater, and the Japanese took full advantage of the situation by expediting their drives south and east.

Roosevelt, who now realized there was no need for Chinese coastal bases, blamed himself for concentrating on opening the Ledo Road to China. Stilwell was recalled to Washington October 18. The President told Chiang that he would not appoint another American officer to command Chinese armies, although he was appointing Wedemeyer as his chief of staff for the China theater. Further complicating a confused and tragic situation was division of the China-Burma-India theater into two parts. Wedemeyer was given command of American forces in China, and the India-Burma theater was given to Lieutenant General Daniel I. Sultan, whom Chiang asked to be placed over the Chinese forces committed to the Burma offensive.

LeMay had wisely kept himself apart from these political moves, but he continued to resist requests to use his B-29s in support of purely China operations. He was upset, therefore, when Wedemeyer strongly endorsed a B-29 strike against Hankow. Wedemeyer justified his stand by citing the imminent threat to Kunming by Japanese ground forces, and the fact that the original Joint Chiefs' guidelines for the Matterhorn project provided for such emergency action. He asked LeMay for an attack involving 100 Superfortresses.

The bomber command head was in a quandary because he was committed to other attacks for the month of December, and he challenged Wedemeyer's authority over his command. Wedemeyer went over LeMay's head and referred the matter to the Joint Chiefs, who, after due deliberation, upheld him and LeMay was told to make the attack.

After conferring with Chennault and Wedemeyer, LeMay agreed to a coordinated strike with the Fourteenth Air Force for December 14. The Fourteenth was assigned to bomb airfields in the Hankow area an hour after B-29s were scheduled to drop incendiary bombs on targets. Supposedly, attacks on Japanese airfields would catch Japanese fighters refueling on the ground. B-29s were given the dock and storage areas along the Yangtze to bomb. Knowing that bombing such targets created a vast amount of smoke after the first formation dropped its incendiaries, it was planned to release in four formations, each with a separate bombing area and a different type of incendiary. Operations officers hoped that with the predicted north wind, follow-on formations wouldn't find targets obscured.

The first date couldn't be adhered to so the mission was reset for December 18. Although Wedemeyer had asked for 100 B-29s, LeMay promised only 60 initially because older B-29s with un-modified engines were being withdrawn from combat, but, as it turned out, LeMay was able to get 94 airborne on that date although 10 failed to bomb.

Chennault upset the carefully laid plans a few hours before B-29s were ready to take off by asking that the command send its bombers 45 minutes earlier. This was the first step in creating an unnecessary foul-up because 40 crews didn't get the message over the primitive communications system. As a result, the carefully prescribed order for B-29s to approach the targets could not be adhered to. Three for-mations dropped bombs out of sequence so later formations found their aiming points obscured by smoke. The net result of this mix-up was that 33 planes in the first three formations hit targets, while a few B-29s flying alone made their own runs. Tragically, with smoke obscuring the target area, some bombs were dropped on civilian areas. Despite the foul-up, between 40 and 50 percent of the target area was burned out, and Chennault claimed that Hankow was de-stroyed as an effective supply base, which seriously handicapped the Japanese Army's drive inland.

After the war, Chennault claimed this Hankow raid was the first mass fire raid the B-29s flew, and gave Le May the idea months later to change from high-altitude, daylight strikes against Japan to night fire raids. Although Chennault liked to take credit for such ideas, his facts were completely wrong. Fire raids against major urban areas had been in the planning stages for a long time, awaiting only the time when sufficient B-29s were available in quantity to make such raids worthwhile on a mass scale. Actually, one such incendiary attack had been made against Nagasaki, but on a small scale. The previous September the Committee for Operations Analysts had studied the possibility of future incendiary attacks against six large Japanese cities. And, in November, LeMay's and Arnold's staffs had actually drawn up plans for such an attack on Nagasaki but it was never made because of the early withdrawal of the B-29 command from China.

# CHAPTER 12

# B-29s Withdraw
# from China

LeMay's problems with the B-29 multiplied because so many of them were the original airplanes, and over 100 separate modifications had been made. Engines always had been a problem but now a shortage of spare parts aggravated the situation. During the three missions to Formosa, three losses were caused by engine and propeller failures. Also, those that aborted did so because of malfunctioning engines.

Despite these difficulties he still owed Arnold a maximum strike at Omura. Previously, he had stipulated that only Superfortresses with modified engines would be used on the Omura mission. He had to change his mind, however, and use some of the older airplanes to get even 36 off on December 19. The mission was a failure insofar as the primary target was concerned because it was covered with heavy clouds, and only 17 aircraft were able to bomb by radar. Other planes bombed docks and warehouses at Shanghai but two planes were lost.

LeMay did his best to get another strike ready for Omura but the weather wasn't cooperative. Instead, 48 Superforts headed for Mukden again. Through the group commanders at briefings, LeMay issued orders that under no circumstances were crews to consider landing in Siberia despite any emergency because the Russians weren't acting like allies. If they got in trouble, he told commanders, they should fly into China as far as possible and bail out. He assured commanders that the Chinese underground would do everything possible to save them and bring them out. He reminded group commanders that the Chinese had often brought crews from as far as a thousand miles, often suffering serious retaliation to their communities for helping the Americans.

LeMay had made a deal with Mao Tze-tung, the Communist leader, who controlled a vast area in North China. He had sent a staff officer and crew in a C-47 transport up to Mao's mountain headquarters not knowing how they would be treated, but hoping to enlist Mao's aid. B-29 crews frequently flew over the Communist-controlled north so the Communist leader's help with downed crews would be welcome. Mao greeted his representative warmly and when the problem was outlined to him, he readily agreed to establish communications with the XX Bomber Command.

With B-29s roaming the breadth of China in almost all directions, any such assistance was valuable. The Japanese controlled all of China's large cities and its railroads and rivers. Thus only a decreasing area in the south was still held by Chiang Kai-shek but an increasing area in the north was coming under Communist control in their battles with the Japanese field forces.

Mao agreed that, when a B-29 went down in his area, he would radio the bomber command and make arrangements to pick up the crew, or he would bring them out to a place where they could be picked up.

LeMay was pleased with the success of his special mission and assigned two officers and some communications experts to handle radio equipment at Mao's headquarters. LeMay, as a further gesture of goodwill, sent a C-47 load of medical supplies to Mao, whose army had been up there for seven years without any medical supplies at all. They made a big hit, LeMay learned, as the Chinese doctor stayed up all night checking over the supplies, which included the new sulfa drugs. LeMay sent these supplies to ensure that his own men would have them when they came down in the area and, as he said later, "to make a little hay with Mao."

The Communist leader was so pleased that he sent LeMay a Japanese sword, and some woodcuts that had been made by his people. LeMay, in return, sent him a pair of binoculars and some other items for Mao's personal use.

Mao was so enthused over his arrangements with LeMay that he offered to build bases in northern China for B-29s but LeMay turned him down because he was having enough difficulty supplying the ones around Chengtu. He did say that it would be helpful if the base around the Communist headquarters was improved and Mao agreed —even working on the field himself one day a week.

It was an excellent arrangement for the XX Bomber Command in more ways than one. First, several combat crews were saved; and one just made it off the Yellow Sea to crash in Mao's area. The Chinese Communist leader immediately wired LeMay that he had saved all but one crewman from the Japanese, and he had salvaged the aircraft's four engines. LeMay told him to forget the engines but to get the men back. Most important for future operations, a weather station was set up and manned by American specialists. The Russians had refused to share their weather forecasts so the one LeMay established in North China gave the only reliable weather forecasts from that part of the world, and it was maintained after the command was withdrawn from China and proved invaluable for operations out of the Marianas.

Between frosted windows and smoke pots obscuring the Mukden target, it was another mission failure. This time Japanese fighters were up in force, contesting every mile of the way to the target. There were two air-to-air collisions, and in one both a B-29 and a fighter went down. The B-29 managed to escape destruction in the second collision, but the fighter was destroyed. Another Superfort was lost when it was hit by a phosphorus bomb. The mission was one of the least successful ever flown due to many factors. Two formations inexcusably released bombs four to nine miles from the target.

One of the few worthwhile results of the Mukden mission was unintentional. Robert Burman's crew lost an engine on the way to the target so they headed for Port Dairen to hit a target of opportunity so bombs wouldn't be wasted. Most of the run was on radar but during the last seconds the bombardier caught sight of a Japanese freighter in the harbor, made quick corrections, and dropped his bombs.

A reconnaissance airplane, routinely checking the area later, reported that a mast of a sunken freighter stuck out of the harbor and a group of buildings onshore were demolished.

After the war, one of the American prisoners held at Mukden reported that the Japanese were absolutely flabbergasted because they had established a secret headquarters along the waterfront at Dairen just a few days before Burman's plane dropped its bombs and, at that moment, the buildings were full of high Japanese officials. They couldn't understand how American Intelligence had so quickly found out about the meeting and sent a bomber to destroy their top brass.

In early November, MacArthur had called a conference at his head-quarters in Hollandia to discuss strategy among the various commands in the Pacific. Previously, Admirals King and Nimitz had changed their minds about a campaign to capture Formosa. Instead, they now favored attacks against Iwo Jima and Okinawa after Luzon was secured. The new schedule called for the Mindoro invasion December 5, Luzon December 20, Iwo Jima January 20, and Okinawa March 1, 1945, and it was agreed that the Twentieth Air Force would lend support by bombing enemy bases on Formosa, while Chennault's Fourteenth Air Force would make attacks on Hong Kong. Arnold, LeMay, and Wedemeyer were concerned about the ground situation in China now that the Japanese had moved into eastern and southern China. They objected to such assistance because fuel for B-29s was becoming critical. Wedemeyer proposed a cut for December, and another for January, which forced LeMay to change his operational plans. He had exceeded his allotment during October in support of Pacific operations, and a further reduction in fuel supplies would reduce such aid even more in the future. As the ground situation in China worsened during November, Wedemeyer was forced to use precious fuel to airlift Chinese ground forces, thus adding to the problem.

LeMay promised to do what he could in support of MacArthur's Mindoro invasion. Unexpected Japanese resistance forced MacArthur to change his schedule for moving northward so Mindoro was rescheduled to December 15, and the Lingayen invasion to January 9.

The Mindoro invasion went smoothly but Allied leaders knew that the invasion of Luzon would be a major one. The Joint Chiefs directed Wedemeyer to allot sufficient tonnage for 250 B-29 sorties in support of MacArthur's forces at Lingayen.

At Hollandia in November, LeMay had been told to make a double strike against aircraft installations in northern Formosa. These targets were so small that LeMay argued against B-29 strikes there. Instead, he sent planes against the Tachiarai Machine Works on Kyushu, an aircraft assembly and repair plant. The all too familiar cloudy weather prohibited the strike at Tachiarai but 28 did bomb the secondary target at Nanking on mainland China, but nine missed the target by six miles. With one B-29 lost, and absolutely no help whatsoever to MacArthur's forces, the mission was a tragic failure.

When MacArthur's invasion fleet moved into the Lingayen Gulf, Japanese air attacks were vicious, particularly the kamikaze suiciders who were making life a flaming hell for many ships. MacArthur sought LeMay's assistance in attacking Japanese airfields, and he quickly agreed although he had doubts about finding suitable targets. Not only was the weather bad over the target areas, but the fuel supply in China was completely inadequate for two strong support missions. He had only enough fuel for 75 B-29s so he sent an urgent appeal to Wedemeyer, who promised substantial aid.

Wedemeyer called in Brigadier General William H. Tunner, head of the Air Transport Command's India-China Division. Tunner agreed to deliver 2,700 tons of gasoline by January 16. Between ATC planes, and those of the bomber command, almost 7,500 tons were brought to China. It was a remarkable feat because weather over the Hump was miserable most of the time, and many crews were lost.

MacArthur's main concern was that Japanese fighters and bombers would use bases in Formosa for attacks against his forces at Lingayen. Although weather continued to disrupt B-29 missions, attacks against Formosan air installations were successful for the most part, particularly against the airplane modification center at Kagi and the airfield installation at Shinchiku, which was completely leveled.

These missions were effective because few enemy planes were able to make antishipping strikes during the crucial first days at Lingayen Gulf. Certainly, these few attacks were nothing compared to what MacArthur had feared following the concentrated attacks of January 6. Although Arnold and LeMay had serious doubts about using B-29s in such purely tactical roles, they tended to agree that losses off Luzon beachhead may have been kept to a minimum because of their efforts, and the work of the Navy's fast carriers. Certainly, the long-range photo-reconnaissance B-29s were most helpful to MacArthur and his command and he expressed his gratification.

In the summer of 1944, LeMay had told Arnold that the fields in China badly needed resurfacing. The original work with crude manual labor wasn't expected to hold up for an extended time, and now the runways were breaking down sooner than expected. Arnold said at the time that the command could expect only nine more months in the theater, so further expenditures on the runways were not justified. He asked LeMay if he needed more B-29s but, under the circumstances, LeMay declined. He was frank in telling Arnold that operations out of the CBI could be justified only until bases in other theaters became available. He told Arnold that he hoped the Joint Chiefs would consider a XX Bomber Command move to another theater earlier than previously projected.

In November, the Japanese overran Liuchow and Nanning, so B-29 operations in the Chengtu area would soon be curtailed regardless of what decision was made at the highest level. Wedemeyer gave Arnold a realistic description of the Chinese ground situation. And, now that he'd had a chance to deal directly with Chiang Kai-shek, he told Arnold that he agreed with Stilwell's criticism of the Generalissimo. He recommended that the XX Bomber Command be removed from China, and reiterated this conviction even after the situation stabilized in mid-December. He told Arnold that the advance of the Japanese had been halted primarily because of bad weather and overextended supply lines, and not because of Chinese counterattacks.

On January 12, Wedemeyer again wrote Arnold and Marshall that the bomber command should be removed no later than the first week of February. He said the command's removal would increase supplies for Chinese forces, and he could augment the Fourteenth Air Force by new units from India. He added that B-29 bases could be used by B-24s, and that the 312th Fighter Wing could be put to better use than its present inactive status as a defense wing.

The Joint Chiefs decided January 15 to withdraw the XX Bomber Command to India and continue operations there, while plans were formulated for its later move to the Marianas.

Brigadier General Lauris Norstad, Twentieth Air Force's chief of staff, was sent to Guam in the Marianas, and LeMay was ordered to meet him there. At their meeting, LeMay was told that the Joint Chiefs of Staff had decided to move the B-29s out of China at the earliest possible time and station the 58th Bombardment Wing in the Marianas. Also, Norstad told LeMay that he would be transferred from his present command in India, which later would be deactivated, and would assume command of the XXI Bomber Command, replacing Hansell, who would be relieved.

Hansell was urged to stay on as vice commander but he asked that he not be so assigned. There were no quarrels or bad feelings between the two men. On the contrary, they had served together in the Eighth Air Force and Hansell had every confidence that Le May shared his views on strategic air warfare. He turned down the vice commander's job because he didn't think LeMay needed a vice commander, and he knew he would be unhappy as a figurehead. It was a wise, and generous, decision.

General Arnold really didn't have much choice in making the change regardless of any dissatisfaction he may have had about Hansell's performance because the XX Bomber Command had to be moved out of India and China, and the Marianas was the only logical place to move it. In such a move, with LeMay the senior man as a major general, it would have been perfectly normal to expect that LeMay would get the top job.

There's no question but that Arnold was dissatisfied with what Hansell's command had achieved but he did personally urge Hansell to stay on as vice commander, so it's apparent Arnold's disapproval wasn't total. Actually, Arnold sent Major General James Fechet, former chief of the Army Air Corps, with Norstad for the express purpose of explaining to Hansell that he was not being relieved for cause or failure to perform.

LeMay had repeatedly reported to Washington that hauling supplies by air over the Hump for his command, Chennault's, and Chiang Kai-shek's armies was impossible, and kept insisting that no more B-29s be sent to India and China. He had explained that it took seven trips by B-29 tankers over the Hump, plus those by cargo planes, to get enough fuel to the forward area for one mission over Japan. Now that the decision was made, he was pleased that the Joint Chiefs of Staff had followed his recommendations.

Once the decision was finalized the transfer of B-29s from China to India was expedited January 20. The only B-29s left in China were attached to a photo-reconnaissance unit that hadn't completed its work on behalf of MacArthur's command.

LeMay brought Brigadier General Roger Ramey back with him to Kharagpur as the new head of the XX Bomber Command to, as he told him, "bring you up to speed before I leave."

LeMay had been dissatisfied with the results of most missions ever since he had come to the CBI. Even before the command returned to India he had set up a series of targets out of those rear bases so crews could improve their skills in formation flying and the technique of dropping bombs through integration of the radar system and the bombsight. In a sense, these were training missions to prepare bomber crews for the more exacting tasks of attacking targets in Japan once they moved to the Marianas, but they also were run to help the ground forces in Burma. The first such mission was flown before the command moved out of China when the Malagan railroad yards at Rangoon were attacked November 3 in association with planes from the Eastern Air Command. These yards had gained in importance because the rail system in Burma had been seriously damaged by previous attacks, so destruction would hamper Japanese forces on the front lines. For the first time, the command was able to carry a maximum bombload of 10 tons per aircraft because of the short distance. The attack was so successful that damage to rolling stock and trackage was extensive, and the roundhouse, which served as the aiming point, was demolished. LeMay called it the command's first job of precision bombing. To add to his satisfaction, all crews returned safely although one plane was lost during a ditching en route to the target.

Stratemeyer congratulated LeMay and immediately asked for another on November 27; this time an attack on the Bang So marshaling yard at Bangkok. These yards were even more important to the Japanese communications network because they fed trains from French Indochina to the Burma front, northern Thailand, and Singapore via branch lines radiating from this hub. Again the command destroyed its aiming points, and tracks in every direction were cut. This time a B-29 was lost on its way back to base.

While the command flew the maximum number of missions out of China in late 1944 with the fuel available in the forward area, it continued to support Allied forces in Burma with attacks against rail systems.

The 1,500-foot steel Rama VI railroad bridge over the Chao Phraya River had long been considered a prime target despite its small size because it was a vital link in Burma's rail system. Bombers went out December 14 to try and knock it out but the weather was bad so the Central Railroad Station in Rangoon was selected instead.

When crews of the 40th Group went out to their airplanes to prepare for the mission, they howled with protest when they found that 500-pound bombs, with a new explosive called Composition B that was far more powerful than TNT and much less stable, hung on racks below the 1,000-pound bombs. Some crews threatened to refuse to fly the mission, claiming the bomb loading was in violation of the field order from Bomber Command. They said these lighter bombs had a different ballistic coefficient than the half-ton bombs hanging over them and they might collide when released from the bomb bay. With their instantaneous fuses, they told Group Commander Colonel Blanchard, the danger was high of an explosion beneath the aircraft.

Blanchard threatened court-martials for those who refused to fly the mission, so they reluctantly agreed to go.

Lieutenant Marion Burke navigated the airplane leading the low element as it headed for Rangoon. An extra pilot was along because the mission was considered a "milk run" but it would give the new arrival experience over a combat target.

As the formation droned toward the target, they could see anti-aircraft fire ahead but it didn't appear near them.

After bombardier Joe Levine dropped their bombs, Burke felt their B-29 rock violently.

The tail gunner screamed, "My God! The sky's turned red."

They immediately suspected that bombs had collided under one of the planes and had blown it up.

Burke turned back to his navigation table but it was gone! Something had come through the plane and wiped out his desk. He blanched. If he had been facing that desk, he would have lost both arms.

He glanced behind him to note with horror that the bomb bays were on fire.

Then the flight engineer yelled, "Number three's gone!" It had been torn completely from the wing, and now the wing itself started to crumple.

"Abandon ship!" the pilot called.

They had lost communication with the crew in the rear so it was hoped they had received the signal.

Burke glanced at radio operator Richard Montgomery and was shocked to find that the sergeant's left hand was hanging only by a tendon. There was no time for emergency aid with the airplane breaking up so he shoved the operator into the nose-wheel well. The sergeant tried to climb back into the airplane but Burke jumped on his shoulders and pushed him out just as the plane started to spin. He followed quickly.

They landed near a Burmese village not far from Rangoon in the middle of a large Japanese troop-training camp for men bound for the Burma front.

Bombardier Levine and Burke got the radio operator's arm bandaged but there was no hope of saving his hand. At first, they thought they might escape but it wasn't long before Japanese troops found them, along with two others of their crew.

They learned later that four of their group's 11 aircraft had gone down after one of them exploded over the target, showering debris throughout the formation. Two actually crashed into the city of Rangoon, and part of the bombs, or one of the planes, killed 753 Japanese on a troop train. They learned the figure later from British prisoners who had been called upon to bury the Japanese soldiers.

The Japanese, never sparing on brutality when it came to American airmen, particularly B-29 fliers, went to work on the new prisoners. They had to stand in the jungle all night, with their hands tied behind them, and the Japanese didn't even spare young Montgomery, who was suffering from pain and shock from the loss of his hand. Any time one of them started to slump, he was kicked.

Next day, a Japanese general interrogated them while his men beat them unmercifully. There were frequent blows to the head by the back end of a samurai sword. This interrogation under various Japanese went on for 48 hours. Then they were loaded on a truck, with guards grinning at them with their weapons cocked and pointed at their heads. They were sure they were being taken out to be shot but, instead, they were transported to an old British prison in the northwestern part of Rangoon which had been taken over by the Japanese. There, they found their crew was still intact, the only one of the four planes downed over the target to survive in its entirety. They were fortunate because there were no survivors of the plane that blew up, and only a few survivors of the other two planes.

Their ordeal had just begun. The Japanese singled out copilot Lionel Coffin because he refused to answer any questions. In punishment, he was placed in a small cage outside in the sun where he could neither sit nor stand erect and they kept him there for three days without food or water. The spirit of this man defied the Japanese and, when he refused to crack, they finally gave up on him.

Another five of the crew were placed in an eight-foot-long, six-foot-wide cell where they received water but no food for several days. From the date of their capture December 14, 1944, until

Christmas they were given no food at all. That day they were given some raw meat, which they ate wolfishly.

All during this time they were interrogated daily, beaten constantly with teakwood clubs, rifle butts, hands, anything that could inflict bodily harm.

One favorite stunt was for several Japanese to come into their cell, pick out one man, and beat him about the face until the man's face swelled up.

The extra pilot on the crew, Lieutenant Robert F. Darrington, a tall, lean Texan, will be forever remembered in their hearts and minds. He was selected for the facial pummeling one day but he just lifted his chin and the Japanese swung and missed, tumbling to the floor to his immense mortification. Two Japanese then forced him to the ground and beat him within an inch of his life.

The Japanese were bad enough but the Koreans and Formosans, in trying to impress their bosses, were the worst of all.

After three weeks of constant torture, they were moved into an open bay instead of their cramped quarters where they had been sleeping on bare concrete floors. There, Burke found a former friend from his hometown in Texas who had been in solitary confinement for two years. This former husky football player was down to 65 pounds. He lived only one more week.

The American fliers were kept separate from ground troops and the worst treatment was meted out to them. They were called Chicago gangsters and daily beatings were commonplace.

Once, a guard outside the compound decided that Burke hadn't saluted him properly. He called the navigator over to the fence and proceeded to hit him in the head with his rifle butt. Then, Burke was forced to climb on top of a narrow seven-foot-high metal fence that had spearlike spikes along the two-inch-wide top. There he was told to straddle the fence at attention. Every time he moved the guard would yell. When Burke could hang on no longer, he fell off. The guard wasn't through. Burke was forced to stand at attention although he was so weak that he was about to faint. Just then a Cockney British enlisted man sneaked up behind him when the guard wasn't looking, put Burke's hat on his head, and took his place. The guard never noticed the difference but that Cockney probably saved Burke's life because he could have endured no more.

The camp commandant, a Japanese captain, was a sadistic bastard that everyone hated. He had a large, yellow tomcat that was well fed and impeccably groomed. One day the cat made the mistake of taking a stroll through the compound. That night they all had a taste of meat with their rice and it tasted good even though it was cat meat.

Nuka, brand name for a rice that was supposed to prevent beriberi, a degenerative disease that killed many prisoners due to malnutrition, went through them like a dose of salts. Pepsi Cola, which had a popular radio jingle at that time, would have recognized the tune but certainly not the words that the prisoners made up to match the tune. "Nuka, Nuka, hits the spot. Two full cups is a helluva lot. Twice as much in the binjo, too. Nuka Nuka is the food for you." The binjo was the little box that they used to relieve themselves.

When there wasn't an English translator around during interrogation, the prisoners would smile toothily but use every epithet in their vocabulary, which, for some, was extensive.

One day, when a translator was in attendance, a prisoner was asked the now familiar question which they had previously refused to answer. "Why do the B-29s outrun our fighters?"

An imaginative type, one young man looked at the interrogator in all seriousness and came closer. In a confidential voice, he said, "Don't you know?" He whispered, "They've got a built-in tail wind."

The interrogator looked at him solemnly, smiled eagerly, and carefully made notes. And that's the way he reported it to his superiors.

Month after month they endured beatings and humiliations, receiving food adequate enough merely to stay alive, but without any medical attention.

One of the translators, a Japanese civilian, took a liking to Burke, keeping him in hard-to-get cigarettes. Whether he was just using different tactics to get information, Burke never found out, but as a chain smoker Burke appreciated the cigarettes. This Japanese civilian was a graduate engineer of the University of Washington who had gone to Japan before the war when he found it impossible for a Japanese to get an acronautical job in the United States. He had left his family in California so he had one constant refrain. He had been told, as had the other Japanese, that their country occupied the West Coast of the United States. He continued to inquire of Burke what the situation was like there and Burke never did convince him that the United States mainland had not been invaded. Still, the translator, obviously worried about his family, pressed Burke for information as to whether he thought the Japanese had killed all Americans on the Coast.

For a time they could bathe once a day in a water trough outside which was also the source of their drinking water. When the Royal Air Force bombed the water mains coming down from the hills, that ended the water trough. Now they were given just enough water to drink. Their food continued in short supply, but the bullocks roaming just outside their fences were evidence that the Japanese weren't going hungry. Their rations were cut even further when the Royal Air Force bombed a river barge that brought their food. They had been getting a cup of rice for breakfast, rice with a few vegetables for lunch, and another cup of rice for dinner. Once in a great while they'd get some fish heads, and even rarer—meat.

In April 1945 they were all taken out to see who was fit to walk. Burke was one of those who couldn't so he was left behind and the others were force-marched to a town farther from advancing British troops.

With Japanese civilians as guards, things eased up a bit. One night, five days after most prisoners had marched away, they noticed these guards were gone. Two of the more agile were boosted over the fence to check the guard shack. There they found the Japanese had left so hurriedly their food was still on the table. They grabbed all the food in sight and gorged themselves for the first time in months. They had to lock the gates to keep the starving Burmese out because there was no more food. After a search, Burke and Joe Levine found weapons, including some of their own .45s, with plenty of ammunition.

Two days later, the Royal Air Force dropped Army rations and there was enough for everyone.

An Australian wing commander, who had been captured just before the Japanese left, tried to impound the rations, saying he wanted to save them because he didn't know how long they would be needed.

Some prisoners had been there three years. They broke into the warehouse and ate all the impounded rations.

When the wing commander threatened them, one American flier stuck a .45 automatic in the commander's face. With his hand tightening on the trigger, the American said, "Shut up or I'll blow your head off." That Aussie never knew how close he was to death.

Indian troops, with their British officers, rescued them a few days later and they were taken down the river to Rangoon by hospital ship and then on to India.

Whether the bomb loading caused the tragic accident that killed so many, and made prisoners of others, or whether a stray Japanese shell exploded in the bomb bay of one of the B-29s, blowing three more out of the sky, will never be known. Not one member of the crew of the exploding bomber survived. The episode still lingers in the minds of some survivors with a bitterness that will never be erased.

The strike by all groups was one of the best ever flown for bombing results but it cost the 40th Group five B-29s and their crews. Of the 750 or so Japanese troops known to have been killed on the ground, Burke and the others didn't consider their losses a fair exchange but they were grateful their sacrifices were not all in vain.

A B-29 reconnaissance plane spotted a Japanese task force of two battleships and a seaplane tender at Cape St. Jacques, French Indochina, December 20. LeMay quickly set up 49 B-29s but before they could be dispatched the warships left the area. With airplanes loaded with eight 1,000-pound bombs, LeMay put crews on standby to hit the Ywataung railroad yards near Mandalay but bad weather made such a mission impossible. Still trying to get them off on a mission, he had the groups change fuses and they headed for another attack on the elusive Rama VI bridge. This time a direct hit was made, with several near misses, plus a number of hits on bridge abutments. At last the railroad bridge was put out of service; at least for the time being.

Christmas Eve of 1944 Japanese bombers penetrated the defenses around Calcutta and four planes strafed and bombed command headquarters at Kharagpur. The bombs caused only a few injuries but several planes were damaged.

Farther north, Captain Matthew J. Farrelly, base defense officer for the 462nd Group, was at dinner when the alert sounded at Piardoba. He hurried to the tower where Captain B. K. Thurston was on duty. En route, he could clearly hear a plane overhead but he couldn't see it. He was out of breath when he asked Thurston, "Has that plane identified itself?"

"No, it hasn't, despite our challenges."

Farrelly was in a quandary. Should he authorize the British antiaircraft batteries to open fire? They were trained crews who had fought in the Battle of Britain during the blitz, and their radar was locked on to the airplane overhead, and the gunners were eager to open fire. Still he hesitated, reluctant to give the final word until some overt action was taken. He checked the perimeter defense posts by phone and learned that the Gurka guards with their heavy, sharp knives were in position and ready for anything. He realized he was violating his own defense plan by not giving the order to fire with an unidentified plane overhead during an alert. While he agonized over the decision, the plane left the area.

Next day Farrelly thanked God for his indecision because he learned the plane was an American C-46 cargo carrier that was unable to establish radio contact with the ground due to a malfunction of the plane's radio.

A total of 28 Japanese bombers penetrated the Calcutta-area defenses from bases in Burma, and British fighter pilots shot every one of them down. The British deliberately didn't announce the destruction of the Japanese bombers so their commanders would wonder whatever happened to them.

General Arnold passed the word to LeMay that the Japanese Navy had suffered grievous losses in the last few months. In effect, the Japanese fleet, as an effective fighting force, had ceased to exist. The loss of 1,500 Japanese carrier fliers during the Allied invasion of the Marianas and the Battle of the Philippine Sea was particularly acute.

Singapore had fallen almost intact into Japanese hands in February 1942, and since then had been developed as the best naval station outside the home islands. Arnold stressed that, with extensive damage inflicted on the Japanese fleet, dock and repair facilities at Singapore should continue to have top priority. LeMay's planners objected because Singapore was at the maximum range of B-29s, forcing them to carry three bomb-bay tanks and only a ton of bombs. Despite command objections, Arnold insisted and LeMay sent B-29s November 5 to strike at the King George Graving Dock, the largest dry dock in the area.

Photographs taken later by a "recon" plane showed that the gate was out of operation, and analysts said it would remain out for at least three months. Postwar investigations proved their analysis remarkably accurate.

Arnold reported that the Joint Chiefs were anxious for another attack. He said, "Because the Japanese fleet is in such a crippled condition, repair facilities such as those at Singapore continue to have first priority." Other priorities intervened so it wasn't until January

11, 1945, that a follow-up attack could be scheduled. The Admiralty IX Floating Dock and the King's Dock at Singapore were selected for a divided attack but no hits were scored, and two B-29s were lost.

Captain Albert Bores and his 468th Group crew almost became the third casualty. Their aircraft was caught in a down draft just as they started across the Malay Peninsula. The huge bomber was whirled up and down like a yo-yo. As Bores tried to hold the aircraft straight and level, a strong force hurled them upward at express-train speed and bombs sheared off their shackles and crashed through the bomb-bay doors. The pilot fought to keep the Fort out of a spin after the airspeed dropped from 310 mph to 180 mph. At last, he established some measure of control and headed back to home base in India.

# CHAPTER 13

# LeMay Transferred

Brigadier General Roger M. Ramey, an experienced bomber man from Hansell's staff, replaced LeMay as head of the XX Bomber Command at Kharagpur. Some of LeMay's top personnel went along with him to the Marianas, including Colonel Blanchard, commanding officer of the 40th Group, so personnel were promoted. Colonel Henry R. Sullivan served temporarily as new commander of the 40th before he was replaced by Colonel Kenneth Skaer.

After LeMay was transferred, the XX Bomber Command no longer served under Arnold's direct command. For the next few months, Lord Mountbatten was in charge and he sent B-29s against targets in the Rangoon, Bangkok, and Singapore areas.

Arnold's original insistence that bomber crews be trained to maintain their airplanes without ground personnel now paid off again. The first group of ground personnel left their bases February 27 for Calcutta from which they were shipped to their new base on Tinian in the Marianas. Others followed at prescribed intervals. Despite the loss of maintenance personnel, missions were flown and their monthly totals actually increased as crews kept their own planes in commission with only a ground-crew chief to help with difficult maintenance problems. Arnold had often been criticized for his insistence that aircrew personnel have both combat and maintenance specialities. Undoubtedly it was costly but the practice paid off in airplanes downed at non-Air Force bases in China, Ceylon, and now the command's ability to undertake extensive operations by keeping their aircraft in commission.

* * *

Mine laying, which had not been stressed after the mining of the Moesi at Palembang, now received major attention. New areas were added such as Saigon, French Indochina, which was a major shipping point between Japan and Singapore; Camranh Bay, northwest of Saigon, and a harbor used by both Japanese naval and merchant ships; and Phnom Penh, a river port up the Mekong from Saigon.

For the first time there were large numbers of new crews that had to be trained, so these missions were ideal for learning techniques that would be used later.

Ramey sent out the mine-laying B-29s during the full moon of January 25 and 26 because Superfortresses had to make their drops between two and six thousand feet. U.S. Navy officials were complimentary about these missions to Singapore, Saigon, and Camranh Bay. So successful was the mine laying of the river leading up to Saigon that its port was closed to the Japanese for several months.

The next full moon was February 27 and B-29s went out again to mine the Johore Strait at Singapore.

After the Fourteenth Air Force lost its forward bases in China, its mine-laying operations were restricted to the upper Yangtze due to range limitations of its bombers. Chennault's bombers laid more than 300 mines in this area, including mines that were designed to drift downstream and, hopefully, help to destroy river boats and barges along this important Japanese supply route.

Although the Fourteenth Air Force did an outstanding mining job, Chennault realized that only B-29s could completely block the entire river so he offered some of his limited stock of aviation fuel if Ramey would sent his B-29s to China to mine the mouth of the river. Ramey agreed and 12 B-29s, operating out of Luliang, mined the river February 27. The next month another group mined the mouth of the Hwangoo and the south channel of the Yangtze. Crews had become so expert at this time that no B-29s were lost and their experience was most useful in the training of the 313th Wing, which later was used as a specialized mining unit out of the Marianas.

Mining missions were sandwiched in between regular bombing attacks, including a maximum effort against the Admiralty IX Floating Dry Dock at Singapore. Hits were scored on a ship inside the dock, and on the dock itself. Both ship and dock later sank. The mission was even more worthwhile because extensive damage was caused to the nearby naval base.

Ramey was all set to send crews out again to Singapore February 6 but Stratemeyer told him that Mountbatten had ordered that naval installations at Singapore and Penang were not to be attacked again. Mountbatten gave as his reason that the British wanted these valuable facilities preserved for use after the Japanese were driven out of Singapore. Such a statement caused raised eyebrows, and some bitter words were expressed against this British attempt to save installations and equipment that were valuable to the Japanese war effort.

While Ramey held up the mission, he asked Arnold for guidance. He was advised to cease such attacks for the time being until an investigation could be completed, and turn to other targets.

Ramey arranged an appointment at Kandy with Mountbatten, who specified priority targets in the Kuala Lumpur area, and some at Singapore. Mountbatten told him that oil dumps and commercial port facilities could be bombed if care was taken that no bombs fell on dock areas that he had specified as off-limits areas.

Superforts bombed a navy yard and an arsenal near Saigon and Bangkok February 7 by radar and many bombs landed in residential areas so Mountbatten put these targets off limits.

The Rama VI bridge, which had been attacked before and temporarily put out of commission, received the attention of the 40th and 468th Groups which bombed it in small formations. Four direct hits destroyed the northeastern approach and 65 percent of the central span collapsed. At last, this difficult pinpoint target was out for good.

The huge military dumps in the Rangoon area, where 75 percent of all Japanese supplies were stored, now were considered prime B-29 targets after they had scored so heavily against the transportation system. At the request of the Eastern Air Command's Strategic Air Force, Ramey was directed to coordinate his operations with B-24 groups. The attacks were successful but it was difficult to assess which groups did the most damage, although the B-29s, with their greater bombloads, undoubtedly accomplished the most destruction.

For the first time, the bomber command used a technique that would later be mandatory for getting formations assembled before the final run on targets over Japan. The lead aircraft dropped a specifically colored smoke bomb and all B-29s assigned to that leader assembled around him.

Mountbatten was planning an invasion of the Malay Peninsula for early fall of 1945, so B-29s made the remainder of their attacks in support of his contemplated invasion. Actually, the war ended before his amphibious forces were ready to make their landings. At the time, however, great destruction was caused to railroad repair shops at Kuala Lumpur; the Empire Dock area at Singapore, the only worthwhile target that wasn't out of bounds, had 39 percent of its warehouse area burned out; and the shop and warehouse area of the naval base received much new damage. The latter attack was made with Mountbatten's stern admonition that the King George VI Dock was not to be touched despite Admiral King's communication that cited the command in a "well done" message for its previous attacks. Two other missions hit oil-storage areas at Singapore, and the 49th and last mission of the XX Bomber Command went in low to fire-bomb targets at Bukum Island. This night mission was flown primarily to establish a tactical doctrine for later fire raids against Japanese cities but it was hardly a forerunner of what was to come because little damage was done.

If one group of men deserves to be called "unsung heroes" those who flew the B-29s on photo-reconnaissance missions must rank high on the list. When the bomber command first came to Asia, information and photographs of Japanese targets were almost totally lacking, and what information there was couldn't be relied upon because it was so dated. The early reconnaissance airplanes were converted bombers, and poorly equipped for the job. Despite such shortcomings, they mapped most of Asia, flew surveillance and search missions at sea, and provided up-to-date information and photographs for MacArthur's command. No other aircraft at the time had the range to do such an extensive job of intelligence gathering. And some remained behind to carry on their high-altitude missions after the command moved to Tinian. Theirs was a lonely, extremely dangerous job because they had to fly straight and level for minutes at a time on a run, oblivious to flak and fighters, because that was the only way suitable photographs could be obtained. Many planes were lost. Some went out and were never heard from again.

Prior to Admiral Halsey's carrier strikes against Okinawa, B-29s photographed the entire area, not only to spot targets for Halsey's fliers, but to find possible sites for future air bases. The work started during the summer of 1944 and continued on into October.

MacArthur sought their assistance prior to his landings on Leyte, and despite the loss of two airplanes, vital photographs of northern

Luzon were taken and wet prints rushed to MacArthur. Their dangerous work was accomplished against great odds, not least of them the engine problems of early B-29s.

It wasn't until late November 1944 that the first true photo-reconnaissance B-29s were delivered to the Far East as F-13s, and were assigned as Flight C of the 311th Wing's 1st Photo Reconnaissance Squadron. Their initial job was daily coverage of Kyushu, and they flew despite the weather any time Pacific commanders sought their assistance. These units remained at Hsinching, China, after the bomber command pulled out to map Manchuria, Korea, and North China. They also did extensive mapping and photo coverage for Mountbatten. Their flights averaged 15 hours, and along with boredom their greatest hazard was Japanese fighters who were well aware of what they were doing, and considered them prime targets.

With a naval observer aboard each F-13, it was standard operating procedure that any time a ship was seen visually or on radar that an open-ended radio broadcast was made to the U.S. Naval Receiving Stations so intelligence about Japanese ship movements was enhanced.

Combat B-29s of the 3rd Photo Reconnaissance Squadron also flew photographic missions out of India on behalf of Mountbatten, and later moved to Guam. Despite attacks by Japanese fighters, photographic strips were made around Georgetown and another area farther south so that maps could be made for Mountbatten's proposed invasion of the peninsula. The war ended just as his fleet was ready to land troops.

By March 30, the command was out of strategic targets. After the last mission, crews were ordered to fly to Tinian individually in two increments of 90 Superfortresses. The first was scheduled to arrive April 1 and the latter May 1. They staged out of Luliang, China, and so battle tested were they that not one life was lost or B-29 destroyed in 18-hour flights from India to the Marianas.

While the XX Bomber Command remained behind at Kharagpur under Brigadier General Joseph Smith, former chief of staff, Ramey was made head of the reactivated 58th Wing and went to Tinian.

A small number of combat crews had been sent home, the majority went to Tinian. Although combat personnel had been overseas for a year, there still was no rotation policy as in other theaters. They weren't told anything, but commanders were advised that only if a crewman's effectiveness would be jeopardized by continued combat duty would he be considered for rotation. Crewmen joked that if you could crawl out of bed in the morning you were considered fit for further combat duty. Many individuals were sent to rest camps at Darjeeling, Madras, and Kashmir, but for those who didn't go anywhere for a rest there was considerable bitterness. Trained crews were at a premium and there were insufficient replacements, and some personnel found it difficult to understand why they couldn't fly a certain number of missions and qualify for return to the States.

The last of the original group commanders, Colonel Alva L. Harvey, was named deputy commander of the 58th Wing under Ramey and went to Tinian, while Colonel James G. Selser took the 444th to the Marianas.

Personnel of the XX Bomber Command didn't leave for Okinawa until early July. There they were assigned to the Eighth Air Force. The Eighth was converted to a very heavy bomber outfit after VE-Day. The XX Bomber Command went out of existence after its arrival, and its personnel were assigned to other organizations.

In the autumn of 1944 a special Air Force board had been set up by Arnold to evaluate the Matterhorn project. The gist of its findings was contained in a weasel-worded statement that "there is no question but that strategic bombing pays big dividends and perhaps the diversion of such logistical effort to the XX Bomber Command is more than justified in the big picture all of which can not be seen from this theater."

After the war, the U.S. Strategic Bombing Survey's report minced no words. It flatly stated that the operations out of China were not decisive in the Japanese surrender. Other analyses were equally unfavorable. Those who compiled the survey ignored the realities of the B-29's presence in China. It was the *only* area at the time capable of handling B-29 operations against Japan. Arnold never expected that its operations would be decisive. The XX Bomber Command did prove that Japan's homeland could be hit, and hit hard, and despite Chennault's belief that the Twentieth was a liability in China, there's no question but that the morale of the Chinese people was sustained by its presence during a very bitter period when large areas of their nation were being occupied by the Japanese. China was kept as an ally, and most important of all, the B-29 was debugged and the tactics developed for the highly successful attacks yet to come that would bring Japan to her knees begging for peace.

Few of the attacks against Japan proper were effective. Weather was one of the prime reasons for failure of crews to destroy more targets. In steel production, the damage to Yawata resulted in a very small decrease in production because it wasn't known at the time that the Japanese had production capacity that wasn't even being used. At Anshan, the series of attacks proved far more successful than was thought at the time. B-29s dropped 550 tons of bombs on the steel plant, causing the loss of 425,000 tons of steel and iron production. This loss didn't affect Japan's total production too much because it was already limited by a tight shipping situation due to the loss of so many of its merchant ships.

Omura was a frustrating target because weather was bad so much of the time. Only the mission of October 25 caused appreciable damage when half the building area was destroyed or damaged. Almost six months of production was lost, and there were heavy casualties of crucial plant personnel.

Attacks against Formosa and Hankow were worthwhile missions but outside the guidelines established for B-29 operations. So were missions against targets up and down the Malay Peninsula and in Burma, and the early mining missions in French Indochina.

After the war ended, Japanese civilians were interrogated about B-29 operations out of China. Many said these B-29 raids against Kyushu created doubts about Japan's invincibility because the government found it difficult to explain them. Japan was forced to divert some fighters to the homeland for defense against the B-29 attacks, although the number amounted to only 5 percent of Japan's total fighter strength. Still, other combat areas did benefit.

No theater in the world could have been a rougher proving ground for the B-29 than the CBI. Much of the Superfortresses' later success derived from lessons learned in this theater, so improvements could be incorporated into later airplanes operating out of the Marianas.

As for the B-29, for pilots, in particular, it was not love at first sight—or first handling. These men had been handpicked for their experience in four-engine aircraft like the B-24 and the B-17. The command historian put it most succinctly: "Their conversion was born in fact, fancy, pride, legend—but most important, of actual performance under combat conditions."

The Superforts' equipment was so new that crew members, regardless of their background, found they had to learn everything all over again. The central fire-control system proved not only accurate but dependable once they learned how to use it. The radar equipment, although primitive in comparison to what would come later, was useful in spotting bad weather, for navigation, and, certainly once it was used properly, a great aid to bombing. The B-29 really came into its own as a very long-range bomber once crews mastered cruise-control techniques. The cruise-control lessons learned in India and China proved invaluable later in saving crews, and improving the B-29's capability by increasing its bombloads.

The bombing survey said that B-29s could have been used more effectively in coordinating with submarines for search missions. They were used effectively that way out of the Marianas, but there wasn't the need in the CBI for such operations. They also talked about low-level attacks against Japanese shipping but there were many far more useful airplanes, particularly Navy carrier bombers, for such work. And, lastly, it was their judgment that mining attacks should have been started sooner, although the most valuable mining missions were later flown from bases in the Marianas where such operations paid vital dividends.

These target systems were considered by the Committee of Operations Analysts, and some were rejected after suitable discussion. Arnold had insisted from the beginning that strategic bombers should strike at the heart of an enemy's industrial power and not be diverted by theater commanders who would use this magnificent aerial weapon only as a tool to further their own limited ends. Within less than five months of the bomber command's departure from India, Japan would be destroyed by strategic airpower. That fact alone says more for Arnold's critics than anything else.

The bombing survey took up the matter of whether the fuel and supplies expended by the Twentieth Air Force might have been put to better use if they had been turned over to Chennault's Fourteenth Air Force. Chennault later developed strong opinions about what he would have done with these supplies, but the strategic bombing survey disagreed, saying that the loss of these supplies to Chennault's operations had been overemphasized because the Fourteenth wasn't all that effective. While the XX Bomber Command attacks against Formosa, as well as individual bombings of secondary or last-resort targets in China, were deemed only of limited value by Chennault, with the possible exception of the fire raid on Hankow, the survey said these attacks were of value to Chinese resistance to the Japanese in the ground war.

The bombing survey said also that the thousands of tons of fuel and supplies that were flown in from rear bases in India for Chinese ground troops all too often went to units that never fought significantly against the Japanese during the entire war.

After the war, LeMay said that the greatest contribution the XX Bomber Command made to the war effort was proving the B-29 in combat, and making recommendations to improve the airplane. He conceded that in relation to the success of operations out of the Marianas once the Twentieth Air Force really got going, that actual physical damage caused by XX Bomber Command attacks on Japanese targets was not too great. "Based on what they got done in China and India with all their supply and maintenance problems they accomplished a hell of a lot," LeMay said.

Chennault and Stilwell were incorrect in their assumptions that Japan could be defeated only from bases in China. In a few short months it would be shown how tragically wrong they had been all along, and how right Arnold had been from the start.

# PART TWO

# CHAPTER 14

# B-29s Hit Tokyo

Guam is the largest of 15 lush, tropical islands in the Mariana's chain in the Western Pacific. It had been a territory of the United States since 1898 until it fell to invasion forces from nearby Japanese-controlled Tinian and Saipan after World War II was declared. Last of the main islands to be captured, following Army and Marine landings in July, Guam was finally back in American hands August 10, 1944, after a bloody battle.

Saipan was invaded first on June 15, and for two weeks fighting was bitter with losses high on both sides. The worst fighting occurred July 6 when the Japanese launched an all-out banzai attack along Saipan's northwest shores. U.S. lines were breached but GIs managed to regroup and before the day ended 4,311 Japanese lay dead along and above the beaches. When the entire island was occupied three days later, all but a handful of the almost 32,000 Japanese Army and Navy men were dead—ten times the number of Americans killed.

Saipan's loss resulted in the downfall of General Hideki Tojo's cabinet, which fell July 18, 1944, reducing for the first time some of the dominant control that the military held over the Japanese Government.

The invasion of Tinian proved not as tough a nut as Saipan to crack although resistance was fierce. In what has been called the most successful amphibious operation of World War II, over 9,000 Japanese were killed after Marines invaded the island through shark-infested waters July 24 and 25. U.S. losses were 328 killed and 1,571 wounded, and the island was declared secure August 1, 1944, although approximately 1,000 Japanese remained holed up in caves around the island. In the months ahead, they frequently charged through tent areas jabbing knives into as many sleeping American bodies as they could find.

As American air, sea, and ground forces prepared for the final round against the Japanese homeland, new organizations multiplied almost daily. It was apparent to the Joint Chiefs that reorganization of the various Pacific commands must be completed quickly.

Arnold placed Major General Walter H. Frank in charge of a special mission April 20, 1944, to prepare the groundwork for introduction of Hansell's XXI Bomber Command and follow-on B-29 units after the Marianas were captured. In coordination with Nimitz' staff, requirements for the '29 commands were agreed to in a spirit of cooperation.

Brigadier General Charles E. Thomas headed the advance echelon of the XXI Bomber Command and established temporary headquarters at Hawaii's Hickam Field in late May.

In a later development, Lieutenant General Millard F. Harmon was placed in charge of Army Air Forces for Pacific Ocean areas July 10, and reported to Nimitz in regard to all operations of his forces. Harmon was a man of vast experience because he previously commanded the United States Air Forces in the South Pacific. In keeping with the intent of the Joint Chiefs that the Twentieth Air Force must take its orders only from Arnold, Harmon was designated deputy commander of the Twentieth but reporting to Arnold and not Nimitz in that capacity. In effect, Harmon's position was comparable to the relationship of top Air Force commanders in the European theater. In other words, while Harmon was responsible to Nimitz as theater commander for air operations, he remained under administrative control of the commander of U.S. Army forces. In the Central Pacific, that commander was Lieutenant General Robert C. Richardson. It was an odd relationship that caused many start-up problems for the new B-29 command but in the final analysis Arnold still called the shots.

General Frank recommended that B-29 groups, and their supporting units, be assigned to the Mariana Islands with a wing assigned to each of five fields.

Nimitz gave Vice Admiral J. H. Hoover the job of constructing two fields, plus an air depot, on Guam, and two fields on Tinian, with another on Saipan. Guam also would be headquarters for the XXI Bomber Command, and Harmon's forward headquarters.

Harmon took over his new command August 1 in Hawaii and immediately set to work to get fields constructed. Work on them had been slow because of other priorities for shipping and construction personnel and he had a fight on his hands although Nimitz was understanding and did his best to help despite a multiplicity of demands from other critical areas.

The Japanese caused some delays in getting the fields started by their fighting tenacity on Tinian and Guam, which upset earlier timetables by a month. Heavy summer rains added to the problem, and frequent enemy air raids didn't help.

Meanwhile, the XXI Bomber Command completed its training in Colorado, Kansas, and Nebraska. Unlike the XX Bomber Command, which went overseas with a minimum of training, the XXI had the advantage of the early command's experiences in India and China, and the airplanes had been modified so that their worst faults were largely eliminated. Also, the new command was able to make long, simulated flights over routes that were similar to those they would fly from Saipan to Tokyo. The first round trip from Kansas to Cuba, where practice bombs were dropped near the island, was a fiasco because weather forecasters made an erroneous forecast and the airplanes encountered serious engine problems. Formations used up so much fuel that B-29s had to land at bases all over the southeastern United States.

General Hansell took one of the first crews to Saipan in October. Major Jack Catton, the crew's regular airplane commander, relinquished his seat to Hansell. When they were taking off from Mather Field, Sacramento, for the long hop to Hawaii, Hansell snubbed the brake pedals to stop rotation of the wheels. Unfortunately, the airplane wasn't fully off the ground and Catton said later, "It felt as if a giant hand had shoved the airplane in the nose." For a moment, Catton turned white, thinking their time had come, but Hansell expertly got "Joltin' Josie, the Pacific Pioneer" airborne after an unusually long run.

The airplane performed perfectly on its flight across the Pacific to Hickam Field, Hawaii. There, Admiral Nimitz expressed an interest in coming out to see the airplane. The admiral literally gave the B-29 a white-glove inspection, and he was complimentary of the airplane and its crew when he talked to Hansell. Nimitz was impressed by the size of the airplane, which he was seeing for the first time, particularly the large bomb bays and their payload capacity. When Hansell described the remotely controlled, computing gunsight system, the admiral was fascinated, saying it was somewhat like the gun-control system aboard Navy ships.

Hansell explained his mission to Nimitz, and the command arrangements that called for operations from bases under the admiral's command. He told Nimitz that the Joint Chiefs had given him responsibility for their construction, bulk supply, and defense but that he would not be under Nimitz' command.

"I don't approve of this organization and command arrangement," Nimitz said frankly, "and if I had understood it more clearly I would have opposed it to Admiral King. But, since it is approved by the Joint Chiefs of Staff I will go along with it. You may be assured that I will give you every help and support. Now, you're going out to the forward area where my commander, Vice Admiral John Hoover, breaks admirals and throws them overboard without the slightest compunction. God knows what he'll do to you. Good luck."

Hansell was slightly shocked, but Nimitz was as good as his word and, to his great relief later, Hansell found Admiral Hoover a staunch supporter.

After they landed at Kwajalein Island, they parked alongside the coral runway. The B-29 was still highly classified so a sign was put up in front of the airplane saying that no one was permitted in it.

Near the Superfortress a B-24 Liberator was parked, and its crew painted a large sign that said, "This is the B-24 Liberator—a proven combat airplane. Everybody welcome."

A Navy Corsair fighter, bound for Eniwetok, flew alongside "Joltin' Josie, the Pacific Pioneer" to avail himself of the navigation expertise of the B-29's Lieutenant John W. Campbell.

As they approached Saipan, two P-47 fighters escorted them to the former Japanese Aslito air base, now renamed Isley Field in honor of a U.S. Navy flier who was shot down over Guam. Hansell brought the first B-29 in for a perfect landing October 12, 1944. Men of all services crowded around it and there was hope in many of them that this mighty new aerial weapon would end the war in the not-too-distant future without an invasion of Japan. For the Marines and Army men who had battled for Saipan's rocky shores at great cost that hope was greatest of all.

It was originally planned to provide two bases, each with two 8,500-foot runways, for each wing. One of the bases on Saipan was not suitable for heavily loaded B-29s so the entire wing was concentrated on only one base. This proved suitable although it caused much crowding and increased the vulnerability of the B-29s on the ground to Japanese air attack.

Four aviation engineering battalions were needed to complete Saipan's Isley Field after Hansell arrived. It was an incredible job of literally blowing hills out of the way and building 200 miles of roads through cane fields and across rolling ground where coral from the shaved hills was used to fill gullys. Japanese buildings were torn down and hundreds of new structures emerged in record time. The six-foot, four-inch Major General Sanderford Jarman kept engineers going at all hours and they got little sleep. They built one mile-long airfield in 12 days while bullets whipped around them as Japanese were routed from their defensive positions.

Tinian already had two small Japanese airfields so it was decided to expand them. The North Field runways were completed ahead of schedule but some paving and facilities weren't completed until June 1945. The delay was caused by the decision of the Joint Chiefs to base the 509th Composite Group on North Field. This was the outfit that was undergoing training to drop the atomic bombs, and they needed special facilities.

Tinian is shaped somewhat like the island of Manhattan so streets were named after many of those in New York City, including a Broadway that ran north and south.

Roosevelt became more and more concerned as he perused memorandums from the Joint Chiefs about expected casualties during the scheduled invasion of Japan, and he pressed Arnold for a step-up in B-29 operations.

Hansell's command had about the same amount of training that the XX Bomber Command had received. This situation was caused by changing the command from a night-bombing outfit to a daylight-bombing organization six weeks before the command was moved overseas. The state of training and efficiency, by Hansell's own later evaluation, was deplorable.

The XX Bomber Command in India was going through so many

changes under LeMay that little of value could be gained from their operations. The fact that Hansell and LeMay were training their commands along identical lines for daylight formation attacks was understandable because both had worked together in England to devise such tactics.

One of Hansell's problems was maintenance because the depot that had been shipped so carefully for easy assembly was completely lost during the invasion of Guam. The Navy's harbor master insisted that the ship carrying the depot clear out of the harbor within 24 hours during a Japanese counterattack. Depot supplies and equipment were hastily dumped into the jungle and never recovered. After that, maintenance supply had to come by air all the way from California. Then, when the depot was finally established, its control was taken over by General Harmon despite Hansell's vigorous protests.

Arnold's staff in Washington was aware that Hansell's command faced far tougher opposition than the XX Bomber Command in India. There were serious doubts among some Twentieth Air Force staffers about bombing targets over the main islands of Japan without fighter escort. Hansell was convinced such attacks were feasible because the B-29 could operate above 30,000 feet and make runs at high speed. A topnotch pilot, Hansell not only had commanded an air division in England, but had flown combat missions over Germany. He was disturbed, therefore, when he arrived in the Marianas without a single target folder and had to wait until reconnaissance missions were run to procure photographs and maps. Still, Hansell was confident because Saipan-based B-29s could reach all important industrial targets in the home islands. Unlike operations out of India and China, his XXI Bomber Command had a shorter supply line of only 5,000 miles from San Francisco, and ships brought in what was needed on a regular basis.

After Brigadier General Emmett "Rosey" O'Donnell brought his 73rd Wing to Saipan, Hansell ordered him to set up a series of combat training missions. Three missions were sent to Truk, formerly one of the great bastions of the South Pacific, but now a bypassed stronghold of limited value to the Japanese. Still an important submarine base, Truk was a legitimate target but B-29 attacks against submarine pens did little damage.

Colonel John B. Montgomery, Hansell's operations officer, went with one of the new crews on a mission to Truk. During approach, that crew lagged behind and their B-29 was jumped by Japanese fighters.

Montgomery watched as two Japanese fighters turned in for head-on attacks. "Fighters at 12 o'clock!" he called.

When he heard no firing, he looked around. Members of the crew looked shocked and not one gunner reached for his gunsight.

Montgomery yelled, "Aren't you going to shoot?"

As front gunner, the bombardier reached for his gunsight controls. Then he stood up, pushed the controls aside despite the fighters closing in, and picked up something from the floor. Montgomery couldn't believe his eyes. The bombardier was studying the oncoming fighters through binoculars.

Fortunately, the fighters swept by without doing any serious damage although the plane was shot full of holes.

Montgomery turned to the young man. "Son, why didn't you shoot at them?"

The bombardier replied, "I was told to make positive identification before I fired my guns."

Montgomery shook his head in disbelief. "In the future, when a fighter flies toward you, shoot him!"

The airfields on Iwo Jima had been hit by Navy carrier planes and by B-24s, but O'Donnell decided to strike at them because Japanese bombers had hit Isley Field November 2 and it was believed they had staged out of Iwo. Two missions failed to cause appreciable damage and one Superfort was damaged slightly by a phosphorus bomb.

Hansell was perturbed by their lack of success against these training targets. He was even more upset when the last mission to Truk resulted only in minor damage to the submarine pens despite perfect visibility.

Truk continued to be a training ground for new units arriving in the theater for the rest of the war, and 32 missions in all were run. These missions gave crews a chance to strike an enemy target that was poorly defended by outmoded fighters and a small number of antiaircraft guns. Besides the training, crews kept the Japanese from rebuilding installations destroyed previously by Navy carrier planes and Air Force heavy bombers so the effort was worthwhile.

Hansell had committed himself to start operations in November. At a meeting with General Marshall, and in accordance with joint campaign plans, the middle of November had been set with all in agreement that the first attack should be against Tokyo, which hadn't seen Allied bombers since the Doolittle raid in April 1942.

Now that the steel industry was no longer considered top priority, mining, urban industrial areas, and the aircraft industry were selected as primary targets. Although the Joint Chiefs were still convinced that an invasion would be necessary to force Japan to quit, there were a number who believed that air and sea attacks might end the war without an invasion. Therefore, the Joint Chiefs agreed to concentrate on targets directly associated with the Japanese war effort. First in importance, it was decided, was the aircraft industry, dominated by four large firms that produced two thirds of all military aircraft. Actually, three companies led the field, including Nakajima, Mitsubishi, and Kawasaki, and they were concentrated in Tokyo, Nagoya, and Osaka. The fourth firm, Tachikawa, was smaller but still important.

The Committee of Operations Analysts recommended that urban attacks and mining should be deferred for the time being, and Arnold and his chief of staff, Brigadier General Lauris Norstad agreed.

Hansell received his first target directive November 11, which stated that he should give first priority to the destruction of aircraft engine and assembly plants, and major overhaul and repair facilities.

During this period the XX Bomber Command in China continued to strike such facilities on Formosa and Kyushu. Arnold made it clear both to Hansell and LeMay in India that the Twentieth Air Force must support Pacific operations and run test incendiary attacks against urban and port areas.

Hansell was directed by Arnold to make his first attack against Nakajima's Musashino-Tama plant in the suburbs of northwest Tokyo,

The 3d Photo Reconnaissance Squadron from Guam sent its first F-13 over Tokyo November 1 at 32,000 feet. After being in the air for 14 hours, the F-13 returned with first-rate target photographs.

The Musashino works was the number one target in Japan because it produced almost half of all Japanese combat engines. Intelligence experts set up the mission under code name San Antonio I. At the time, they believed there were 500 fighters in the target area but actually there were only 375 fighters in all the home islands. The projection of 150 heavy guns proved accurate. Elaborate preparations were made to rescue downed fliers at sea and five submarines were positioned between Iwo and Japan while destroyers were stationed between Iwo and Saipan. Finally, all search planes were placed on alert for November 17.

Late delivery of B-29s from the States had held up this first mission because Arnold and Hansell both wanted to get at least 100 over the target.

The Navy's fast carriers planned to strike the Honshu area between November 12 and 17, and Hansell scheduled B-29s to arrive the last day, supposedly at a time when Japanese fighters would be exhausted. Hansell welcomed the Navy diversion but then Japanese Navy operations against Leyte Gulf threw the Navy time schedule off. Halsey had to cancel the Navy strikes against Honshu, and he and Nimitz recommended that the XXI Bomber Command attacks be canceled also, or postponed until the Navy was ready. When Hansell received this word he notified General Arnold that he was prepared to launch the mission alone without help from the Navy. He didn't want the impression to spread that his command could operate only with Navy assistance.

For Hansell, a series of events and problems combined to create a command crisis as the day approached for the first mission from the Marianas. He had hoped to lead the first mission but Arnold prohibited him from doing so. Therefore, the plan that he had evolved with the assistance of his 73rd Wing Commander Rosey O'Donnell and their two staffs had to be passed along to O'Donnell for execution.

There was still only one operational runway, and it had no lights for returning aircraft, only smudge pots, instead of the four runways Hansell had expected when he arrived in the Marianas. The next nearest runway was 1,200 miles away at Kwajalein and he knew that if there was a mishap on that single runway that all remaining aircraft returning from the mission would be lost.

Both he and O'Donnell had no illusions that the wing's Superfortresses would be operating over Japan against defenses that would fight back desperately. Experiences over Germany had demonstrated how costly such an operation could be.

It was still impossible to stretch the range of the B-29 to meet reasonable requirements for formation flying over enemy territory and Hansell needed more experience with cruise control to guide his decisions. The Air Transport Command, despite his pleadings, had refused to permit the 73rd Wing to move its units from the United States to the Marianas in squadron formation in order to gain some experience with cruise control. ATC officials theorized that the airplanes lacked the range to fly in formation from Sacramento to Hawaii, a distance of 2,400 miles, without a bombload and with excellent communications links and weather forecasts.

Now, to carry out the first mission over Japan, the B-29s would have to fly 3,200 miles with a bombload, with primitive communications, virtually no accurate weather forecasts, and still have to fight their way in and out. It was a prospect that sent shudders through Hansell's thin frame.

At this stage of the war, rescue services over the hostile Pacific were meager. For a B-29, even minor battle damage that resulted in loss of performance or fuel could be fatal. With the thought of adding more fuel, Hansell authorized overloading the bombers to 140,000 pounds—an increase of 10 tons over the original design weight of the aircraft!

Although there had been a few practice missions for the early crews, Hansell's command faced its initial mission over Japan just five weeks after arrival of the first B-29.

Hansell's anxiety increased when Arnold forwarded a letter that General Kenney had written to him which vehemently castigated Hansell's operational plan and predicted failure. Kenney told Arnold that the B-29s couldn't make it and that a daylight attack in formation would result in the Japanese simply shooting them out of the sky.

Since MacArthur's air boss had far more experience than Hansell in fighting the Japanese, his words were dismaying to say the least.

Even worse, Arnold added a postscript in his own hand that his senior and most experienced advisers agreed with Kenney and that he, Arnold, was inclined to agree. He said that if he still believed his command could make it, "Good luck, and God be with you."

To cap the whole situation, Hansell received a handwritten, personal letter from Rosey O'Donnell expressing doubt that the 73rd could carry out the mission as planned without excessive losses, and recommended that the first assaults against Japan should be made at night by single aircraft. In the letter, Rosey catalogued the familiar troubles and said he felt that the hazards and the lack of training produced risks which exceeded the limits of prudent military judgment. "Failure of the mission," O'Donnell wrote, "would produce a disaster which far exceeded any military advantage that would accrue from success." In recommending temporary abandonment of the daylight mission, and adoption of night operations, O'Donnell said the command would have a chance to build up its competence.

High command is a lonely job, but Hansell, his sharp features now more pronounced than ever as tension mounted, felt about as alone as any commander in history. No one seemed to offer anything but criticism.

They met alone to discuss O'Donnell's recommendation. He told Rosey that he agreed with everything he said, acknowledging that night operations would be far less risky from the tactical point of view, which was the proper limit of O'Donnell's responsibility. He saw that O'Donnell was unhappy that he had to make such a recommendation, but he assured his wing commander that he was clearly within his proper sphere in doing so and that he owed it to himself, the 73rd Wing, and to him. Hansell was aware that if the situation resulted in disaster, and O'Donnell had failed to warn him of his convictions, that he, Hansell, would have had every right to say "Why didn't you tell me?"

The problem wasn't that simple for Hansell because he had strategic considerations to weigh which not only included but transcended the tactical problems.

Just before Hansell had departed for Saipan, Arnold had sent for him, saying General Marshall wanted to see him. At their meeting, Marshall reminded Hansell that the first operation of the Twentieth Air Force in the Pacific was a joint operation, coordinated with the surface operations of the Army and Navy. He stressed the importance of carrying out the XXI Bomber Command's mission on time.

Marshall asked point-blank, "Can you carry out your share?"

Hansell told him unequivocally that they would do so.

Now, on the eve of the command's first mission, if Hansell ordered abandonment of his command's prescribed part, and changed the missions to night operations against Japanese area targets, he knew this would be an open admission that the Twentieth Air Force could not do the job for which it was created. Such a decision would destroy at one blow all the Air Force arguments for a strategic air command dedicated to destruction of targets in Japan—targets whose destruction the Joint Chiefs of Staff had approved. The structure of the Twentieth was shaky at best. Theater commanders continued to make strong demands for control of the B-29s. Hansell had to consider that the whole concept of strategic air warfare as a war-winning strategy, carried out by a unified air command, was hanging in the balance.

With these thoughts in mind, he told Rosey of his deep concern with the dangers involved, and shared them with him, but that the strategic considerations outweighed the tactical obstacles. He said, "I am determined to go ahead with daylight attacks against our prescribed targets."

He studied O'Donnell's face thoughtfully. "Are you reluctant to lead your wing on the forthcoming mission?"

Rosey hastened to assure him that he was not. He expressed his willingness to lead the mission although he had felt impelled to voice his concern.

Hansell accepted that position and each returned to his headquarters.

Later, O'Donnell asked for a second meeting with members of both of their staffs. At this session, O'Donnell recommended minor changes in the operational plan as conceived originally in order to simplify it and enhance its chance of success. Hansell agreed to all proposed changes.

Hansell set the morning of November 17 to send the B-29s on their first strike against Japan but a typhoon at Saipan prevented the takeoff. For a week of on-again, off-again, schedules the crews waited impatiently for the weather to clear. It finally did so on the 24th.

"Dauntless Dottie," with General O'Donnell and Major Robert K. Morgan, pilot of the famed "Memphis Belle" B-17 in the copilot's seat, took off at 6:15 A.M. O'Donnell had to use every foot of runway, and some of the ground beyond before "Dauntless Dottie" decided to take to the air.

Another 110 B-29s followed with 277.5 tons of bombs. The typhoon, which had grounded planes for a week, now lay between Saipan and Iwo Jima so all planes had to fly a western route instead of two routes that would converge from east and west on Tokyo.

After forming up after takeoff, the line of squadrons with nine airplanes in each loose formation headed for Japan on the 1,500-mile trip. B-29s soon began to drop out because of overheated engines and head back for Saipan until 17 returned.

Close to landfall on Japan the formations started to climb to

35,000 feet and now engine troubles increased, particularly during the last 5,000 feet.

The black-haired, blue-eyed Irishman from Brooklyn, General Rosey O'Donnell, led the wing over Tokyo. Weather was bad over the target as formations tried to get through at altitudes of 27,000 to 35,000 feet. Wind velocities of 150 mph raised downwind ground speeds to 445 mph, making it almost impossible for the 24 bombardiers who could spot the target to synchronize.

Major Jack Catton led his 498th Group as it turned on its initial point over Mount Fujiyama. He and his navigator, Lieutenant Campbell, noted the tremendous right-hand drift during the turn into the downwind leg toward the target. They were experiencing the jet stream for the first time although it wasn't known by that name. Few airplanes had ever flown at such high altitudes so they were caught by surprise. Once the wind was behind them they rapidly approached the target at a speed so high that bombardier Robert Canfield barely had time to identify the target before the indices on his bombsight crossed and the bombs headed earthward.

Catton hadn't expected fighters at their altitude but as they pulled away from the target and headed for Choshi Point he heard the cry, "Fighters at 11 o'clock!" They attacked almost head-on with cannon and machine guns on a perfect interception and several shots struck home before they were over the Pacific and out of reach of those murderous guns.

The plane piloted by Lieutenant Sam P. Wagner was raked by guns of a Japanese fighter shortly after it left the target. Other planes in the formation tried to ward off another attacker as a "Tony" (Japanese fighter) headed in for the kill while the guns of three B-29s zeroed in on the fighter. Hits were so effective that the fighter's guns were silenced but, to the horror of all those watching in the formation, the Tony crashed into the tail of Wagner's plane and both headed down with the B-29 plunging almost vertically to the ground. Eyewitnesses anxiously searched for parachutes but there were none. Wagner's crew was the new command's first loss over Tokyo.

Six B-29s failed to bomb due to mechanical difficulties but other Superforts bombed dock and urban areas of Tokyo when they couldn't see the target through the undercast, and 35 crews had to drop by radar.

Once away from Tokyo, crews breathed more easily because Japanese fighters had not put up a strong defense. The heavy guns that had been predicted were there but their fire proved light and inaccurate.

En route back, one crew was saved by the Air-Sea Rescue Service after ditching. Only two B-29s were lost and eight others damaged but the bombing of the primary target was very poor, amounting to destruction of only 1 percent of the building area.

Fighter and antiaircraft opposition proved far lighter than anyone expected but crews learned their first bitter lesson about the unpredictable weather over Japan. Masses of clouds could form quickly once a cold front out of Siberia moved in to clash with the warm, moist Pacific Ocean air. Oftentimes, weather fronts covered thousands of square miles and remained stationary for days, ranging to 40,000 feet and higher with towering black thunderheads blazing with forked lightning, and with up and down drafts that whirled B-29s about like toy airplanes while they were drenched with rain that tested the mettle of the most experienced pilots.

After this mission, Hansell instructed pilots to fly individually through such fronts and not try to maintain formations.

In Washington, Twentieth Air Force Headquarters released a statement by Arnold that substantial bomb tonnages had been dropped on a plant on the outskirts of Tokyo, and upon other selected targets. "Tokyo's war industries have been badly hurt," Arnold said, "and only two aircraft failed to return."

Arnold went to the White House to brief President Roosevelt. He'd had a long ordeal to justify his faith in the B-29 program. He told the President, "No part of the Japanese Empire is now out of range."

Militarily, the mission achieved little but it did prove that Hansell had been right all along because the feasibility of conducting daylight precision strikes against military targets in the home islands had been proven without a doubt. If for no other reason, the mission could be called a success because the command's bombing of Tokyo was crucial to the ultimate achievements of airpower in the winning of the war.

Bombing accuracy was awful, and Hansell was the first to admit it, but the 73rd Wing had proved to itself, and others, that successful and decisive air warfare would be carried out from the Marianas. In time, with experience and improvement in techniques, Hansell's faith in strategic air warfare would be fully vindicated. At the time, Hansell increased efforts by his lead-crew school to improve bombing accuracy, using 10 percent of his total supply of Superforts in an intensive program.

The second mission to the same target November 27 was led by O'Donnell's chief of staff. Colonel Walter C. Sweeney, Jr., encountered winds of 220 mph as he led his formation from Mount Fujiyama to the target. The navigator clocked their ground speed at 580 mph, much too high to synchronize the bombsight properly and the Musashino plant again emerged unscathed.

Despite Arnold's glowing reports to the President and the press, the B-29s couldn't have done a worse operational job and, unfortunately, results would continue to be poor for some time to come.

# CHAPTER 15

# A Pattern for the Future

Although the first two missions against Tokyo targets achieved no military goals, their impact on the Japanese people was great, resulting in disillusionment with their military leaders' ability to protect the homeland.

Hansell's command concentrated on daylight, high-altitude precision attacks against aircraft factories but still found time to make more strikes at Iwo Jima's airfields, and experimental incendiary attacks against Tokyo, Nagoya, and Kobe.

A third attack against the Musashino-Tama aircraft plant again resulted in failure.

The Japanese struck back at Isley Field on Saipan and in two raids destroyed four B-29s on the ground, seriously damaging six others, and causing lesser damage to 22 more.

General Harmon, Commanding General of the Army Air Forces in the Pacific, and Deputy Commander, Twentieth Air Force, thought at first he would be the field commander for the Twentieth. Harmon's job was difficult because he had to deal with various commands to get Twentieth Air Force units established in the theater. He couldn't have done it without the wholehearted support of Admiral Nimitz.

Shortly after taking command, he pressed Arnold for a clarification of his responsibilities, saying they were involved and difficult at best. "Any lack of clarity in regard to the Twentieth Air Force will but add to the confusion," he said.

Later, he sent Arnold a long memorandum that suggested he control the Twentieth in the field but Arnold never approved. Instead, Arnold wrote September 22, "Nothing must be done to affect the approved concept of a strategic air force whose operations are controlled from Headquarters, Twentieth Air Force, Washington." Arnold added that he was desirous of decentralizing controls so he had asked the War Department to give Harmon administrative authority over B-29 units in the area. He was emphatic, however, in stating that Harmon's headquarters was not in the Twentieth's operational chain of command.

Harmon was an outstanding general officer and he wanted command of the Twentieth because, as a professional, it would help to advance his career in the postwar Air Force. Although his motives were perfectly natural, and his desire for the job understandable, Arnold now made it crystal clear that such was not to be the case.

Arnold's reason for maintaining tight control of the Twentieth was his fear that the Navy would gain control of the B-29s. He was thinking ahead to the postwar era when a drive could get under way to promote an independent Air Force. So, he continued to fight those in the War Department and the Department of the Navy who resisted such an independent status. Arnold won an important round when he was given specific administrative control of the Twentieth on November 22 which he, in turn, delegated to Harmon as his deputy.

Harmon still fought for more than administrative control, seeking authority over combat operations, which Arnold continued to exercise out of Washington.

Nimitz helped his cause December 6 by giving him operational responsibility over all Army and Navy land-based bombers and fighters in his capacity as commander of the Strategic Air Forces, but Arnold still remained adamant about operational control of B-29s.

Brigadier General Richard C. Lindsay tried to placate Harmon by giving the air staff's appraisal of the problem. "Having the fullest confidence in you personally and recognizing Admiral Nimitz's fine cooperative spirit, Arnold is apprehensive of the compromising action that could be taken by CINCPOA's staff with relation to the operation of the Twentieth Air Force units should you and your staff be placed in the direct functional channel of operational control."

Hansell shared Arnold's apprehension about falling under the command of Admiral Nimitz, despite his admiration for the man. He was still hypersensitive about theater command of strategic air forces because General Eisenhower had demanded and received "temporary" full command of the Strategic Air Forces in Europe. He got command two months before D-Day and kept it for four months after D-Day, which was six precious months taken out of the combined bomber offensive.

Admiral Nimitz already had authorization from the Joint Chiefs of Staff to take operational control of the XXI Bomber Command in an emergency. Such an emergency occurred when the Japanese Navy sortied during the Leyte Gulf operation. At that time, Hansell had only 45 B-29s on Saipan, certainly not enough to launch a diversionary attack on Tokyo. Still, he had them loaded with one-ton bombs and placed on alert. Hansell then notified Admiral Hoover, Admiral Nimitz, General Harmon, and General Arnold that his command was standing by to assist the Navy upon request. Hansell took this action for three reasons. First, he wanted to help. Second, he didn't want it said that his command was idly ignoring an emergency. Last, he wanted to forestall any formal request from Nimitz for temporary control of his command which, once placed under the admiral, might take months to get free again. Therefore, by putting his command at Nimitz' disposal he hoped to avoid a formal request, and leave the way open to return to his main job.

General Harmon was not at all appreciative and Hansell got a theoretical rap on the knuckles and was told to get back to his own business. At the time, Hansell believed that Harmon would have preferred to take such action himself, and believed later that Harmon probably was quite justified in thinking Hansell's act was presumptuous. Actually, the Joint Chiefs never gave a directive to the command to report to Admiral Nimitz.

During this period the Joint Chiefs were involved in realigning responsibilities of the independent commands under MacArthur and Nimitz. Arnold's actions in regard to Harmon's requests for greater authority over the Twentieth Air Force were motivated by his strong conviction that the Air Forces should have coequal status in the Pacific.

Harmon had recommended that 20 B-29 groups be sent to Okinawa once the island was secured and bases built for them. Arnold told him that two new wings, the 315th and 316th, were definitely planned for the Philippines as the XXII Bomber Command, and that no new wings would go to the Central Pacific. Harmon voiced vigorous objections, citing the advantages of using the Marianas and Okinawa for mass bombing of Japan. He urged Arnold to delay plans to send B-29 wings to the Philippines until he could get Nimitz' approval to add two more wings to the Marianas. After a talk with Nimitz, the admiral refused to expand B-29 operations in the Mariana Islands because there were shortages of service troops and shipping facilities. He told Harmon such shortages were undermining his ability to carry out operations already authorized by the Joint Chiefs for early 1945.

Harmon continued to seek expansion of the Twentieth in the Marianas and on December 26 the Joint Chiefs did assign two more wings although the 316th was later assigned to the Eighth Air Force on Okinawa.

The Joint Chiefs authorized transfer of the 58th Wing from India to Tinian's West Field in April at a January meeting and scheduled the 315th to Northwest Field, Guam. Personnel of the 313th Wing began to arrive on North Field, Tinian, in December and became fully operational in February.

Hansell reviewed his operational plans for Arnold, telling him that he would make maximum strikes against top-priority targets in daylight when weather permitted, and radar attacks when weather wasn't suitable for precision bombing.

He sent his bombers out at night to bomb the dock and industrial areas of Tokyo November 29 but the results were negligible. Wind velocities exceeded 180 mph over Tokyo when Superfortresses tried again to destroy Musashino December 3. It was a futile mission because target damage was small and losses heavy with six Superfortresses down and six damaged.

Colonel Richard T. King led the 500th Group on this mission. He watched in amazement as 15 Japanese fighters leveled off above their altitude of 32,000 feet. From his vantage point on the jump seat behind pilot Major R. Goldsworthy, he watched the fighters turn gracefully in the sky in front of them and then roar at them with a rate of closure that was frightening. The 12-plane formation closed tightly around the lead plane and several Japanese fighters exploded spectacularly as the massed firepower of the formation's guns concentrated their fire. For a moment he thought they'd survive the onslaught but over the intercom he heard that their left wing had been hit, and gasoline was pouring out in streams from the punctured fuel tank. In seconds, the wing was on fire and Goldsworthy ordered everyone to bail out.

King caught a brief glance at the altimeter just before he dropped through the nose-wheel well. They were at 29,000 feet and going down fast. After his chute opened, he counted the parachutes around him. There were at least eight, and possibly another in the distance.

The colonel landed in a field and collapsed his chute. For the first time he felt pain in one leg and on his face, and was surprised to find that he had been burned. When he heard the roar of aircraft engines above, he glanced up to see Japanese fighters diving at him so he hurried over to a grove of trees. There he collapsed in a state of exhaustion. Japanese civilians quickly found him, and he was bound with his parachute's shroud lines.

King survived the tortures of imprisonment but Colonel B. E. Brugge from Headquarters, 73rd Wing, who had flown on the mission as an observer, died shortly after his capture.

Captain Donald J. Dufford's crew on Long Distance sustained 131 fighter attacks and, through superb gunnery, the intrepid crew managed to survive even after a Tony rammed their B-29, tearing out its number three engine.

Captain Francis J. Murray's crew from the 498th Group fought back in as savage an encounter with the enemy as any seen that day. Their troubles started before the target when ice formed on windshields. Despite the danger of leaving the protection of a large formation near a target, Murray had no choice because he couldn't see and he feared a collision.

No sooner was the plane away from the formation than Japanese fighters pounced on the straggler. Murray was shocked to hear the severity of the damage reports from crew stations as fighters swarmed around his plane. The B-29 was quickly riddled, and gas tanks were punctured. As if that wasn't enough, after they salvoed their bombs one bomb-bay door wouldn't close. With guns firing continually, Murray turned the huge bomber back to sea and, incredibly, the attacks ceased and the stricken bomber headed home.

With the open bomb-bay door, the drag increased the amount of fuel needed to keep the airplane flying but Murray kept her in the air for six hours. He would have made it all the way except that 1,200 gallons of fuel couldn't be transferred because of damage to the system.

Once he heard the engines start to sputter from fuel starvation, he headed toward the ocean. Rain pelted the crippled bomber as it hit the water at 120 mph, rolled forward for a few seconds, and then broke in half. With practiced skill, the crew got the life rafts inflated and the survivors huddled in them. Copilot Lieutenant Ray Keller went down with the wreckage when he couldn't get out in time.

Murray directed that the rafts be tied together so they could more easily be spotted by search planes. Rescue was days away, however, and their emergency rations were soon gone. They managed to catch two fish, which they ate raw. Later, Sergeant Charles Dean killed a sea gull with his .45 automatic and this was cut into 10 pieces and eaten.

On the tenth day, a Navy PB4Y was spotted about 10 miles away. Murray ordered release of a dye marker and the firing of two flares, but the plane failed to see them and they watched it turn away with a sinking feeling amounting almost to despair.

There was just one flare left but it had a bad primer and had refused to fire in the past. Dean placed it in the gun and hit the plunger with all his strength. This time it worked, with the flare soaring high into the sky, and the crew of the rescue plane spotted it and headed back, dropping a note that a rescue ship would pick them up shortly. They were jubilant, pounding one another on the back, as they awaited the ship. They didn't have long to wait because a destroyer approached within an hour and picked them up 300 miles from Saipan.

That was the last mission of the command for 10 days.

In the early part of December, O'Donnell assembled his group and squadron commanders and the lead crews. There were about 200 men present, including Hansell and members of his staff.

Hansell listened with amazement as O'Donnell reviewed their progress and complimented them for the great job they had done, and how heroic they had all been.

Then, O'Donnell called upon his boss to say a few words. Normally a forward-looking optimist with a sense of humor, Hansell wasn't amused now. His narrow face was pinched with anger. He and O'Donnell were such divergent types that it was inevitable that conflicts would arise between them.

Hansell stood up and faced the assemblage. "I'm in sharp disagreement because in my opinion you people haven't earned your pay over here. Unless you do better, this operation is doomed to failure."

Most of the men would rather have remembered Rosey O'Donnell's words but Hansell was right. O'Donnell was mixing emotions and leadership in his appraisal of their operations. Now Hansell had balanced this out properly and directed their thinking in the proper direction.

In a joint Army–Navy attack, B-29s struck at airfields on Iwo Jima, an operation approved enthusiastically by General Arnold, who was more and more concerned by the loss of B-29s on the ground at Saipan. These were damaged or destroyed by Japanese bombers staging out of Iwo.

With MacArthur's campaign to retake the Philippines behind schedule, Hansell set up an attack December 13 against the Mitsubishi Aircraft Engine Works at Nagoya, one of Japan's top producers of aircraft engines. Such a strike wouldn't have an immediate impact on MacArthur's operations but the plant's destruction would reduce the number of fighters and bombers his troops would ultimately have to face. Two days before the Mindoro invasion, 71 B-29s made excellent patterns on the target and destroyed much of the plant's covered area, thereby reducing engine production from 1,600 to 1,200 a month. Most important, this raid convinced the Japanese to start moving equipment to underground sites, which further reduced production. Opposition to the raid was strong, resulting in four B-29s lost and 31 damaged. Bombing was the best yet with 16 percent of all bombs within a thousand feet of the aiming point. It would have to be hit again, but this was a good beginning because the plant produced over 44,000 engines during the early prewar years and the war years.

Hansell's bombers weren't as effective December 18 when they bombed the Mitsubishi Aircraft Works, a large assembly plant in Nagoya that used the engines made at the other plant. At first, damage to the roof area appeared severe and analysts overestimated total damage, which was far less than that caused by the December 7 earthquake.

The Mitsubishi Engine Works was attacked a second time December 22 but this time incendiaries were used. Arnold and his staff had long advocated use of incendiary bombs because of the highly flammable nature of Japanese targets. The small fire raid on Tokyo the night of November 29–30 had proved disappointing so they hadn't been used again until now.

The XX Bomber Command's successful burn-out of the Hankow, China, storage areas December 18 had proved how potent such fire bombs could be so General Norstad, the Twentieth's chief of staff, told Hansell to prepare for a fire raid on Nagoya as soon as he could muster 100 B-29s. He said he was anxious to get data for planning purposes so they would know how to plan for large-scale fire raids later against Japan's major cities.

Hansell told Norstad, "We have with great difficulty implanted the principle that our mission is the destruction of primary targets by sustained and determined attacks using precision-bombing methods both visual and radar. Now that this doctrine is beginning to get results on the aircraft industry, you are exerting pressure to divert my forces to area bombing."

He reminded the chief of staff that such a drastic change would undermine the progress already made. He made it clear that he would order such a mission only if Norstad modified his original directive.

Norstad softened his approach. He told Hansell that the aircraft industry continued to have overriding priority, and that the fire raid was simply a test for future planning.

Hansell agreed to run the mission just as soon as other scheduled missions were out of the way. Only 48 out of the 78 taking off on the daylight mission December 22 dropped incendiaries by radar when the target proved to be cloud covered and little damage was done.

The last mission in 1944 was a return visit to the Musashino plant near Tokyo December 27.

Major John E. Krause piloted "Uncle Tom's Cabin" as an element leader while a nine-plane formation turned on Mount Fujiyama and headed for the target. Just a minute before bombs-away Krause noted a Tony coming head-on at 12 o'clock high with all guns firing. The fighter's bullets raked the top of the fuselage and the central fire-control blister exploded, killing the gunner inside.

Krause felt the impact as the Japanese fighter smashed into the right wing, opening a huge gash out of which fuel poured in a stream. Desperately, he tried to remain in formation but seconds later he momentarily lost control of the bomber as it slid away from formation. Horrified eyes peered out of sighting stations in the other B-29s as Japanese fighters bore in relentlessly. With disbelief, they watched as another Tony rammed the right side of the bomber, ripping off both engines on that side.

While they stared, they could tell that Krause was desperately trying to maintain the airplane in level flight, and every turret was pouring streams of shells at the persistent fighters. Just when it seemed as if the brave crew would regain control, another Tony rammed the crippled bomber from underneath. "Uncle Tom's Cabin" went into a spin but Krause unbelievably managed to bring her back under control while he flew a parallel course below the rest of the squadron. The Japanese fighters continued their attacks as crew members in the other Superfortresses watched 30 more fighters tackle the bomber that refused to die. These attacks proved beyond the capabilities of the crew to fight off and, after seven minutes, Krause's plane headed straight down from 20,000 feet and crashed northwest of Tokyo Bay. There were no survivors. Later, it was confirmed that at least nine Japanese fighters had been shot down by Krause's gallant crew.

This mission proved tragic in other ways because most of the bombs set a hospital on fire. The Japanese had a field day calling the American fliers devils who were interested only in destroying hospitals, schools, and homes.

Hansell set up another incendiary attack on Nagoya January 3.

The first "Battlin' Betty" was destroyed on the ground at Saipan by Japanese bombers. Major Gerald G. "Robbie" Robinson now had his second airplane of the same name over Nagoya and, for a time, he thought he'd lose this one, too.

Over the city, a fighter came head-on, his 20-mm shells shattering the Plexiglas nose, wounding the bombardier, and knocking out the number one engine. With loss of pressurization, the temperature dropped to 40 below zero as he and his copilot, Lieutenant Colonel John H. Griffith, fought to control the airplane.

When he saw that his bombardier had been hit, he turned the controls over to Griffith and pulled Lieutenant Paul O'Brien into the pilot's compartment, noting with concern that one of O'Brien's feet seemed almost severed. The pilots removed their heavy clothes and tucked them around the bombardier to keep him from freezing.

Robbie looked frantically for his heavy gloves but they'd been lost in the shuffle, and he had to fly the airplane bare-handed. Once they got beyond range of fighter attacks, he lowered their altitude to 4,000 feet and flew the 1,500 miles to Saipan on three engines.

Lieutenant J. D. Bartlett's "American Maid" was also heavily attacked over Nagoya. Crew members reported hits in the tail but, worst of all, the left gunner's blister blew out and Sergeant James Krantz almost went with it at 29,000 feet. Fortunately, he had designed his own harness to prevent such an eventuality. Although he remained secured to the plane, most of his body, with the exception of his right leg, had been sucked outside the airplane as it decompressed. With the outside temperature at 40 below zero, and his oxygen mask torn off, he was in danger of freezing to death or dying from lack of oxygen. Frantically, Krantz got his mask back on and tried to crawl back into the airplane. The pressure of the air was too great despite his efforts. In three minutes, he was unconscious.

Two gunners tried and failed to pull him back in, and even with the assistance of the radar operator they couldn't budge his body. When the copilot responded to their frantic calls for help, the four of them were able to pull Krantz's limp body back into the airplane. The gunner had been in that frigid air for 10 minutes and he was suffering from frostbite. After pure oxygen was administered, Krantz recovered.

The only other casualty was the tail gunner's loss of a finger, which was shot away. The incendiary attack on Nagoya caused inconsequential damage to the city so Norstad had no reliable data on which definitive plans could be drawn for future fire raids.

Hansell was disillusioned with incendiary attacks and sent his bombers to Musashino again January 9 but strong winds were so severe that formations were torn apart and another six B-29s were lost with only slight damage to the target.

A mission against the Mitsubishi Aircraft Works at Nagoya proved equally fruitless. These missions were frustrating to crews for many reasons. Pilots found the change from tropical conditions on Saipan to the freezing temperatures at bombing altitudes a physical and emotional strain. Airplanes frequently couldn't stand the drastic change in temperatures and all kinds of problems developed. The long haul to Japan, without friendly fields to fall back upon going or coming back when trouble developed, created constant pressure on crews that was worse than Japanese opposition. The number of B-29s bombing primary targets kept declining and crews either bombed secondary or last-resort targets or salvoed their bombs and returned to base.

It was a discouraged command that set out January 19 to bomb a new target on the Inland Sea west of Kobe. The Kawasaki Aircraft Industries Company in 1944 had delivered 17 percent of Japan's airframes and 12 percent of its engines. For a change there were no losses as 62 Superfortresses bombed the target. Intelligence experts estimated that 38 percent of the roofed area had suffered major damage. This was small comfort to Hansell, of course, because he now learned with surprise and shock of his removal. What Hansell and his staff didn't know at the time, and learned only after the war, was that every major building in both the engine and airframe areas had been hit hard with production cut 90 percent. Not only was the damage far more severe than known right after the strike, but Kawasaki moved usable machine tools to other, more protected areas. Although the plant was repaired, only limited assembly of aircraft was accomplished for the remainder of the war.

Chief of Staff Norstad had written Hansell December 7 in regard to the first mission over Japan in response to his concern about Arnold's reaction. "I knew you would worry about the Chief's feelings at that time since you know him well enough to realize he would be very much keyed up until the first show was over. He was impatient, but his impatience was directed against the circumstances and not against you. You were not 'on the pan' at any time. I think I can illustrate his attitude by telling you his reaction to the fourth and fifth postponement. After he had indicated he was disturbed, I made a statement to the effect that I didn't think it a good thing to put the heat on you under the circumstances. He replied, 'Who said anything about putting the heat on Possum?' in a rather irritated manner."

Norstad had been dispatched by Arnold January 6 to tell Hansell he was through, LeMay was ordered to Guam for a conference, and the latter was directed to take over the command January 20—the day after the Kawasaki strike. If Hansell could only have known the true facts about how successful his last mission had been he might have felt some measure of vindication for his long fight to prove the efficacy of precision bombing. The meeting was embarrassing for all concerned because they were friends, so formalities were quickly dispensed with. Hansell requested a minor job in the training command back in the States, which was granted, and one of the Air Forces' most imaginative planners lost a coveted job to a younger man who had once served under him as a group commander in England.

Before Hansell returned to the States he went to Saipan to pay good-bye to the crew with whom he had flown overseas. There were no dry eyes as they said good-bye to one another because they all had grown to like one another so much. Major Catton's plane "Joltin' Josie" had been named for his wife, Josie. When Hansell joined the crew for the flight overseas, he had added "Pacific Pioneer" to the title. Before the crew went on a mission, Hansell often flew down from Guam to wish them luck.

Now, in parting, he had a special gift for their crew chief, Master Sergeant Hancock. He gave him a swagger stick, with a stiletto inside, which a friend in the Royal Air Force had given to the general.

Catton and his crew were choked up when Hansell walked away. They had found him to be one of the warmest, most compassionate men they had ever known, and along with many others in the 73rd Wing they would remember him with affection.

When the 38-year-old LeMay took over, he demonstrated again that he was a "doer" and an outstanding manager by selecting only topnotch officers for his staff. He chose as his chief of staff Brigadier General August W. Kissner, who had learned to fly with him at Kelly Field in 1929. Colonel James D. Garcia, the dark, fastidious officer who had already proved himself with the XX Bomber Command, was placed in charge of intelligence operations. For deputy chief of staff for operations, LeMay selected the energetic 33-year-old Colonel John B. Montgomery. The slim Montgomery had flown as LeMay's copilot during the classic interception of the Italian liner *Rex* in 1938 when a B-17 piloted by LeMay demonstrated airpower's ability to intercept ships 600 miles at sea.

LeMay was only too happy, therefore, to accept Hansell's strong endorsement of Montgomery, who had been Hansell's deputy chief of staff for operations.

Colonel C. S. Irvine, the bluff, tireless man who did more to win the Battle of Kansas than any other man, was the oldest of LeMay's staff at 46, but no better man could have been picked to be in charge of supply and maintenance. An Arnold intimate, Irvine had served in World War I as a Signal Corps private.

LeMay found the XXI Bomber Command about in the same condition that he had found the command in India. He quickly realized why he had been selected by Arnold to handle operations in the Marianas. He was senior in rank and his combat background was more extensive, in comparison to Hansell's, with almost two years in England, first as a group commander then later in command of an air division. Hansell had been a wing commander for only a short time in England, and had flown a number of missions, but his combat-experience level wasn't as extensive because he had been called back to Washington where his talents as a superb planner were needed even more.

LeMay had improved operations out of India and China so he was now given a chance to show what he could do on a much larger scale. Changes were needed quickly to get some payoff for all the things Arnold had fought for in getting a semi-independent strategic air force into combat.

When his new staff grumbled about controls from Washington, he told them, "I don't have the impression that officials in Washington are breathing down my neck. I've got more freedom of action than any air commander in this war. It's my chore to see that we make this command pay off. Once Arnold made up his mind to consolidate the B-29 commands because the one in India couldn't be supported, I'm sure I was chosen over 'Possum' because I had the most combat experience."

In parting from the Marianas, Hansell wrote Arnold a letter. In previous correspondence, he had made no bones about his dissatisfaction with his command's performance. Now he said that a review of statistics showed that the record of the 73rd Wing compared favorably with the 58th Wing during their first combat months. For the record, he listed four major problems. He said originally the 73rd had been trained for radar night bombing and then switched to precision bombing for which they were not as qualified. Bombing accuracy was deplorable, he said, and he was making progress in improving it, and the rate of aborted aircraft was getting better after it peaked at 21 percent of all B-29s airborne. One of his primary tasks, he told Arnold, had been to reduce the number of aircraft ditching, and setting up procedures to improve air-sea-rescue operations. In conclusion, Hansell said he believed progress had been made in rectifying these problems and that his main fault was in driving his crews too hard.

Escort fighters were assigned to the Twentieth in late January, and Harmon objected strongly. He wanted to retain control so he could make maximum use of fighters wherever they were needed most.

LeMay was just as adamant that he should have absolute control, and sent a strong message to Washington supporting this stand. Arnold upheld LeMay but gave Harmon operational control of fighters during the upcoming assaults on Iwo Jima and Okinawa.

Harmon refused to accept defeat and took off with his staff on a trip to Washington to press his case personally at the highest level. After his plane departed Kwajalein for Johnston Island, it disappeared and was never heard from again.

Harmon's loss, and the deaths of his top staff members, was serious but, fortunately, most major decisions on employment of the strategic air forces had been made. Major General Willis H. Hale was assigned temporarily to fill Harmon's position. He was replaced in early May by Lieutenant General Barney M. Giles.

Harmon's hopes of commanding B-29 forces in the field would never have been realized despite his capabilities because Arnold would not have permitted the Twentieth to come under Admiral Nimitz. If Harmon had been given command of the B-29s as part of his responsibilities as Commanding General of the Army Air Forces in the Pacific, Nimitz as theater commander would have exercised control of the Twentieth Air Force.

# CHAPTER 16

# Japanese Concentrate Fighter Forces

Those who expected a dramatic turn-around with LeMay in command were disappointed. The next two missions against aircraft plants in Nagoya and Tokyo were no more successful than those under Hansell.

LeMay realized from the start that he had another "rabble" on his hands like the inexperienced people he had inherited in India so he started a training program similar to the one he established when he took over the XX Bomber Command.

In studying the reports of missions, he noted that most had been flown at 35,000 feet. He knew enough about the B-29 to realize that the bulk of their losses were due to mechanical failures rather than Japanese resistance. The first thing he did was to bring formations down to lower altitudes over the targets, where engines and other equipment wouldn't be under such a severe strain. He justified this action by saying that winning the war would cost less in lives by better bombing results at lower altitudes. Arnold, merely directing target priorities, kept hands off operations as LeMay went ahead with plans to retrain the command.

LeMay often argued with the members of the target committee in Washington. They were experts of all kinds but all too often they didn't know what was possible to accomplish in the field, particularly under the bad weather conditions that existed almost daily. LeMay was aware of the limitations of the present radar system but he was even more concerned because few operators seemed to know how to get the most out of their equipment. Navigators had found it useful when there was a land-water contrast on the radar scope and they could interpret such a "picture" but the radar sets hadn't proved useful in bombing. As a result, most bombing of targets had to await days when visibility was good. After studying weather patterns over Japan, LeMay realized that in the best weather month of the year only two to seven days were clear enough for visual bombing while the rest of the time was what LeMay called "stinkin'." He told his staff, "The worst part is that you have to forecast those days accurately, and then make sure you're over those targets on those specific days." He was thankful that he had made arrangements with Mao Tze-tung for the weather station in North China because they weren't getting any other worthwhile weather forecasts except those from the command's own reconnaissance airplanes.

He had insisted that B-29 bombing altitudes be lowered below 30,000 feet because the jet stream over Japan made accurate bombing impossible unless you went upstream, and then airplanes were practically sitting still and getting shot at for what seemed like forever before they could get away. Downstream, he knew, the Norden bombsight couldn't synchronize because the run was too short. Crosswise to the wind proved equally impossible because the bombsight wasn't designed to correct for such wind velocities.

Earlier, Hansell had recognized the limitations of the Norden bombsight and, despite the howls of protest from crews, had directed that bombing be done upwind in spite of the added risk in an effort to put the bombs on the target. He had placed his highest hopes on a new radar set, the APQ-7, which was far superior as an aid to bombing than the present APQ-13. Unfortunately, it wasn't ready until the closing months of the war when its accuracy under all-weather conditions in selective bombing was a marked improvement.

Maintenance problems assumed such dimensions that LeMay devoted as much time to their solution as anything else. He told his staff, "Prior to the war we had a combat group and alongside it a service group. This service group was supposed to do second-echelon maintenance—the supply, support and housekeeping work. The base commander was head of the service group and the combat command just lived on his base so it became a question of priorities. When the combat commander wanted to emphasize flying, the base commander was often more interested in mowing lawns so his base would look pretty. So, we mowed lawns.

"After I got to England with the 305th Group, the service group that was supposed to take care of my planes reported not to me, but to the service command. If I gave them an airplane to fix, it became their airplane and not ours. Consequently, I was rather reluctant when we were short of everything to give them an airplane because they never had our sense of urgency.

"When I got to India, I took the service group and put it under the combat commander. I went even further and insisted on centralized maintenance, and set up a production line."

One of the first thing that "Bill" Irvine came to see LeMay about after he took over on Guam was to outline his ideas on maintenance, which Hansell had previously approved. LeMay listened as Irvine described a program that was identical to the one he had set up in India. He didn't know whether his maintenance chief knew of his organization in India but he was pleased they were in agreement. LeMay just nodded his head. "Go ahead and do it."

Aircraft losses rose to 5.7 percent of all B-29s dispatched on 22 missions during January. They resulted from a concentration of Japanese fighter forces and the long over-water flights, which were costly in planes once they got into mechanical trouble or tried to return after being badly shot up.

Typical of the opposition during January was the experience encountered by Lieutenant Lloyd Avery's crew in "Irish Lassie" January 27. En route to the target, gunners knocked down three fighters before a "Zeke" (Japanese fighter) dove on their B-29 from above while streams of fire zeroed in on him. With breathtaking suddenness, the Japanese pilot never pulled out of his dive and his airplane bounced off the B-29's left wing, ripping off eight feet of the aileron and part of the landing flap. Even worse, the fuel tank for the number one engine was slashed open and gasoline streamed behind the wing. The engineer quickly transferred fuel from that tank until it was below the level of the damage.

Avery stayed with the formation despite the serious damage to his airplane. Fighter attacks increased and a "Jack" (fighter) moved in on the tail despite the concentrated fire of the tail gunner. Pieces of the tail assembly were ripped off by savage bursts, and then the Japanese fighter smashed into the tail, tearing out the entire left side of the tail gunner's position and entombing him.

When the tail assembly was so seriously damaged, the pilot's control cables were severed. After bombs were dropped, the damage the airplane had sustained now presented almost impossible problems for the pilots because "Irish Lassie" went out of control and started to descend in lazy spirals.

The copilot didn't realize at first that his controls were still good. After the plane had fallen 8,000 feet, he managed to get the airplane under control and headed for home despite continued fighter attacks. Even with the loss of the tail guns, and all guns on the left side of the airplane, the gunners made every bullet count, and finally, over the Pacific, Japanese fighters called it quits.

Avery sent five men back to the tail gunner's compartment to free him, and they were at last successful.

On approach back to the base on Saipan, the copilot desperately tried to keep the airplane from falling off as he approached the cliffs where the runway began. He put his feet on the instrument panel and hauled back on the wheel with all his strength, and the nose of the airplane, despite the serious damage to the control surfaces in the tail, responded reluctantly just as the bomber hit the runway. Then the nose wheel collapsed, and a wing caught on an embankment and spun the airplane in a vicious pinwheel while one engine caught fire and ripped off and the fuselage cracked in the middle.

It was an incredible ending to a mission that had seemed hopeless over the target. Remarkably, only two crew members were injured in the landing. Nine of the 11-man crew were decorated for valor against almost impossible odds.

LeMay was particularly disappointed that only half of all planes on each of the January missions were able to bomb the primary target. He was aware that the command's poor showing was due, in part, to inexperience, particularly poorly trained aircraft mechanics and shortages of almost everything. During this period, maintenance facilities were inadequate and most missions had to be flown from a single runway because the second hadn't been completed. This single-runway operation resulted in delays in getting each wing off the ground, so assembly of formations was more difficult.

After studying intelligence reports covering missions during the last two months of 1944, LeMay found only one plant had been crippled by B-29 strikes. The Mitsubishi plant at Nagoya and the Nakajima plant at Ota evidently had lost some production capacity, but the number one target, Musashino-Tama, on the outskirts of Tokyo had suffered only 4 percent damage after 835 B-29s attacked it in a series of missions. He hated to admit it but Navy planes had done more damage in a single strike.

What LeMay didn't know at the time was that the slowdown in production during the latter part of 1944, particularly production of aircraft engines, was due primarily to dispersal of plants underground or into the countryside because of fear of B-29 attacks, and not the attacks themselves.

After loss of the Marianas, Prince Higashikuni, commander in chief of Japan's Home-Defense Headquarters, realized the war was lost when B-29s came to the Marianas. He said after the war, "We had nothing in Japan that we could use against such a weapon. From the point of view of the Home Defense Command, we felt that the war was lost and said so. If the B-29s could come over Japan, there was nothing that could be done."

Arnold, with his customary impatience to get on with the job, pressed LeMay to improve operations. Privately, LeMay told his staff, "with those jet-stream winds over Japan, you could go on forever trying to get up to a target. General Arnold has crawled out on a dozen limbs a thousand times to get the physical resources and funds to build these airplanes and get them into combat. Now he finds they're not doing well. He's determined to get results out of this weapons system. The turkey is around my neck. I've got to deliver."

Before he was removed, Hansell had worked zealously to improve defense tactics over Japan, and to cut operational losses by improving rescue services for crews downed at sea. He knew that much of the problem of losses at sea would be solved once Iwo Jima was in American hands. It was midway between the Marianas and Japan, and would be a haven for badly shot-up Superfortresses, provide a site for navigation aides, and afford a base to station fighter escorts and rescue aircraft. Also, greater bomb tonnages could be carried to targets in northern Japan if B-29s could refuel there.

LeMay continued to run the type of operations during February that Hansell had started, while he concentrated on training inexperienced crews. He set up the same kind of lead-crew training he had initiated in England and later brought to India for the XX Bomber Command.

Losses remained high in early February as 360 B-29s went out on a series of missions that achieved little. These flights at above 20,000 feet may have offered some protection to crews under fire from antiaircraft guns, but the strong winds aloft often made the bombers sitting ducks for Japanese fighters, which frequently couldn't be beaten off despite electronically controlled gun turrets.

Bombing results remained poor not just because of failure to hit aiming points, but because the weight of bombs had to be reduced from 10 to 3 tons because of the fuel needed to fly at high altitudes. An average B-29 used 7,650 gallons of gasoline on a mission, or over 500 gallons an hour. LeMay made it clear to his operations officers that using over 22 tons of fuel to drop 3 tons of bombs, or even less, didn't make sense. Even worse, he told them, was the fact that only the best crews seemed able to make such a round trip to Japan with a safe fuel reserve. Those who couldn't ended up in the ocean, particularly if they lost an engine.

Reports of shot-up airplanes with half a tail gone, or part of a wing shot away, were common after each mission. Such damage was not unusual in Europe, but in the Pacific a return flight of 1,500 miles under such conditions was often fatal.

Takeoff weights shot up to 138,000 pounds for an airplane originally designed for 120,000 pounds. Power settings had to be increased for the long climb to altitude, creating an additional strain on engines that already had enough problems.

With losses mounting, LeMay switched to less heavily defended targets than those at Nagoya and Tokyo. He decided to attack the Mitsubishi Aircraft Works at Tamashima and sought Norstad's approval. The Twentieth's chief of staff gave it reluctantly, suggesting that an incendiary attack on Kobe might offer more rewards because it was an important port city, with concentrations of shipbuilding yards and plants for marine engines. It also was an important rail junction with strategic industries.

A more modern city than most in Japan, Kobe's factory districts were congested and highly vulnerable to fire bombs. The heart of the city was so congested that it housed 100,000 people to the square mile.

LeMay decided to abide by Norstad's recommendation and set up two wings despite the fact the 73rd was still short of airplanes, and two groups of the 313th Wing hadn't completed their training. They went out February 4 but only 69 of 129 bombed the target. Swarms of fighters met them, numbering at least 200.

"Devil's Darlin'," with Lieutenant Maurice L. Malone at the controls, fought off one fighter after another over the target. Malone's problems were compounded by failure of the bomb-bay doors to close because a bomb-bay tank, which had inexplicably been released from its shackles, dangled out of the airplane.

Now the fighters were on them in earnest and Malone was killed instantly as cannon fire exploded in the cockpit, and the radar operator was seriously wounded.

Copilot Lieutenant Robert U. Burton took over the controls. He found that the instruments for the right engines had been shot out, the left flap had fallen partway down, and the tail had received serious structural damage. He decided to dive into cloud cover in an attempt to escape the fighters but, in doing so, he accidentally feathered the number two engine and immediately the plane was in desperate flying condition. He quickly rectified his mistake, just as Major Joe Kramp peeled out of formation with his B-29 and instructed his gunners to fight off those Japanese fighters who were continually making attacks at Burton's plane.

Once they had a respite, the navigator helped to remove Malone's body from the pilot's seat and joined Burton at the controls as the number three propeller spun off and Burton needed assistance.

Burton called Kramp on the radio and they agreed on a speed that could be maintained.

Flight engineer Lieutenant William Silk had his hands full as Burton had to feather the number four engine and now there were two engines out on one side.

"Devil's Darlin'" limped home and there were only 15 minutes of fuel remaining and 60 miles to go so Burton decided he would crashland at Isley's number two field about midnight. Such was not to be for this 498th crew because it wasn't long before the number one engine began to sputter and the second engine quit. It all happened so quickly that Burton didn't have time to call people to their crash stations and they were only 50 feet off the ocean. With moonlight silvering the wave tops, the plane settled gently into the water. Four men were injured but all those who remained alive were rescued, although the body of the plane's commander sank with the airplane.

One B-29 was shot down over the target and 35 other Superfortresses received varying degrees of battle damage. The industrial southwestern section of Kobe suffered substantial damage with 5 of the 12 most productive factories hard hit. One of two shipyards received so much damage that its production capacity was cut in half. Fabric and synthetic-rubber plants were completely wiped out.

In advance of the invasion of Iwo Jima, LeMay sought Nimitz' approval to hit the Musashino plant at Tokyo on D-Day to discourage air reinforcements from the mainland to the island. Nimitz agreed because Navy carrier planes were scheduled to do the same two days before the invasion.

The strike was a familiar story. A weather front prevented B-29s from forming and only 33 bombed the target, with insignificant results. Most crews dropped bombs on the port of Tokyo and the city itself, resulting only in damage to a spinning mill, a railroad yard, and a bridge across the Sumida River.

Two days before Iwo's D-Day, Navy carrier planes struck Musashino with small bombs and rockets and caused considerable damage, much to LeMay's chagrin.

The amphibious assault against Iwo Jima began February 19. Lieutenant General Tadamichi Kuribayashi had organized his defenses in depth and Marines had to pry Japanese out of their strongholds. The stench of death hung heavy over the tiny island as American Marines and Japanese fought for yards day after day until the island was secured March 27, although pockets of heroic Japanese held out even longer. The cost was heavy with V Amphibious Corps losses, which didn't include the losses of the Navy task force, amounting to 4,590 killed and 301 missing, with almost 16,000 wounded. Japanese losses were over 21,000 dead and only 212 captured. It was a battle the likes of which Americans had never fought before, and, although the cost was high, Iwo Jima's capture saved hundreds of lives of B-29 crewmen once fields were established. By the end of the war, 2,400 B-29s and 25,000 airmen made emergency landings. Admiral King, chief of naval operations, said he believed the lives saved exceeded the lives lost in the island's capture.

Once the island was secured, work was started to convert the central field into a huge base with two B-29 runways, two fighter strips, and a combat service center. Heavy rains delayed construction and the 9th Naval Construction Brigade's Seabees worked two 10-hour shifts daily to construct runways on top of the volcanic rock. It wasn't until July 7 that the first 8,500-foot runway was completed, although the entire base was never finished before the war ended.

When Iwo became operational its air base was, in LeMay's words, "used right up to the hilt." Cruise-control techniques had been refined so that crews could get to Japan and back with an adequate reserve of fuel but flight procedures had to be used properly, something new crews learned the hard way. Each mission was planned knowing that the most inefficient crews would have to land at Iwo because they were short of fuel. LeMay knew precisely how many missions the average new crew had to fly before they got it into their thick skulls that they had to fly the airplane the way they were briefed, otherwise they'd run short of fuel. He planned to saturate Iwo with gas-shy airplanes and cripples each mission.

With Iwo denied to Japanese bombers, attacks practically ceased against bases in the Marianas. In the previous six months, the Japanese had sent more than 80 bombers against Saipan and Tinian and lost 37 of them but had caused the destruction of 11 B-29s, with many more damaged.

The Nakajima plant at Ota now had the highest priority because it manufactured Japan's best fighter, the Ki-84 or "Frank." It had produced 300 fighters in December but it wasn't known until after the war that in the first part of 1945 its production had declined to one third that number due to plant dispersal.

On February 10, B-29s, with mostly high-explosive and a few incendiary bombs, struck the Ota plant in perfect weather, but the bombardiers were decidedly less than perfect, although 74 Franks were destroyed in one building. Most damage was caused by incendiaries and Ota officials told Americans after the war that a heavier concentration of fire bombs would have destroyed the plant. B-29 losses were severe, with 12 down and 29 damaged as Japanese fighters contested the airspace around Tokyo.

LeMay and officials of the Twentieth Air Force in Washington still believed that fire raids against major cities would pay off but they knew that each force had to be large enough to be effective. Norstad reminded LeMay February 12 that the two previous incendiary attacks had not been productive, and he strongly recommended another fire raid to procure additional data. Nagoya received his endorsement although such a mission was given a lower priority than destruction of the two leading aircraft and engine plants.

The Air Force had built a typical village in Utah that was attacked by a new fire bomb made of jellied gasoline called napalm. It was developed with the assistance of the Standard Oil Company, chemists at DuPont, and the National Research Defense Council. The village had fire-fighting equipment comparable to types used in Japan. Training attacks on the simulated village proved that once napalm set fires in the village fire fighters were helpless to stop them.

Another futile try to reach the Musashino-Tama plant near Tokyo in late February was frustrated by clouds, and B-29s were diverted to the secondary target. After the mission, LeMay's operations officer, Colonel John B. Montgomery, went to his boss. "Our whole campaign will fail unless something is done to get a better delivery of bombs on the target. We can bomb secondaries forever by radar and it would have little significant impact on Japan."

LeMay agreed. He told Montgomery that he was considering lowering bombing altitudes to 5,000 feet and using incendiaries to attack urban areas. He said that Brigadier General Thomas S. Power and Colonel Hewitt T. Whelass had come up with a plan for a low-level attack that would use radar to direct planes along the east side of Tokyo Bay, and then on to Tokyo. Each plane, he said, would have its own heading, fly at a predetermined speed and altitude, and bomb at a specified time. LeMay said he liked the idea, and they had given him an overall plan within 24 hours.

"What do you think about it, Monty?"

"It has great advantages of going against highly inflammable urban areas at low altitudes that will assure vast destruction. However, there are several points that concern me. Bomb loads would increase by a factor of three to four because we won't have to lift the airplane to altitude, thereby saving fuel."

LeMay respected Montgomery's judgment because, as operations officer, he had done an outstanding job of supervising the preparation of mission orders, and had flown a number of missions to learn at firsthand the problems they faced. Before the war, Montgomery was not only a superb pilot, but he had been trained as a celestial navigator, and was the number one bombardier in the old Air Corps.

Montgomery continued. "In my opinion, the natural dispersion of bombs due to the greater accuracy of bombing at lower levels, at night by radar, will give us pretty good coverage if the aiming points are selected properly. Further, the increase in bomb load will give us a new approach to this whole thing. I'm not so sure about the availability of incendiary bombs. They are in short supply. We might mix high-explosive bombs with incendiaries which would have the added advantage of obstructing firefighters on the ground. I must admit," he said candidly, "that I'm concerned about losses."

LeMay disagreed. "The Japs won't be ready for this kind of attack."

LeMay knew he hadn't done any better than Hansell, and he had to take drastic action, otherwise the whole B-29 program would fall apart. The Navy was disgruntled about hauling all their tonnage to the islands, saying the Twentieth was dropping everything the theater had on nothing, and the Navy was expected to drop nothing on everything. He knew Nimitz, in particular, was getting to the point of demanding some changes. LeMay was well aware that some general had to come out there and face the Air Force doctrine of bombing selected targets at high altitudes. If he failed, and came up with nothing else to get on with the job, he was expendable. LeMay had no doubts about what action Arnold would take.

His thoughts were interrupted by Montgomery. "A while back I had an idea that we could come in with two forces—one trailing the other. The first would drop flares at night, and light up an area, so the second would have enough light to use the Norden bombsight to pinpoint an industrial target."

LeMay nodded. At the time, he thought the idea was a good one. After a mission was run to the Mitsubishi plant in Nagoya, in which Montgomery personally participated, they found that the target did get lit up and the interval between the two forces was correct. However, bombardiers found the light so diffused in their bombsight telescopes that they couldn't see the target well enough to bomb accurately. So, the whole idea was called off.

In preparation for the low-altitude missions, LeMay ordered Montgomery to set up a training mission to Kito Iwo, a small island just off Saipan that would be attacked by 12 bombers in columns of three at 50 feet with delayed-action bombs. Montgomery tried to talk LeMay out of it but his boss couldn't be budged by arguments, saying only that he had his reasons.

Montgomery sent word by teletype to the 73rd Wing at Saipan to set up the training mission for the first of March, giving precise details.

Back came a message. "Altitude in error. Two ciphers missing."

Montgomery messaged back. "No. Altitude correct. Five zero feet."

There was a pause. Then another message. "General O'Donnell would like to communicate with Colonel Montgomery."

"Here, Rosey."

"What's going on down there?"

"LeMay's orders."

"I'll be right down."

Montgomery passed along the word to LeMay. With a slight grin on his face, LeMay said, "Set up a round table for me, you, Kissner, Blanchard, Garcia, and Rosey."

About an hour later O'Donnell came in, and LeMay waved him to a seat. "Well, Rosey, what is it?"

"I cannot fly that mission."

There was dead silence, with all eyes on LeMay. He took his pipe out of his mouth and looked directly at Rosey. He said softly, "You will fly that mission." Their eyes locked and there was such an implacable look in LeMay's hazel eyes that it was O'Donnell who dropped his eyes first. LeMay knew that O'Donnell was close to General Arnold but that didn't faze him one bit.

O'Donnell squirmed in his seat but said nothing more.

"Anything else?" LeMay said.

"No," Rosey said, walking stiff-legged out of the room.

After the mission was flown successfully, there were wild, untrue rumors that flooded the Marianas. It was told and retold how some bombs hit the ground and almost jumped into the bomb bays of the airplanes following in line. One prize story was that a bomb came up even with the horizontal stabilizer and flew formation with a B-29.

Now Montgomery understood. With the rumor widespread among the crews that LeMay would make them drop their bombs over Japan at 50 feet, 5,000 feet didn't seem at all bad. It was a masterful lesson in psychology.

For the low-altitude runs over Tokyo, LeMay selected a point of departure on the east side of Tokyo Bay. From this point, incendiaries could be dropped on the city after a predetermined number of minutes and seconds according to the speed of the aircraft over the ground.

LeMay called in Dr. Gould, a Massachusetts Institute of Technology radar expert assigned to the command. "I want you to go to Saipan, fly with half a dozen of the worst radar operators, and find out if they can fly by radar over this tit of land on the northern part of Saipan at 6,000 feet."

Gould confirmed LeMay's worst misgivings when he came back shaking his head. "I didn't realize how bad the operators are. However, with some training I think most of them can identify that tit of land at 6,000 feet on their radar sets."

LeMay didn't blame the radar operators. They had received practically no training because the sets hardly ever worked properly in the States.

He weighed the risks of bombing Japan's cities at low altitudes. If he agreed to authorize such missions, he was aware that he was committing his entire command where failure might mean the loss of most of the command's crews and hundreds of millions of dollars worth of airplanes. If the plan was successful, the destruction of Japan's war industries would shorten the war by months or even years, and save thousands of lives by making a costly invasion of the Japanese homeland unnecessary. In the past six weeks, he had sent crews on 16 missions and only one had caused appreciable damage. In these raids, over 5,000 tons of bombs had been dropped and not one important target had been destroyed. He knew his popularity among the men had gone down in direct relationship to the failure of each mission. As he told a concerned aide, "Hell, I wasn't sent out here to win friends and influence anyone but the Japanese!"

In reviewing the past six weeks, he noted that only one day had been suitable for visual, high-altitude bombing. His weathermen had predicted March would be little better. He knew that, weather permitting, crews had reached such a peak of efficiency that they could hit targets, but he recalled a comment of Rosey O'Donnell who said, "You can't hit 'em if you can't see 'em."

He agreed with Rosey, telling him, "We're still going in too high, still running into those big jet-stream winds upstairs, and weather is almost always bad."

His analysis of radar bombing from 25,000 to 30,000 feet showed that at most only 5 percent of bombs landed within a thousand feet of a target. All too often the percentage was less than 1 percent. Therefore, he ruled out high-altitude radar attacks. The stickler was that low-altitude strikes, to get under the heavy cloud layer over Japan, had to come in at 5,000 to 6,000 feet. At those altitudes, LeMay believed hits could be doubled because target winds would be light, elimination of the long climb to high altitude would save over 5,000 pounds of gasoline that could be traded for bombs, and the service life of engines would be lengthened.

The nagging worry in the back of his mind was that such a drastic change could be suicidal. He knew that sending bombers over Germany at 6,000 feet would be murderous, but he was convinced that Japan's antiaircraft defenses were nowhere near comparable. Most important, he expected to surprise the Japanese by the first attacks. He knew you could never surprise the Germans but he believed you could surprise the Japanese and he was willing to take the risk.

He had carefully studied all the aerial photographs of Japanese targets available with photo interpreters. He wasn't satisfied with the little he found so he authorized reconnaissance planes to get more. He looked particularly for low-altitude antiaircraft batteries but he found few concentrations that would pose a problem. In comparison to the Germans, he had little respect for Japanese fighter pilots, and he noted their aggressiveness had declined by the end of January. Most of the good fighter pilots had long since been killed, and the shortage of gasoline in Japan prohibited extensive training of new pilots.

He noted that only 78 B-29s, a rate of 4 percent, had been lost since operations began in the Marianas. This total included a third of the losses that were due to mechanical failures. The crew loss of 60, or 3 percent, was even less, whereas the peak loss in the European theater had been 25 percent per month.

He was convinced from analysis of Japan's defenses that they were strongest at high altitudes, but had almost negligible defenses at low and middle altitudes.

While making up his mind, he told Norstad what he had in mind. "I'm thinking about doing a little gambling to really get something done. I don't know General Arnold or his traits and characteristics. Would he go for something like this?"

Norstad was noncommittal and LeMay knew that he and he alone must make the momentous decision, and not rely on a staff officer to help him.

LeMay faced the lonely decision but it took him only a few days. He realized he had to do something, and quickly. The B-29 command wasn't getting anything done because weather was the ruling factor. He knew Arnold had to have results and it was up to him to try and get them. If he made the wrong decision, the responsibility would be his alone. Therefore, he deliberately avoided asking Arnold permission to make low-level night fire raids. He reasoned that, if he failed, Arnold could remove him and try someone else until a successful way was found to destroy Japan from the air. The more he reviewed his options, after studying all data available, the more convinced he became that night fire raids were a good risk, and he didn't believe the loss rate would be too high.

He decided the first raid would be a night, low-altitude fire raid on Tokyo. After Dr. Gould had assured him that the least efficient radar operator could locate a small tip of land off Saipan, he directed that a similar tip that stuck out into Tokyo Bay should be used to start a run into the target areas on prescribed compass courses for so many seconds and bombardiers would unload their fire bombs.

For the Air Force, LeMay's decision was a drastic change in the classic doctrine of daylight, precision bombardment. When the general's aides learned of his plans, some tried to talk him out of such a step. He refused to reconsider.

LeMay knew he had reached the point of no return. Further procrastination was useless. He had weighed the alternatives so he went ahead with the decision that had been forming in his mind for days. Now was the time for action, not further words, and he demonstrated again the flexibility that set him apart from most other field commanders. In the final analysis, his ability to turn away from established procedures once they proved ineffective, and try something new, was the key to his success as a top commander. He didn't have to be told that the Air Force doctrine governing strategic bombing hadn't worked to the fullest in the Pacific. This was due, in large part, to the B-29's limitations. Now he devised a totally new strategy that promised a better chance of defeating Japan, and with fewer American losses.

They all knew of the flammability of Japanese cities so incendiary attacks had long been considered. During tests, incendiaries dropped from high altitudes with the number of airplanes available in the early days were not effective due to a lack of concentration and total tonnage. However, all tests indicated that ideally an attack should have at least 400 B-29s, and that the bombing accuracy had to assure the proper concentration. LeMay knew that if radar-bombing accuracy could be improved, then his crews could fly at night, or in bad weather, and utilization of his command would be increased.

Also, by bombing from low altitudes the bombload would be increased. By using a point of land on Tokyo Bay that was easily identified by radar, even untrained radar operators would have little difficulty in finding it.

LeMay knew that the incendiary attack he set up for February 25 against Tokyo couldn't possibly achieve maximum damage because there were only 231 Superfortresses available for the mission. However, "Tom" Power's 314th Wing on North Field, Guam, swelled the total to the largest force ever sent over Japan.

The 313th Wing's 6th Group was led by Captain Edgar McElroy. This was his second attack on Tokyo. He had participated in the Doolittle raid April 18, 1942. The night before, Tokyo Rose announced she knew about the coming attack and McElroy's participation in it, along with the name of the plane he would fly. She said the Japanese had a special welcome waiting for him. So, western style, he strapped on his pearl-handled .45 and went on the mission. Tokyo Rose's boast didn't materialize and he returned unharmed.

However, 59 B-29s didn't make it all the way. The rest of the force dropped 450 tons of fire bombs and a square mile of the huge city went up in flames. The results exceeded all expectations with 27,970 buildings destroyed or damaged, and B-29 losses were minimal.

The Musashino-Tama plant near Tokyo remained virtually intact after another attack failed March 4 for the eighth time when cloud cover forced B-29s to drop by radar on Tokyo's urban areas. This attack marked the end of the most difficult phase of trying against impossible odds to use B-29s primarily as high-altitude, precision bombers.

Two days later, LeMay's information officer, Lieutenant Colonel St. Clair McKelway, came to his office to get a story. LeMay was blunt and McKelway got one that he wasn't about to release. "This outfit has been getting a lot of publicity without really having accomplished a hell of a lot in bombing results."

# CHAPTER 17

# Fire Blitz Devastates Japanese Cities

LeMay summoned his wing commanders to meet with him at his quonset headquarters on Guam. He told them he was encouraged by the February 25 incendiary raid on Tokyo, and that his experts calculated the industrial heart of Japan's 20 largest cities could be burned out with M-69 fire-bomb clusters. He said tests run in the United States on typical Japanese structures were promising but not conclusive so he had waited until the command had sufficient B-29s to saturate targets with incendiaries.

He was frank in admitting that his contemplated low-altitude night attacks might increase losses prohibitively but that high-altitude release of fire bombs had proved inaccurate. Some of the command's flak experts, he said, considered low-altitude attacks at 5,000 to 6,000 feet, particularly over Tokyo and Osaka, as suicidal. He said he disagreed because Japanese antiaircraft defenses were far less accurate than German defenses, which were controlled electronically, because the Japanese relied heavily upon searchlights and inefficient gun-laying radar. He estimated flak losses would not exceed 5 percent. When he saw skepticism on some faces, he reminded them that only two Superfortresses were known to have been lost solely to antiaircraft fire.

Initially, he said, the attacks at low altitude would have the advantage of surprise. When asked about enemy fighters, he discounted their effectiveness. He had been informed by intelligence officers, he said, that there were only two units of night fighters in all the islands, and that their operations were primitive by American standards.

"That's why," he said, "I'm sending B-29s in without ammunition."

General O'Donnell gave a low whistle, and the others seemed stunned at first.

"Frankly," LeMay said, "I'm removing the ammunition because I'm afraid crews will be shooting at each other more than they will Japs. Then, too, we'll save about 3,000 pounds by eliminating ammunition which will give us another ton and a half of bombs."

He said he had long favored night missions because conditions in the Pacific were so unlike those in Europe, although he realized few crews had been trained for such operations. "It is my hope," he said, "that these night missions will reduce losses at sea because returning B-29s will be over Iwo in daylight." This decision demonstrated again his flexibility, which was the key to LeMay's success as a commander of bomber forces.

In conclusion, he told them that he was inaugurating an all-out effort before the Okinawa invasion, and a series of strikes would be made against Japan's major cities.

His wing commanders agreed with LeMay's assessment of the situation, knowing, as he did, there was a calculated risk, and if losses were heavy their whole strategic campaign would be crippled. Once LeMay weighed the alternative of sending bombers at high altitude over Japan only to find targets cloud-covered while crew and plane losses mounted with no significant results for their efforts, he didn't hesitate. It was his decision, and he asked no one to back him up. Not for one moment did he worry that failure would destroy his own professional career. He knew that if Japan was to be destroyed by airpower, this was the only way to do it.

The first city on the schedule to be blitzed was Tokyo, with Kobe, Nagoya, Nagasaki, and Osaka scheduled for the same treatment during a 10-day period. It was the most massive incendiary attack ever conceived and, before it was finished, the missions would use every incendiary bomb in the Marianas, with more not available until the first week of April.

In justifying the tight schedule, LeMay told staffers, "I want to get in and out of the Empire before the Japs make things too costly for us."

Before he sent wing commanders back to their bases, he charged them with training crews prior to the first mission. He insisted they practice with maximum takeoff loads and make instrument bombing attacks on tiny Rota in the Mariana's chain, which was still occupied by a few Japanese. He even called for flights to Truk so that crews would learn how to form a bomber stream at night. In insisting upon careful preparation, he said, "We must seek maximum compressibility to confuse and saturate Japanese defenses."

Operations officers figured for days how to get B-29s off on the first mission because only one B-29 could get off each of five runways every minute. That left a 400-mile spread in the bomber stream from the first to the last B-29. To complicate matters, Guam-based B-29s had to start 40 minutes earlier to place themselves in the proper lineup over Japan.

The risk of collision was high because B-29s would fly singly to Japan, and bomb targets individually. Any differential in the time sequence would be highly dangerous, bringing B-29s in on collision courses.

Perhaps the heaviest burden fell on Colonel Irvine, who had to scrounge short supplies and organize maintenance teams to cover emergencies at all bases. He said his job was a "helluva lot worse" than planning a maintenance schedule for an airline. "When you send a combat wing out," Irvine said, "you get some mean jobs."

LeMay was relentless as wings prepared for the first big fire raid against Tokyo March 9, making sure that nothing was left to chance. For those who were appalled that American bombers would resort to bombing cities, and Nimitz was one of them, LeMay patiently explained that Japan's industries were concentrated in major cities where tens of thousands of household shops fed the big factories. He reminded doubters that target specialists estimated that the main industrial areas of 20 of Japan's principal manufacturing cities had half the numbered precision targets on the Twentieth's master list. Civilian casualties might be high, he conceded, because these cities contained over 16 million people, or 22 percent of all Japanese in the home islands. What it came down to, he said, was that fire-bombing of these cities, brutal as it was for noncombatants, was the only way to destroy Japan's ability to wage war—a war that she had provoked by her sneak attack on Pearl Harbor.

Japan's cities were firetraps, despite some reinforced concrete buildings in Tokyo and Yokohama. Poorer sections of Tokyo were the worst, where practically all buildings were one- and two-story wood-frame houses. Japanese cities had had conflagrations before, with Yokohama suffering 20 or so in the twentieth century. The new incendiary bombs, like those filled with napalm, were deadly when used against such construction. Clusters separated in the air through the action of a time fuse and six-pound bombs plummeted through roofs splattering walls with flaming dabs of jellied gasoline. Other incendiary clusters pierced concrete and metal roofs, burning like acetylene torches.

The British pioneered fire raids over Germany. The most devastating was a night attack against Hamburg in 1945 when a huge conflagration almost destroyed the city.

For 36 hours prior to takeoff March 9, 1945, 13,000 men worked night and day to prepare the B-29s for the mission. Bombs had to be hauled from jungle hideaways to the flight lines, their fins and fuses attached, and then hoisted up into bomb bays. Then, just prior to takeoff, crews received their kits and were briefed with final details.

LeMay was on hand with his chief of staff, Kissner, at Guam's North Field to watch General Power and his 314th Wing take off.

Power told LeMay just before takeoff that a squadron maintenance officer had stormed into his office because his men had worked 36 hours straight to get an airplane in commission and his squadron operations officer told him he was a few minutes too late. Power said the captain was furious. He was dirty, unshaven, and red-eyed for want of sleep. The general ordered a crew rounded up and the plane made the mission although it was 45 minutes late in taking off. LeMay appreciated this kind of dedication and made a note to extend his thanks to the captain and his men.

Rain had fallen during the day and now at dusk the tropical vegetation was bright and sparkling as the last rays of the setting sun caressed trees and shrubs. Fluffy cumulous clouds lay to the north as coral dust whipped into the air as the rapidly churning wheels of the heavily laden B-29s roared down the runway.

LeMay watched the departing Superfortresses, a cigar clamped tightly between his teeth while his eyes checked each airplane's departure. Finally, still lost in his own thoughts, he turned away and headed back to headquarters for a long, lonely vigil until the first reports came in.

Fifteen hundred miles away thousands of people went about their usual routines never suspecting that death rode on wings for thousands before dawn of a new day as 324 Superfortresses flew parallel in three long streams en route to Tokyo. They carried almost 2,000 tons of fire bombs, an average of six tons per airplane.

Pathfinders were ahead to light up specific points in the city so those who followed would know exactly where to drop.

The commander of the 314th Wing, General Thomas S. Power, went in first to drop his bombs, then circled the city at 10,000 feet to observe the results as Superforts from three wings streamed in. From his grandstand high in the sky Power watched as small fires erupted and then seemed to flow into one another until huge areas were engulfed in flames. Power watched in awe as fires spread. Weather was perfect and pathfinders had marked the heart of Tokyo well. At first, Power couldn't believe how little antiaircraft fire sought out the bombers as they came in, dropped their fire bombs, and left almost unmolested. Only an occasional fighter rose in protest, and he was astonished that there weren't hundreds trying to interfere with the steady stream of bombers. Power looked down almost in disbelief as surface winds increased and spread the flames, which leaped over rivers and fire breaks and raced through a rectangular area three by five miles. The tremendous updrafts from the heat generated by the fires tossed his B-29 violently and he noticed that the bombers at 5,000 and 6,000 feet were hurled skyward at the rate of hundreds of feet a minute. It had taken only 30 minutes before fires were out of control. Power noted the level of his fuel gauges indicated he'd better head home and he was glad to do so because he was shaken by the horror of what he had seen, knowing thousands had died or were homeless. His tail gunner reported he could see the glow in the sky 150 miles from the city.

LeMay waited up in Operations to hear the first reports. Power had sent a flash that they were bombing visually, with large fires started, and that flak was light to moderate, with few enemy fighters.

LeMay said, "It looks good." There was a ghost of a smile on his tired face but he wouldn't say more until he'd seen the reconnaissance photos.

Power's plane landed at 8:30 A.M. There were dark circles around his eyes and he badly needed a shave. He told LeMay, "It was a hell of a good mission."

The Japanese had been caught off guard, and fighters attacked only when a B-29 was bracketed by searchlights. As the strike progressed, flak increased in accuracy and 14 B-29s were shot down with another 42 damaged. Five crews were saved, however, by air-sea rescue teams that picked up their distress signals.

It was apparent that the fire bombs had been so concentrated that

Japanese fire fighters were overwhelmed, and thousands of people were trapped. The destruction was appalling. Panic caused many of the 83,793 dead as one fourth of Tokyo dissolved in flames, with 267,000 homes destroyed and over a million people made homeless. So intense was the heat that water boiled in the canals, and liquid glass rolled down the streets.

Radio Tokyo made no pretense of minimizing the destruction of life and property, calling the raid "slaughter bombing." One broadcast said, "The sea of flames which enclosed the residential and commercial sections of Tokyo was reminiscent of the holocaust of Rome caused by the Emperor Nero."

This devastation was far greater than the much smaller city of ancient Rome had undergone and 22 industrial targets were destroyed along with thousands of home factories. Unlike Nero, LeMay wasn't fiddling with joy because he wasn't the kind of man to rejoice over the suffering of hundreds of thousands of people.

After the war, an official of the Home Affairs Ministry reported, "People were unable to escape. They were found later piled upon the bridges, roads, and in the canals, over 80,000 dead and twice that many injured. We were instructed to report on actual conditions. Most of us were unable to do this because of horrifying conditions beyond imagination."

By midafternoon of March 10 an area of 15.8 square miles had been gutted, including 18 percent of the industrial area, 63 percent of the commercial area, and the heart of the congested residential district.

When final reports were in, LeMay called the mission a "diller." It wasn't for several days that reconnaissance photographs could be taken because of the pall of smoke that hung over the city. When LeMay and Power finally saw clear photographs, they stared at them in disbelief. Although familiar with stricken cities in Europe, they had never seen such damage. Even the famous Ginza District, with its luxury shops and hotels, was completely burned out.

One of the pathfinder pilots was assigned the Tokyo Electric Power Company as his aiming point. The crew hit the target right on the nose.

In the fall of 1945, this pilot came to Victor Agather's office on Wall Street with a bundle of securities that he had inherited from his father, who had died while he was overseas. When Agather opened the roll he found they were first mortgage bonds of the Tokyo Electric Power Company, which had been sold on Wall Street in 1925. Agather referred the matter to the War-Claims Administration in Washington and the young pilot received full payment at the par value of the bonds.

LeMay got the only direct message from Arnold he ever received after this raid. "The results of yesterday's mission," Arnold wired, "show that your crews have the nerve for anything. Congratulations."

Nagoya was next. Japan's third largest city, it was the center of the aircraft industry. LeMay realized that this time the Japanese would be expecting them. Also, after the first big incendiary mission without gunners or guns, the crews voiced their unhappiness because some members would finish their combat tours before others. Before the mission, LeMay relented and allowed the lower turrets to be manned but with orders to shoot only at searchlights to keep from shooting down other B-29s.

Although more fire bombs were dropped than on Tokyo, the all-important surface winds weren't strong enough to spread the fires and they remained widely dispersed. No damage was caused to the aircraft plants, and only two square miles of the city were gutted.

LeMay realized that one of the problems was spacing of the incendiaries 100 feet apart, or twice the distance separating fire bombs dropped on Tokyo, which prevented concentrations of fires. These less than optimum results, LeMay believed, were the direct result of being too greedy and trying to cover a larger area by increasing the bomb interval. After this mission he ordered a return to the original bomb spacing.

The city of Osaka had not been hit so it was set up for fire-bombing March 13. A city of more than two million people, it lay at the head of oval-shaped Osaka Bay at the eastern limits of the Inland Sea. An important transportation center, Osaka produced ships, electrical equipment, and one third of Japan's machinery and machine tools. In addition, its Army Arsenal produced 20 percent of the Japanese Army's ordnance needs.

LeMay's target specialists warned him that it would be a difficult target to destroy because the city had numerous firebreaks throughout its congested areas because it had undergone natural disasters through the years. Then, too, many of its major buildings were made of fire-resistant materials.

Concentration of bombs was the keynote that LeMay left with crews prior to their departure. Weather wasn't cooperative and all crews had to off-set their bombs by means of radar. Fortunately, this procedure served to provide a uniform pattern for the 1,700 tons of fire bombs that were dropped during a three-hour period, and 8.1 square miles of the heart of the city were burned out. Fortunately, the Japanese civilian death toll wasn't too high and 119 major factories were destroyed for a loss of only two B-29s.

The next mission had to wait until March 16 and B-29s were sent across the bay to Japan's sixth largest city. Kobe lay along the south side of Osaka Bay, and was a major industrial city.

LeMay's stock of regular incendiaries was used up sooner than expected so this time he had to use 500-pound clusters of magnesium thermite in four-pound bombs that were particularly effective against heavy industrial areas.

Although over 300 fighters tried to prevent the B-29s from bombing, not one of the three Superfortresses lost on the mission was hit by fighters.

The fierce heat from Kobe's burning buildings created thermals so severe that planes were thrown violently about the sky. Major Jack Catton's airplane was particularly affected because it was flying at 4,500 feet. Just as he was getting the airplane under some measure of control, he felt a huge jolt that sent quivering shocks through the airplane. He thought the tail had been sheared off because he lost complete control. When he called tail gunner Norman T. Roberts, he got no answer. He didn't learn until later that Roberts' mike had been torn from his throat so he couldn't communicate for a time.

After Catton regained control, he admitted to the crew that he'd had the hell scared out of him. After talking with several crew members who had witnessed a huge blast directly beneath them, it was evident that an ammunition factory or arsenal had blown up.

Once the fires got under way they spread throughout the eastern half of the business district, burning an important industrial area. The Kawasaki shipyards, builders of submarines, received heavy damage, and almost three square miles, or a fifth of the city, were turned to ashes.

The last fire raid of the blitz saw B-29s returning to Nagoya on March 19. A change in bomb loading was made to include two high explosive bombs in every third airplane to disrupt fire fighters on the ground. Again radar had to be used for dropping fire bombs and three additional square miles were destroyed, including damage to the Nagoya Arsenal, freight yards, and the Aichi engine works. The top priority Mitsubishi plants miraculously survived again.

These raids gutted 32 square miles of urban area in four key cities, along with destruction of many important targets that otherwise would have had to be singled out for precision bombing. Despite the dire predictions of some on LeMay's staff that the losses would be prohibitive, less than 1 percent of all crews participating in these missions was lost, a rate far less than daylight, high-altitude missions. Combat crews, many of whom had flown all five missions, were exuberant. Maintenance crews also felt a morale uplift but they were too exhausted after working night and day for 10 days to permit much of a celebration.

These maintenance crews had performed a genuine miracle by having 83 percent of all B-29s available for each mission instead of the previous average of 59 percent.

LeMay believed he had now found the answer to the eventual destruction of Japan. In reviewing statistics, he found that 91 percent of all B-29s dispatched on each mission bombed the primary target, instead of the 36 percent average on daylight missions. Most important, he noted with satisfaction, the bombload per aircraft more than doubled, and it was evident that B-29s could fly twice as many missions because engines were subjected to far less strain at these lower altitudes.

He told his Chief of Staff Kissner, "The end result is the same as if the force had been doubled."

It was apparent to LeMay that Japanese cities were even more vulnerable than they had realized, but that fire raids were not suitable for all targets. He planned to continue daylight attacks against aircraft plants whenever weather permitted, but most of the time he would send B-29s with fire bombs to destroy the 33 urban areas selected by the Joint Target Group. This organization listed 22 for a two-phase program, including plants producing ground ordnance and aircraft in the initial phase, with the second phase including manufacturing plants for machine tools, electrical equipment, and those associated with ordnance and aircraft components. The remaining 11 priority targets would be considered at a later date.

LeMay told Nimitz that he would need more supplies because he planned to fly each combat crew 120 hours each month. The request was turned over to the admiral's staff. They scoffed at LeMay's request, saying, "You only flew thirty hours a month in Europe. How in hell are you going to fly a hundred and twenty hours out here? Besides," they said, "we've only planned for a maximum of sixty hours."

LeMay didn't believe they had planned for any such figure so he got mad. "I'm planning to do it," he said. "When I run out of supplies, you explain it to the Joint Chiefs because I'm going fishing."

LeMay said admiringly later, "The Navy really stirred its stumps. How they got the ships and the supplies out there in six weeks I don't know but we never did catch up until the end of the war."

LeMay did fly his crews 120 hours a month and bombs were delivered for the most part just before each mission. Time was so crucial that the bombs were not taken to the dumps but delivered directly to the hard stands and loaded on the airplanes. Everyone pitched in to haul bombs from the ships—Marines, Seabees, all available personnel who weren't otherwise engaged.

Meanwhile, LeMay's lead-crew school was active every day as crews learned the technique of radar bombing. They became so expert with the early radar system that they now could hit an inland target with no land-water contrast in the middle of a thunderstorm.

After the big fire raids, LeMay studied the broadcasts by Japanese radio to the people of Japan. They often verged on the hysterical, and LeMay was convinced his new tactics had the Japanese at a decided disadvantage. He told Kissner, "The Japanese did not foresee the possibilities of strategic air attack. We have them cold."

# CHAPTER 18

# The Nation's Highest Honor

With invasion of Okinawa set for April 1, Nimitz exercised his right to call on the Twentieth Air Force for assistance to bomb airfields and their installations on Kyushu. The kamikaze suicide attacks in the Philippines against Navy ships were still fresh in his memory and he wanted to avoid a repetition as much as possible.

LeMay was reluctant to divert his strategic forces because he believed they would be more effective bombing industrial targets, but he got orders from Arnold to knock out the airfields on Kyushu. He agreed to send B-29s out March 27, while other Superfortresses mined the Shimonoseki Strait that night. Airfields were attacked again on the 30th.

Actually, these raids didn't interfere with fire-bombing attacks because there was a serious shortage of incendiary bombs following the earlier large raids.

After the preinvasion strikes were completed, LeMay went to see Nimitz. "We've been lucky on the weather, Admiral. I'm sure you've seen the photographs I've sent you. We've got everything flat on Kyushu. I believe we ought to go back to strategic bombing. All we can do now is put more holes in the fields, and we can't stop an occasional airplane from taking off that the Japs have hid down the road someplace. We've done all we can."

Nimitz walked over to LeMay, patted him on the back, and then put his arm around him. "You've done a fine job, LeMay. Let's check with Sherman to see what he says."

Admiral Sherman refused to release the bombers. When LeMay

protested, a telegram was sent back to Admiral King in Washington that the Navy would pull off and leave the ground troops on shore if the Twentieth didn't continue bombing the Kyushu fields.

LeMay liked Nimitz and found him most cooperative although he disagreed with him in this instance; he realized all services had to help during an amphibious operation because it is the most difficult of all military operations.

When Marines and Army troops went ashore Easter morning at Hagushi they found little opposition because the Japanese had decided not to contest the beaches and set up first-line defenses farther inland. The Tenth Army held a beachhead 15 miles long and 3 to 10 miles wide by April 4, including two airfields that were quickly put to use by the Americans.

At first, kamikaze attacks were not serious, but April 6 the Japanese sent 335 suiciders over the invasion area, and about an equal number of conventional fighters and bombers. Losses of ships and men mounted to the critical stage. To further complicate matters the giant battleship *Yamato,* and its accompanying warships, slipped out of Tokuyama and headed for Okinawa. Task Force 58 ended this foray by sinking the battleship, the light cruiser *Yahagi,* and four of the eight destroyers.

When B-29 assistance was sought again, LeMay met with Nimitz to protest continuation of the attacks but the admiral, after another talk with Sherman, who told him that invasion ships were under constant heavy attack, turned the general down.

LeMay decided to go directly to Arnold and present his case at the highest level. After Arnold talked to Chief of Naval Operations King, who supported Nimitz' stand, LeMay was advised to do as he was told.

The Russians renounced their neutrality pact with Japan April 5. And, a week after the invasion of Okinawa, the Koiso Cabinet was dismissed and a new cabinet under Admiral Kantaro Suzuki, former navy chief of staff, was formed.

With near perfect weather forecast for April 7, LeMay split his command to hit the two top-rated precision targets. The 313th and 314th Wings attacked the Mitsubishi engine works at Nagoya, destroying 90 percent of the plant. This was the kind of pickle-barrel bombing that Hansell believed in, and had so long advocated. The 73rd didn't do as well with their nemesis the Nakajima Musashino-Tama plant on the outskirts of Tokyo, although their one-ton bombs caused heavy damage to machine shops.

Superfortresses returned to Kyushu April 8 and dropped a variety of bomb types, some with delayed-action fuses, but LeMay still was convinced this was wasted effort, and that B-29s would contribute more to prosecution of the war by bombing strategic targets.

The 73rd Wing returned to Musashino-Tama April 12 and, despite heavy haze that prevented visual bombing, managed to drop 64 tons of bombs on the eastern end of the plant to cause damage severe enough to finally remove the target from the top-priority list. By now, B-29s had flown 11 missions against Musashino-Tama and only the last two were partly successful. Task Force 58's low-level attack the previous February still had done more damage than any Superfortress strike. Such was the continuing destruction, however, that Nakajima officials abandoned the plant, moving machine tools to other areas, and engine production was stopped.

Over a hundred P-51s from Iwo's VII Fighter Command escorted bombers on the April 12 mission, and B-29 damage was reduced to 36 despite vigorous opposition by at least a hundred Japanese fighters. LeMay had sent the 313th and 314th Wings to Koriyama, over a hundred miles from Tokyo, to try and draw fighters away from the capital. It didn't work and P-51s had a fight on their hands. The attack on two chemical plants and an aluminum plant at Koriyama was successful because all three were severely damaged.

Captain George A. Simeral, commander of the "City of Los Angeles," was assigned to lead a formation against one of the chemical plants at Koriyama.

Near the formation's assembly point, 175 miles from the target, Simeral raised his right hand as a signal to radio operator Sergeant Henry E. "Red" Erwin, to release the first colored flare through the chute in the bottom of the airplane to signal others to join on the leader. The pilot watched anxiously as the flak burst around them and fighter attacks pressed close, firing all the way.

While Red waited by the chute for the signal to release a phosphorus smoke bomb, Simeral raised his hand again. Erwin carefully pulled the pin, and inserted the bomb in the chute quickly because once it was armed it would explode in six seconds. To his horror, the bomb exploded at the end of the chute because the last flare had damaged the hinged flap at the bottom of the tube. The bomb blew back into his face, covering him with flaming phosphorus. His nose was burned off and most of his right ear, as the white-hot, burning metal ate through patches of skin on his face and right arm. Almost blinded by smoke, he tried to grab the bomb as it rolled across the cockpit's floor before coming to rest and burning the metal flooring.

Thick black smoke filled the cockpit and the pilot couldn't see his instrument panel. Simeral lost control of the plane and it plummeted to 700 feet above the wave tops. Struggling to fight down panic, Simeral considered jettisoning their three-ton load of fire bombs but he was fearful they would explode beneath the plane at such a low altitude and destroy it.

While the pilot fought to regain mastery of the plane, Erwin groped for the smoke bomb on the floor. Almost blinded, with his clothes on fire, and his flesh burning off his body, Red was oblivious to the excruciating agony as he searched frantically for the bomb until he found it. With his right hand he picked up the flaming phosphorus bomb, almost shrieking in agony as the phosphorus quickly burned the flesh from his hand to the bone. He stumbled across the narrow confines of the forward cockpit, bumped into the upper turret, and then smashed into the navigator's table, which blocked his way. Somehow he had to fold the table back or he'd never get to a window in the pilot's compartment. He tucked his flaming bomb under his arm against his burned body and, using his horribly burned hand to unlatch the table, moved it to a stowed position.

More dead than alive, he almost fell into the pilot's compartment yelling, "Open the window!"

Roy Stables kept trying to tell him that the window was open, until finally Red saw the open window, hurled the bomb out, and collapsed.

It had taken only 12 seconds but it seemed a lifetime to the crew. The pilot now had the plane under control and he pulled up just 300 feet off the water and climbed to a safer altitude.

Red Erwin was a mass of flames, particularly his rubber life jacket, as Gene Strouse grabbed a fire extinguisher and put the flames out while Erwin, uncomplainingly, lay in agony on the floor.

Simeral turned the plane back and at full power headed for Iwo Jima. Erwin was the only one of the crew trained to give first aid, and he had to instruct them how to give him morphine to deaden the pain, and later blood plasma.

It took an hour and a half to reach Iwo and Erwin never lost consciousness, which would have alleviated some of the terrible pains of his burn-racked body.

Near the island, Simeral learned that Iwo was under attack by Japanese bombers. He set the B-29 down while the air battle raged above them.

Doctors fought to save Erwin's life and for four days they weren't sure they could. Taking a chance on moving him, they flew Red to Guam, where a better-equipped hospital could do things the forward hospital on Iwo could not.

Arnold sent Major General Willis Hale from Hawaii as his personal representative to honor Erwin five weeks later and pin the nation's highest honor on the 23-year-old hero. Erwin was covered with bandages from head to toe and he could barely hear the general as he said, "Your gallantry and heroism, above and beyond the call of duty, saved the lives of your comrades." He pinned the Medal of Honor to the bandages on Red's chest.

The Alabama man was the only member of the Twentieth Air Force to be so honored. Arnold said of Erwin's action, "The country's highest honor will still be inadequate recognition of the inspiring heroism of this man."

The Mitsubishi engine works at Shizuoka was struck by 11 B-29s that couldn't make it to Tokyo or Koriyama. So heavy was the destruction by this small force that 86 percent of the factory was damaged.

Despite the number of attacks in support of the Okinawa invasion, LeMay was still able to send B-29s to urban areas. April 13 they hit Tokyo's arsenal district northwest of the Imperial Palace. Three hundred bombers burned out 11.4 square miles that night, and an equal number burned another six square miles along the west shore of the bay two nights later. Other attacks that night destroyed 3.6 square miles of Kawasaki and 1.5 square miles of Yokohama.

While Kyushu's airfields were kept under regular B-29 attack, LeMay interrupted his Okinawa support April 24 to send bombers to attack the Hitachi Aircraft Corporation's plant at Yamato, 20 miles from Tokyo. During bombing runs partially obscured by haze, B-29s went in at 12,000 feet while fighters drove relentlessly at the big bombers, flying right through their own flak. Despite heavy opposition, the engine plant was completely destroyed, but four B-29s were lost and 68 damaged.

The next day LeMay wrote Norstad, the Twentieth Air Force's chief of staff, "I am influenced by the conviction that the present stage of development of the air war against Japan presents the Army Air Forces for the first time with the opportunity of proving the power of the strategic air arm. I consider that for the first time strategic air bombardment faces a situation in which the strength is proportionate to the magnitude of the task. I feel that the destruction of Japan's ability to wage war lies within the capability of this command, provided its maximum capacity is exerted unstintingly during the next six months which is considered to be the critical period. Though naturally reluctant to drive my force at an exorbitant rate, I believe that the opportunity now at hand warrants extraordinary measures on the part of all sharing it."

The Tachikawa Army Air Arsenal near Tokyo was set for attack April 30 but bad weather prevented release of bombs. Some bombs were held for the city of Hamamatsu and dropped with good effect by radar. This raid and the one against the Hiro Naval Aircraft Factory at Kure were coordinated with the invasion of Okinawa and considered of direct assistance.

The 58th Wing made its first strike from the Marianas following its arrival from India when it joined the 73rd for an attack on the Hiro Naval Aircraft Factory at Kure. It was a rough baptism of fire for the 58th but they quickly demonstrated they were professionals of the highest order. With Navy ships firing from the harbor, and bursts rattling like thunder around each formation as it dropped its bombs, the B-29s peeled away to the left for home. The 462nd's Lieutenant Marvin E. Ballard achieved perfect bombing with 100 percent of his formation's bombs on target. The 58th Wing had proved itself again. So devastating was the total strike that the plant's production was cut in half.

Heavy destruction was caused on the day Nimitz released B-29s from Okinawa support when a small force of 15 462nd Group bombers hit the Kawanishi Aircraft Company's Konan plant, which built airframes. Two formations, led by Captains Ralph T. Holland and Dock O. Waller, were able to drop when, at the last moment, their bombardiers found holes in the clouds and were able to synchronize. Destruction was so heavy that the company closed the plant and removed surviving tools to another location.

* * *

The merger of Pacific Ocean Area commands under Nimitz and the Southwest Pacific forces under MacArthur went into effect April 5 and MacArthur was named supreme commander of all Army forces while Nimitz was designated to command all Navy forces. There was only one exception. The Twentieth Air Force remained under Arnold until it was decided whether command of the Twentieth should be transferred to the Marianas. Under consideration for some time was formation of a United States Army Strategic Air Force in the Pacific but such action was delayed until mid-July.

The continued good relationship between the Navy and the Army Air Forces was directly traceable to Admiral Nimitz. There were differences between the Navy and the AAF, but they remained at lower levels. Once they were referred to Nimitz, they were quickly resolved, mostly in favor of the AAF. These differences were natural because the Twentieth Air Force was literally forced upon the theater command for supplies and services, without any authority to direct their operations. In many ways, such a command structure was confusing but somehow it was made to work and the tremendous buildup of the Twentieth Air Force in the Marianas, almost unparalleled in military history, almost always received its share of huge quantities of bombs, fuel, and supplies when they were required. Nimitz was the man most responsible for this cordial state of relations.

A prime example of cooperation was the resolution of the problems associated with the air-sea rescue service. It was a hodgepodge of Navy–Air Force units with, at first, little coordination. The Navy had been using flying boats but they were not adequate for the job. Late in April, converted B-17s with droppable motorboats were placed in service. Most useful of all were converted B-29s, known as Super Dumbos, which could stay on station far longer than other rescue airplanes. Navy submarines played a significant part because they operated within sight of Japan, often snatching crews from the water close to shore. Once air-sea rescue operations were tightened, and new equipment placed in service, B-29 crew losses at sea were reduced by a third.

The Joint Target Group had issued a new target directive for the Twentieth Air Force April 3. When weather prevented daylight strikes, it was recommended that the urban areas of Tokyo, Kawasaki, Nagoya, and Osaka be fire-bombed. This directive was based on the assumption that an invasion of the home islands would still be necessary. LeMay disagreed. After the devastating March fire raids, he was convinced that airpower alone could force Japan's surrender. With buildup of his command proceeding rapidly, with the 58th Wing operational in early May, and the 315th Wing expected to be ready by July, he figured the 2,925 sorties flown in April would be increased to 6,700 by September; fully enough, he believed, to bring about Japan's collapse.

His greatest concern was a shortage of crews. B-29s were being delivered at an ever-increasing rate and he expected the average of 148 aircraft per wing in April to rise to 192 by late summer. His flight surgeon told him crews could average a maximum of 60 combat hours a month for an extended period, but beyond that he wouldn't be responsible for their ability to function effectively. LeMay faced a dilemma. He was convinced his command could end the war in a matter of months, but with an average loss rate of 2 percent, and an anticipated tour of duty of 35 missions for crews, he would be short almost 300 crews by August, which would drastically reduce the bomb tonnage on missions. There was only one solution— one that he didn't like to take. To get the maximum number of bombers on the March fire raids, crews had flown 80 hours that month. He could justify such an excess for one month, but asking crews to continue to fly even more hours month after month was another thing. His flight surgeon was opposed because even 60 hours was greater than the Eighth Air Force had flown. Unlike the Eighth, LeMay knew, most of the Twentieth's hours on missions were not over Japan but on the long ocean flight to and from the target where strain was less.

LeMay figured that, based on the assumption the invasion would go on, his command could fly 120 hours per crew each month through the first of December. Then, he knew, they would fall flat on their faces because they'd be out of crews, supplies, everything. But such a schedule would allow the command 30 days after the invasion for follow-up strikes, so if efforts to destroy Japan before the November 1 invasion failed to achieve its objectives, the Twentieth could fully support the invasion for 30 days after the first troops landed on Kyushu. After December 1 he would have to sharply curtail B-29 operations.

When staff members objected, he pointed out the high morale of crews and maintenance personnel. "Every time we stick up photographs of our reconnaissance photos, the men go wild. They're really gung ho. Strangely enough, the people who are falling by the wayside, and dropping like flies, are those in the 'topo' squadron." These were the men who prepared the target material.

Despite misgivings of many members of his staff, LeMay decided to increase the combat hours each month to 120 per crew. "If Japan can be defeated without a costly ground invasion," he told his staff, "the risk of airmen's lives is worth it."

LeMay continued to press Arnold for an increase in new crews, but they couldn't be trained fast enough in the States, a problem that would continue until war's end. He even offered to take B-17 and B-24 crews and complete their training in the Marianas.

When kamikaze attacks were at their worst off Okinawa, the XXI Bomber Command sent over a hundred B-29s from three wings on each mission. Once land-based air forces were established on Okinawa, the need for B-29s diminished and, the first part of May, only a few bombers from one wing were sent out. There was little fighter opposition to B-29 attacks but 24 Superfortresses were lost to all causes, with another 233 damaged.

Superforts made over 2,000 sorties against 17 air bases on Kyushu and Shikoku from April 17 to May 11, absorbing over 75 percent of the command's total effort against Japan.

Despite crew protests, top headquarters insisted that all scantily clad female figures on B-29s be removed. Photographs taken for publicity outraged some of the folks back home and the paintings were either removed or bare breasts covered.

Lieutenant General Simon B. Bruckner, Jr., commander of the Tenth Army, was one of the casualties of the Okinawa campaign. Marshall selected General Stilwell, who had lost his CBI command due to conflicts with Chiang Kai-shek, to replace Bruckner and head the ground troops for the scheduled invasion of Kyushu.

Nimitz was warm in praise of B-29 assistance when he released them May 11 but LeMay wasn't impressed with their contribution. He told his staff, "No matter how we socked at those airdromes, we couldn't reduce the kamikaze threat to zero." Actually, the Japanese admitted after the war that B-29s caused serious disruption of their air operations because these attacks made it difficult to keep bases in operation as hangars and maintenance shops were hit repeatedly. The kamikaze threat was met by the combined efforts of all services, but loss of ships and men undoubtedly would have been much higher without Twentieth Air Force intervention.

# CHAPTER 19
# *A Hell on Earth*

After VE-Day, Colonel Cecil E. Combs, target specialist for the Twentieth Air Force, advised Chief of Staff Norstad in Washington that fire raids should be intensified to bring the Japanese war to a quicker conclusion.

Arnold agreed when Norstad reported to him, saying we must "capitalize on the present critical situation in Japan." He told LeMay to concentrate attacks on aircraft plants and urban areas. LeMay chose to devote most of the command's efforts to the large urban areas until June.

In two raids, Nagoya was heavily damaged. On the night of May 14, 3.15 square miles of Nagoya were gutted, and Mitsubishi lost its ball-bearing plant. Two nights later, Superfortresses returned and dropped incendiaries on the southern part, where most large industries were located near the city's docks. This time the burned area totaled 3.82 square miles, and included heavy damage to Mitsubishi's aircraft plants. Although there were some precision targets still to be knocked out, Nagoya was scratched from the list of urban areas for future fire raids because 12 square miles of the city had been burned, and most of its industry damaged or destroyed. This raid, and the one preceding it, cost the command 13 B-29s, most of them on the first raid, which was opposed by more than the usual number of fighters.

Jack Catton was transferred from the 73rd Wing to help out on mission planning, although occasionally he still flew missions. He was aware of criticisms by wing commanders of how certain missions were planned, and he resolved to try and meet their recommendations. He was told he had a free rein as long as his plans didn't conflict with LeMay's ideas on how a mission should be run.

With another attack on Tokyo coming up, Catton studied the flak charts and decided to bring the B-29s in on another axis of attack to avoid a heavy flak installation. Wing commanders had complained they were losing their most experienced lead crews to flak batteries.

LeMay always joined the planning staff after lunch the day before a mission. The general listened to the briefing officers without comment until they completed their presentation.

He looked quizzically at Catton. "Who planned this mission?"

"We planned it, sir," Catton said.

"Why did you select this axis of attack?"

"It's a good IP and will give us a good radar return. More importantly, this axis will avoid heavy concentrations of flak batteries."

"Let me ask just one question. Is that the best axis of attack?"

"Yes, sir. I think so."

"No, I don't think you do. I mean from the standpoint of bombs on target, which is the best axis of attack?"

"Well, actually, the other one is. It's a better IP, a better look at the target. Target acquisition would be simpler but we do have extremely heavy defenses because we've been over this route four or five times and . . ."

LeMay interrupted. "Let me explain something to you. We will lose fewer crews and we'll destroy the target far sooner if we use the best possible axis of attack from the standpoint of getting bombs on target."

Catton quickly agreed to change the operational plan. One thing he had learned was that LeMay would listen to suggestions, but you'd better know what you were talking about. LeMay had the reputation for being tough, but he always had the welfare of his crews at heart. He was not only an outstanding pilot, but he had qualified as a navigator, bombardier, and a gunner. He not only knew what his equipment was capable of doing, but he knew what his men could accomplish once they were properly trained.

Superforts returned to Tokyo during the nights of May 23 and 25. A thousand heavy guns, searchlights, night fighters, and rocket-propelled Bakas tried to blunt the attack. The Bakas were suicide craft with a thousand-pound warhead in their noses that streaked across the night sky like a ball of fire with only one thought in the mind of their pilots and that was to ram a B-29. All these Japanese weapons helped to contribute to the loss of 17 B-29s, but an additional 5.3 square miles of the city were burned out.

The city became a sea of flames below them as bombers relentlessly came through a hell on earth as the Japanese threw everything they had into their desperate efforts to stop at least some Superfortresses from pouring liquid fire on their city. Each bomber started fires in a certain area which were spread by surface winds of hurricane velocity until they joined with other fires to become a raging inferno that trapped Japanese by the thousands, mingling their blood with the boiling water in the canals.

When crews returned to their bases, they handed in their reports with hands that shook, with shock and horror still reflected in their eyes from what they had witnessed just a few hours before.

The second night, the bombers hit parts of the financial and commercial districts. So intense was the smoke that many B-29s had to drop by radar but 16.8 square miles were burned, bringing the total in six raids to almost 51 percent. For the average city dweller life was one continuing hell as Japan fought for her very existence as a nation.

James Pattillo, now flying with the 313th Wing, approached Tokyo the night of June 25 at 6,000 feet on a northwest heading. Halfway across Tokyo Bay searchlights caught them and the cockpit was lit up bright enough so he could read a newspaper. He held to their course on the bombing run. He was startled by what looked like 8 or 10 grains of rice flying at them, which seemed to burn out in front of the windshield.

He turned to his copilot, Harold D. Madden. "What the hell was that, Slim?"

"It's a goddamn night fighter."

The same thing happened a few minutes later. Pattillo called his tail gunner "Red" Murphy. "Take a shot at that son-of-a-bitch."

"Who you talking about?" Red replied. The searchlights were so bright he couldn't see a thing.

Once they were over the city, Pattillo watched apprehensively as the bomber streams converged. The raging fires below them lit up the sky and the surrounding countryside. As they neared the bomb-release point, the glow from the fires seemed to pulsate. The searchlights went on and off, remaining on only if they bracketed a bomber, and then antiaircraft bursts swarmed around the airplane until it seemed impossible that it could survive. Often antiaircraft fire was so concentrated that a B-29 didn't have a chance and exploded with a blinding flash while pieces of flaming wreckage rained down to become part of the devastation below.

Pattillo watched one B-29 and his throat constricted as the huge bomber tore itself apart and headed down without a single parachute visible. The thought uppermost in his mind was "Will we be next?" The thought sent shuddering waves through his body and he felt almost literally that he was sweating blood.

Pattillo waited nervously for the bombs to release. When they did he made slow "S" turns back and forth as automatic-weapons fire surrounded them. He had always been told not to reverse a turn because that only gave the fighter a chance to get in another shot, but this time the fighter fired only a couple more shots and gave up.

Finally, they were away from those disconcerting lights and Pattillo turned the airplane to the northeast to pass Choshi Point before leaving land behind en route home.

Captain John Hechinger, a group intelligence officer, learned following the war some of the horror of these fire raids. His cousin had been captured on Guam in December 1941 and forced to work in the salt mines. He told Hechinger that if the B-29s had burned down any more towns they probably would have killed him. He survived the destruction of three cities. Typically, he said, when B-29s started fires in the center of the city thousands of people would rush by their prison camps. All they could think of, he said, was "My God, don't leave us here to burn." Finally, someone would open the gates and they'd run like hell to get away from the fires but next day they'd be rounded up and locked in another prison camp.

Tokyo, too, was removed from LeMay's list. The command paid a heavy price with the loss of 26 B-29s, while another 100 were damaged, bringing the total loss for both missions to 43 Superfortresses.

LeMay was so concerned about night losses over Tokyo that he scheduled the next mission, May 29, to Yokohama in daytime and sought fighter support from the VII Fighter Command on Iwo Jima. It was a good thing he did because 150 angry Japanese fighters tried to attack B-29 formations but, for the most part, they were unable to do so because of the P-51 Mustangs. Formations turned on Fujiyama and crews gazed admiringly at the famous mountain as it glistened below them in the morning light with its snow ring on top and its lower slopes a dark green.

In perfect visibility, they headed for Yokohama, noting that a pall of smoke still hung over Tokyo after the two-day fire blitz of the Japanese capital. Four hundred and fifty-four bombers dropped incendiaries and a third of the city was destroyed, including an area of 6.9 square miles.

LeMay turned his bombers loose on the center of Osaka next. The bombers went out on schedule June 1 but the fighters ran into an unexpected weather front that was so severe that 27 fighter planes and 24 pilots were lost at sea. Only 27 out of 148 fighter planes got over Osaka. The raid added 3.15 square miles to the previously burned-out areas but it was not as successful as the March raid.

Lieutenant Colonel Thomas R. Vaucher, now operations officer for the 462nd Group, looked up as Major Carl T. "Shorty" Hull walked in. LeMay earlier had indicated that the combat tour of duty would be 35 missions, but he hadn't made it official. Many pilots like Hull had flown their 35 and were grounded until LeMay made up his mind. The rumors had it that the tour of duty might be extended, but there was nothing official.

"Vaucher, I want to go on the next mission," Hull said.

"No!" Vaucher said. "You've got your missions in. And this is certainly not one for you to go on."

Hull persisted. "My wife's had a baby and I'm sitting around driving myself crazy with nothing to do. Anyway, LeMay probably will increase the number of missions, so I might just as well start getting them."

Vaucher was adamant, and refused to assign Hull to the mission. The pilot returned again later and persisted until Vaucher relented and named Hull as deputy commander.

When Vaucher announced at the briefing that they might have to go in at 15,000 feet to get under the clouds, there was an uproar from crew members. They shouted that all guns could zero in at that altitude.

Vaucher was going along himself as 58th Wing commander and he tried to quell the protesters but nothing convinced them. With finality, he said, "I didn't set the altitude. LeMay did. As flight commander, I have no authority to cancel the mission. When I hear from the weather planes en route, I'll determine the actual bombing altitude."

The trip to Japan was routine but all hell broke loose as they headed up the bay to Kobe on the south side. Vaucher sat on the jump seat as they headed up the bay. He had never seen such heavy antiaircraft fire and the gunners had them zeroed in because he could see the red flashes as the shells exploded. He winced as the damage reports came in from the crew and he knew they were hit badly. Hull's plane, on the right, was hit heavily about the same time and started to go down. Vaucher watched in horror as Hull's plane peeled off and eight of his crew bailed out.

Their own plight was almost as critical as they pulled away from the target and headed for Iwo with gasoline streaming from the number three engine. It seemed an eternity until they spotted Iwo Jima. Vaucher listened to the chatter on the intercom as pilots begged for permission to land their seriously shot-up B-29s. To complicate the tense situation, weather was poor over the island as B-29s headed straight in ignoring frantic calls from the tower to await their turn. For some, with two, even three engines out, they had no choice.

Their condition wasn't that desperate but they were short of fuel due to the large quantity they had lost through leakage. Inside the cabin, the smell of gasoline was sickening.

The Iwo tower at last listed them as next to land, and brought them in by radar direction because they couldn't see the island until they were almost up to it. Vaucher stared at the field in disbelief. There were 73 B-29s piled up alongside the runway and, while he watched, another Superfort splashed into the ocean. Vaucher breathed a sigh of relief when their long, torturous trip came to an end with touchdown.

After the airplane was parked, they crowded around it to count the shrapnel holes. There were holes everywhere, and a count later showed more than 400. Vaucher had known they were badly hit, but he looked at the B-29 with astonishment. How it had flown 700 miles in such shape was more than he could comprehend. Incredibly, only one person was slightly wounded. The airplane that had taken such good care of them was now headed for the scrap heap and would never fly again.

It wasn't until the war ended that Vaucher found out what happened to Shorty Hull and his crew. He, and most of his men, landed close to a military compound. They were taken before the ground commander, who immediately held a court-martial and sentenced them to death the same day for their so-called war crimes. They were taken outside and beheaded. Vaucher was heartsick, especially because LeMay later set the number of missions to complete a tour at 35 and Shorty Hull needn't have flown his 36th mission.

Another crew on the Kobe mission also went through hell. Major Kramp's 498th Group formation came under a coordinated attack by six Japanese fighters after they dropped their bombs. Both sides of the formation were attacked, but Lieutenant Robert A. Rochat's plane received the worst of it. The fuselage suffered numerous hits, and the number two engine was knocked out. Kramp watched Rochat's plane fall away from the formation, and Lieutenant Horace S. Rich called Kramp on the radio to tell him of Rochat's plight as they approached land's end. Kramp slowed the formation, hoping Rochat could catch up. It was no use. A "George" fighter moved in on the tail of the crippled bomber.

Rich called Rochat on the radio. "Pull into the formation! Make it quick!"

Rochat didn't answer but it was apparent that he couldn't get enough power to do so. Rich's tail gunner reported that the fighter still tailed Rochat's plane, and there didn't seem to be any return fire from Rochat's tail gunner. Either his guns were out, or he was badly injured or dead.

Rich's tail gunner watched anxiously as the Japanese fighter seemed to play with the bomber like a cat would a mouse before pouncing. Then, deliberately, the fighter pilot rammed the tail of the bomber and promptly bailed out, while Rochat's B-29 staggered along for a few more minutes with its tail assembly badly mauled as Rochat desperately tried to keep the airplane in the air.

After the fighter rammed Rochat's plane, Kramp sent Lieutenant Charles E. Pound back to fly cover because he no longer could jeopardize the rest of the formation at such low speeds.

Pound swung alongside Rochat's plane 13 miles from land's end, and his crew noted a parachute unfolding beneath the bomber. He saw that the nose wheel was down so Rochat must have given the order to bail out.

At 10,000 feet, Rochat's Superfortress dipped down and went into a flat spin. Pound's crew members counted four parachutes before the bomber hit the ocean. He immediately sent out a call to rescue forces and circled above until a Super Dumbo arrived. After the rescue craft told him that survivors had been spotted, Pound headed for the Marianas.

Lieutenants Charles Duveen, John Kesekes, and John Duffy, and Staff Sergeant Arthur Liberi parachuted out of the plane, but as they floated to the ocean a Japanese fighter made several passes as the men dangled helplessly from their shroud lines. Their ordeal wasn't over after they landed in the ocean because they were attacked by sharks, and, if that wasn't enough ordeal, a Japanese plane dropped depth charges trying to kill them. Fortunately, they survived and were picked up within sight of Japan.

Four and a third square miles of the eastern and western parts of Kobe were burned on this June 5 mission so another was stricken from LeMay's list of urban areas to be destroyed. The command paid a heavy price with 11 B-29s lost and 176 damaged.

The eastern and central sections of Osaka, including the Army Arsenal and other industrial targets, were hit June 7. The 58th Wing carried two-ton high-explosive bombs to attack the arsenal, but the others had incendiaries. Most planes had to drop by radar because of heavy cloud cover, so the burned area was only 2.21 square miles.

LeMay was pleased with the success of the daylight raids and he knew the primary reasons for destruction of precision targets was the lowering of bombing altitudes from 30,000 to 20,000 feet—and, at times, even lower. This decision had been a calculated risk but the loss between March 24 and May 19 was only 20 B-29s for a rate due to all causes, and not just Japanese defenses, of 1.3 percent. Those who had protested such low bombing altitudes, insisting that losses would be prohibitive, were effectively silenced.

# CHAPTER 20

# "When Is the War Going to End?"

LeMay's staff had been hard at work for weeks on a new plan to cover the remaining days of spring and the summer months ahead. The doctrine remained the same. During clear days, the aircraft industry would be attacked. When weather was bad, and radar runs necessary, the command would drop incendiary bombs on urban areas. No longer was it necessary to send a maximum effort to one target, so each mission LeMay divided his command to hit separate targets. The "Empire Plan" started June 9 and, as it turned out, served as the governing document for all operations until war's end.

General Arnold flew to the Marianas in early June. LeMay and his staff gave him a briefing on Guam, explaining their operations, and what plans they had for the future.

The staff brought in what they called their "flip" board, which was a roll of butcher's paper on which graphs and diagrams had been drawn. LeMay noted that Arnold was impressed although he didn't have much to say until the briefing was almost over.

He turned to LeMay. "I'm asking this question to everyone I see out here. When is the war going to be over?"

LeMay replied, "We've been too busy fighting to figure out a date but if you'll give me thirty minutes I'll give you an estimate."

Arnold nodded. LeMay took several staff officers aside and said, "Go back and find out when we're going to run out of industrial areas as targets."

Although he didn't tell Arnold, LeMay was using a world almanac to identify Japan's smaller cities for attacks because it was more reliable than the target list he got from Washington.

While they were waiting he explained to Arnold that, in the past, when the concentration was on visual bombing, planes had to be assembled, fueled and bombed, crews briefed, and then they had to wait until the weather was clear enough for bombing. "Now that the command is trained for radar bombing, once we're ready we take off regardless of the weather because we can hit industrial areas without even seeing them."

One of his officers walked in and handed LeMay a note. He turned to Arnold. "We'll run out of big strategic cities and targets by October 1. I can't see the war going on much beyond that date."

Earlier that day Arnold had received word from Marshall that the Joint Chiefs would meet with President Truman June 18 to discuss invasion plans and to brief the President for his mid-July Potsdam Conference with Churchill and Stalin.

Arnold turned again to LeMay. "I want you to go back to Washington and give the briefing you've given me to the Joint Chiefs."

Arnold had always believed that Japan could be defeated by airpower and now he was more convinced than ever and he hoped that a briefing by LeMay might convince the Joint Chiefs to call off the coming invasion, or at least delay preparations for it.

LeMay never had any doubts once his command began to demonstrate its capabilities. At first, it was a matter of timing because they couldn't get the airplanes and they were losing airplanes faster than they were being delivered.

Through a mixup among Washington officials who forgot about the international date line, they couldn't make the first date. LeMay and members of his staff were delayed 24 hours and appeared at the next meeting of the Joint Chiefs. He was all fired up to tell a convincing story but he found the presentation one of the most frustrating he had ever given. The Joint Chiefs sat there in disbelieving silence, for the most part, while General Marshall slept through the entire briefing. LeMay realized he had failed because the President had already approved another course of action. He returned to Guam more than ever convinced that he would prove by actions what they had refused to believe in words.

Later that month, LeMay briefed several magazine writers who asked the now-familiar question of when the war would be over. "Japan has been defeated," he said. "It's merely a matter of time until they can get their leadership to find a way to capitulate. They are totally defeated now. They must surrender. It's just a matter of time."

On Guam's Northwest Field, Arnold and Nimitz later witnessed the christening of a 315th Wing's new B-29 as the "Fleet Admiral Nimitz."* Wing Commander Brigadier General Frank Armstrong told the gathering that the airplane was dedicated in honor of Nimitz for his marvelous logistics support even though the Twentieth Air Force wasn't under his command.

This new wing had B-29s with no gun turrets other than the one in the tail. Its electronic radar equipment was unique because it had the 18-foot airfoil Eagle Antenna System, which permitted greater target identification and made these B-29s look somewhat like biplanes. The "Eagle" system was conceived by Professor Luis Alvarez, and developed by M.I.T.'s radiation laboratory and Bell Telephone Laboratories. It was being used for the first time in the Pacific.

With the dedicated airplane in the background, and Nimitz' name and a five-star flag painted on the side, Arnold spoke to a large assemblage of officers and men from all services. On behalf of the Joint Chiefs of staff, he expressed their congratulations for Nimitz' outstanding use of minimal forces in achieving a continuing advance against the enemy, and in securing the Marianas not only for B-29 bases but land and sea forces. Arnold praised the admiral for his command of United States forces in the Central Pacific since shortly after Pearl Harbor, saying they were now in a position for the final assault by whichever means was necessary to achieve surrender.

When it came his turn to speak, Nimitz said, "The B-29s have had tremendous success in bringing Japan closer to surrender." He spoke frankly of his misgivings when the first eight groups were sent to the islands because they would not be part of his command, and the logistic support would have to be taken from his own forces. "Their success has been so great that I'm welcoming twelve more groups."

After the official ceremony, Nimitz and Arnold inspected the airplane, particularly the APQ-7 radar and the new navigation aides, with Colonel Boyd Hubbard, commanding officer of the 501st Group. At one point, Nimitz asked him what more assistance he could provide and Hubbard mentioned the establishment of a loran site to improve navigation facilities on an island near Japan. He had

* A painting of this aircraft hangs in the Admiral Nimitz Center. It was presented by survivors of the Twentieth Air Force in 1974.

previously requested such a site through routine channels but it had been pigeonholed somewhere. The admiral made a note and it was operational two weeks later.

In parting, Nimitz presented Hubbard with a five-star insignia to pin on the upholstery of the airplane, a case of beer, and a bottle of Haig & Haig pinch-bottle scotch. The insignia he still treasures but the beer and scotch were quickly consumed to celebrate the occasion.

While Arnold was on Guam, the preliminary U.S. Strategic Bombing Survey report on the bombing of Germany was forwarded to him. He noted that it emphasized that strategic bombing had had a disastrous impact on Germany's ability to wage war.

He recalled LeMay's briefing, knowing that if he was correct in his assumption that the Japanese war could be won by bombing, that reconsideration should be given to plans for the invasion. Personally, he was convinced that Japan could be forced to capitulate because he didn't believe she could stand the punishment meted out to Germany. He noted in the strategic bombing report that a group of survey officials had stated flatly that, based on what they had seen in Germany, there was no need to invade Japan.

Arnold was most anxious to expedite plans to set up a headquarters on Guam: one that would command all strategic bombers and not just B-29s. Lower-echelon officers resisted such a move and wanted the new headquarters to be in charge of only the Twentieth Air Force. Such a situation was considered intolerable by Arnold and for a time he considered moving such a headquarters to Manila in the Philippines but that wasn't practical. He sent a message to Marshall asking him to tell the Navy that the strategic headquarters definitely would be on Guam.

During his briefing by LeMay, the matter of bomb supply was brought up and Arnold was told of his concern that B-29 operations could be restricted by the supply of bombs and ammunition that was distributed by the Navy.

Arnold talked to Nimitz and found the admiral agreeable to every suggestion, including the strategic command headquarters on Guam with General Carl A. Spaatz in command. They both realized there were no problems between them at their level and what problems had been encountered resulted in junior officers magnifying problems out of proportion. They realized it was a problem common to both services and each agreed to have a talk with his own people.

During a visit with MacArthur, Arnold was surprised when Mac-Arthur said a strategic air command organization was a mistake, particularly in the hands of General Spaatz. MacArthur told Arnold that he wouldn't object if he kept command with Giles as his deputy, but he was against Spaatz getting the assignment.

The Pacific ground commander conceded that bombing would be helpful in winning the war in the Pacific but that the doughboys would have to march on Tokyo. Arnold tried to explain the plan for destroying Japanese cities and industrial targets, and discussed the Twentieth's operations in detail. MacArthur expressed surprise at the size of the B-29 effort although Arnold didn't believe he really understood the Air Force plan for reducing Japan to impotence.

Before Arnold returned home, he sent Marshall a message. Although he was still convinced that the Twentieth would force Japan to surrender, there was too much opposition in the other services to support such a theory. He told Marshall that he supported the invasion of Kyushu, and requested bases for 40 more groups of heavy bombers. He also recommended an all-out bombing offensive to complete Japan's destruction. He agreed that plans for the invasion of Honshu in the spring of 1946 should go forward but that a final decision should be delayed.

He asked Marshall to tell the Joint Chiefs that emphasis should be placed on a strategic air offensive with a naval and air blockade. He said the air war should be stepped up so that conditions would be favorable for the November 1 invasion of Kyushu with a minimum loss of lives. He estimated the Air Forces would need to drop 1.6 million tons of bombs to destroy Japan's industry and paralyze her economic life. This estimate was far off. Actually, only 147,000 tons were needed.

President Truman expressed his deep concern about the heavy casualties predicted for the invasion, possibly numbering as high as one million. The President also expressed his concern about the length of time it might take to defeat Japan through a blockade and sea and air strikes.

The first of June the Interim Committee on atomic bomb matters had recommended that the bomb be used against Japan as soon as possible but on a military target surrounded by other buildings and without prior warning.

When alternative proposals were presented to the President, invasion plans were allowed to proceed but he withheld final approval. Although B-29s were causing havoc throughout Japan, the Japanese Army was still intact and there appeared to be no possibility of the Japanese surrendering unconditionally. The President relied heavily on Marshall's views and the Army Chief of Staff was adamant that airpower alone would not knock the Japanese out of the war. Mac-Arthur, too, supported Marshall in a lengthy message.

Although Admirals King, Nimitz, and Leahy denied after the war they had supported the invasion, they did approve plans for it, saying the southernmost island of Kyushu would bring increased airpower to bear upon Japan.

Secretary of Navy James V. Forrestal voiced his opinion that the Kyushu invasion was a sound military investment. Secretary of War Stimson tended to agree but he hoped that the end would come by other means. They both agreed that the bombing should be stepped up, and the blockade noose drawn tighter.

Before Arnold returned to Washington he visited the island bases, coming to Tinian June 15 to honor the original B-29 wing.

Captain Denny D. Pidhayny, a squadron radar maintenance officer in the 468th Group, stood in front of his troops as a jeep, driven by 58th Wing Commander Brigadier General Roger Ramey, with Deputy Wing Commander Colonel Alva L. Harvey in the rear seat, and Arnold in the right front seat, approached in view. The large formation had been quickly assembled from units of all groups of the 58th. Some officers were told that General Arnold was coming, and that he wanted to talk to the first B-29ers in action. They were advised, "Don't bother about Class 'A' uniforms. Take 'em anyway they are. The more informal the better."

Pidhayny glanced apprehensively at the ragtag collection of men in greasy coveralls, T-shirts, cook's whites, and every possible clothing combination. They represented most of the group's personnel but many of the flying crews were absent because they were on a mission over Japan.

The "Old Man" approached with a half smile on his face, oblivious to the disheveled men in front of him, but one immaculately dressed brigadier general in Arnold's party did a double-take as they passed in front of the formation and turned back to stare with disbelief at what was undoubtedly the most unmilitary outfit he had ever seen in the history of the United States Army Air Force.

Pidhayny recognized Arnold although he seemed more careworn than pictures he had seen of him. At the time, he didn't know that Arnold was recovering from a serious heart attack.

Arnold stepped along briskly to greet officers and men and the familiar grin momentarily seemed to erase some of the tired lines on his face. Thoughts raced through Pidhayny's mind as he watched the five-star general approach them. Was Arnold thinking back to his own service in World War I when sickness deprived him of overseas air-combat service? Or was his still youthful spirit trying to burst from his erect body despite the slight droop to his head? Pidhayny thought he seemed to lose some of the shackles of age as he said, "I've wanted to see and talk to you for some time, and felt it appropriate to use the anniversary of the first big raid on Yawata to do it." He thanked them for their efforts. "In Washington there are two groups of opinion," he said, "about the end of the war without an invasion." He said he wasn't sure about those who believed an invasion wouldn't be necessary, but he hoped they were right.

He recalled that a year had passed since the first raid on Japan, and that he was pleased to award the 58th Wing with a Presidential Unit Citation for that historic mission. It was the first of three that the wing was eventually awarded.

# CHAPTER 21

# Japanese Cities
# Reduced to Ashes

The Joint Target Group in Washington had listed 33 urban areas for attack. They were concentrated in eight of Japan's largest cities. Yawata was the only one that hadn't been destroyed by June.

Colonel James D. Garcia,* LeMay's intelligence officer, stressed the importance of compressing fire raids within a short period of time and recommended attacks against smaller cities once the larger ones were leveled. He came up with a list for LeMay that included cities like Hachioji with over 60,000 people and Fukuoka with over 320,000, and eventually his list totaled 58. Each of these cities had one thing in common. They were flammable, contained war or transportation facilities, and were highly congested. Garcia believed strongly that Japan's will to continue the war would deteriorate rapidly, through the cumulative effect of one fire raid after another, and force her to sue for peace. LeMay agreed, but he had to finish off the larger cities before he could turn his attention to the smaller ones.

Six targets were hit in the Tokyo area June 10 and heavy damage was caused to the Hitachi Engineering Works at Kaigan and a seaplane base.

Several missions caused damage to the Kawanishi Aircraft Company plant at Narao, which was hit so hard June 9 that the few remaining machine tools had to be moved elsewhere, thus effectively ending its production of Navy planes. The Aichi plant at Atsuta suffered severe damage, but two-ton bombs dropped by radar against

---

* Garcia was killed in an airplane crash on Guam the last day of the war.

Kawasaki's plant at Akashi unfortunately leveled a village instead of the factory.

The Osaka area received LeMay's attention June 15 when nearby Amagasaki, an industrial suburb with synthetic oil refineries, power plants, industrial firms, and the Kawanishi Aircraft factory, was struck by 444 B-29s with over 3,000 tons of bombs. Iwo's P-51s were ordered to protect the bombers over the target but they were warned to return to base because of a weather front. They weren't needed, as it turned out, and another 1.9 square miles of Osaka and a half square mile of Amagasaki were burned out. The fires were widely scattered because so much destruction had been caused by previous raids that it was difficult to get a big conflagration under way.

Later in the month, six targets on southern Honshu were attacked and one of them, the Kure Arsenal, suffered severe damage with destruction elsewhere minor to severe. These attacks did reduce production of "Betty" bombers and "George" fighters.

Phase I of the urban area program ended with all objectives achieved. Japan's six largest cities totaled 257.2 square miles. Since the first of March, 105.6 square miles of these cities had been destroyed—only seven square miles short of the goal set by the Joint Target Group in Washington. These industrial cities had experienced unbelievable destruction, with great factories destroyed or damaged and tens of thousands of small household or feeder plants wiped out. The havoc was the worst ever experienced by a modern nation, with millions of people without homes and places to work. Hundreds of thousands fled the cities, including workers for the factories that remained, so industry came almost to a standstill.

Only after the war was the true state of affairs in Japan made known. Their air-raid system was so primitive that it collapsed very early in the series of attacks. Discipline became an ever-increasing problem as people lost confidence in their leaders and Japanese officials began to consider a negotiated peace.

The Twentieth had sent 6,960 B-29s on 17 maximum-effort incendiary raids with 41,500 tons of bombs for an average mission loss rate of only 1.9 percent or a total of 136 Superfortresses lost to all causes. LeMay was satisfied that the losses, in comparison to the gains achieved, were acceptable. Actually, they were far less than losses incurred on earlier missions at high altitudes.

The weather was better than predicted during the past three

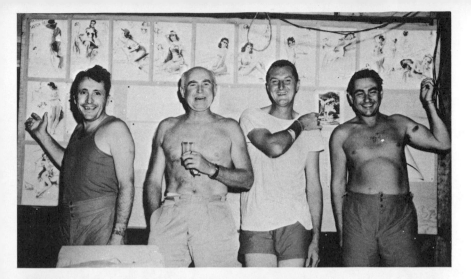

NELSON BIRD DOGS—In a rare moment of leisure, "Hap" Arnold's Saipan-based trouble-shooting crew relax in their office tent among their Petty-girl photographs. From left, Harry Hubbard, who missed the Doolittle Tokyo raid when his plane flew into a flock of ducks at night and one of the birds came through the windshield and badly injured his left eye, was a first-class technical man with an affinity for detail; Erik Nelson, Arnold's personal troubleshooter with authority to use the Air Force chief's name and office judiciously and report back only solutions to problems, gained Arnold's confidence as the only man to fly completely around the world in a Douglas cruiser in 1924 and afterwards credited then Major "Hap" Arnold's fine engine overhauls in San Diego for his success; Captain Arthur Borden, a Princeton graduate known for his unusual organizational ability, who, as administrative officer for the group did all their record keeping, follow-up, etc.; and Lieutenant Colonel Mark Maidel who came up through the ranks from a GI and who was considered by Agather as the best aircraft practical technician he had ever known. In regards to Erik Nelson, Agather considers this self-effacing man the most influential individual in solving the critical operational problems of the B-29.                         (Photo courtesy of Victor N. Agather.)

SAIPAN CONFERENCE—Lieutenant General Millard F. Harmon, center, meets with "Rosey" O'Donnell, left, and Major General Haywood S. Hansell, Jr. prior to forthcoming B-29 attacks on Japan.                         (Photo courtesy of H. S. Hansell, Jr.)

FRIENDSHIP BANQUET—
Lieutenant General Li Tzu,
center, welcomes Lieutenant
Colonel Kenneth E. Hodges, far
right, with a handshake as
Nationalists and American
officers meet at Pengshan to
promote friendship and
cooperation between Allied
forces. To their left is Major
James Pattillo.
(Photo courtesy of the
Pattillo Collection.)

LEAD CREW—Author Captain
Wilbur H. Morrison, bom-
bardier of Major Thomas R.
Vaucher's lead crew, stands
in foreground. Others, from
left: Sgt. James O. Bush,
Vaucher, T/Sgt. Guido J.
Bianchi, Lt. Ralph Todd, S/Sgt.
Isadore Scheinman, Lt. James
F. White, T/Sgt. Albert I.
Carmona, Lt. Michael P. Egan,
Sgt. Norman C. McLeod, and
Lt. Robert C. Albert.
(Photo from the Author's
Collection.)

*VICTOR N. AGATHER—One of "Hap" Arnold's troubleshooters rides in bombardier's compartment on a flight out of Saipan.*
*(Photo courtesy of Victor N. Agather.)*

TINIAN—North Field, home of the 313th Wing and the 509th Composite Group,
is in the foreground. The 58th Wing occupied the field in right center.
(Photo courtesy of T. R. Vaucher.)

DAMAGE TO OSAKA—After the June 15 mission, the principal part of the city
lay in ruins. Dotted areas are those that were thinly populated.
(Photo courtesy of T. R. Vaucher.)

# DESTRUCTION BY FIRE

KOBE CITY OUTLINE

■ OLD DAMAGE
▦ NEW DAMAGE

## KOBE

THROUGH THE EFFORTS OF ALL OF THE UNITS OF THE 58ᵀᴴ WING AND THE MANY SUPPORTING UNITS HERE ON TINIAN, 4.85 SQUARE MILES OF NEW DAMAGE WAS CAUSED ON THE MISSION OF 10 JUNE.

PREVIOUSLY ABOUT 4 MILES HAD BEEN DESTROYED BRINGING THE DEVASTATED AREA TO 56% OF THE BUILT UP SECTIONS.

THE KOBE GAS WORKS IS MORE THAN 80% DESTROYED- THE KAWANISHI MACHINE SHOP IS 100% DESTROYED — THE NIPPON DUNLOP RUBBER CO. IS 100% DESTROYED —

THIS WAS ALL POSSIBLE THROUGH THE EXCELLENT COOPER- ATION OF THE SUPPORTING UNITS. WE OF THE 58ᵀᴴ THINK ITS SWELL TO HAVE YOU ON OUR TEAM.

PREPARED BY TARGET UNIT, INTELL. SECTION, 58TH

GUNG HO!—Pictures like this kept the morale of the exhausted flight and ground crews at a high level. (Photo courtesy of T. R. Vaucher.)

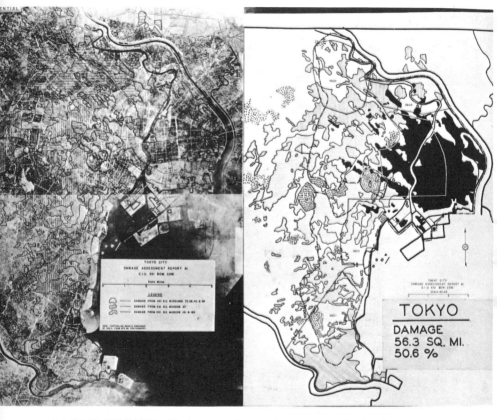

*DAMAGE TO TOKYO—Black area indicates destruction in the first fire raids. (Photo courtesy of T. R. Vaucher.)*

months, permitting LeMay to send five daylight strikes in April, three in May, and four in June. The weather didn't hold by the end of June and it wasn't until July 24 that another daylight mission could be dispatched.

By the end of June the Twentieth was up to full strength with 1,000 Superfortresses and 83,000 men and LeMay set out to throw the full might of his command against Japan. The first attacks against cities in the 100,000 to 200,000 population class were started June 17 as a wing was assigned to each of four cities—Omuta, Hamamatsu, Yokkaichi, and Kagoshima. Omuta suffered the least with only 4 percent destruction and Hamamatsu the most with 70 percent, or over six square miles of the city wiped out along with important targets.

The night of June 29 the 58th Wing was assigned Okayama. Crews crossed Shikoku, flying between layers of thick clouds that offered ideal protection. Late arrivals could see a red glow on the clouds for miles until the clouds parted and what was left of Okayama lay before them. Okayama's destruction was awesome with almost two thirds of its built-up area wiped out. Crews watched in utter horror as the city disintegrated before their eyes while prima chords ripped incendiary clusters apart above the city and individual fire bombs descended in long streams to the holocaust below. Only one B-29 was lost and several crews reported that it was a mass of flames as it slowly fluttered to earth, leaving the sky reluctantly before becoming part of the inferno below.

Almost a month later, Fukui succumbed in a similar fashion as flames quickly formed into one huge mass, rising for thousands of feet before forming a huge smoke cloud.

Multiple incendiary attacks were made on an average of two nights a week and, in general, four cities went up in flames each time. The 315th Wing often integrated its night attacks against the oil industry, while crews from other wings gazed in awe as a huge refinery exploded near them en route to their target cities.

It was apparent as these fire raids went over Japan time after time with little opposition that Japan's air defenses were completely ineffective. The Japanese had never produced a first-rate night fighter, and the ones they had couldn't be controlled from the ground. As a result, only one B-29 was known to have been lost to fighters.

When LeMay saw the opposition against his B-29s was so ineffective he decided to try psychological warfare and drop leaflets on Japanese cities to warn them in advance that they would be fire-bombed. He chose to warn a dozen or so at a time of an impending attack and then hit some of them. Three Japanese officers, who were prisoners of war, volunteered to translate the text for the leaflets. The approved text for the first drop of 660,000 copies said, "In accordance with America's well-known humanitarian principles, the American air force, which does not want to injure innocent people, now gives you warning to evacuate Aomori, Tsu, Ichinomiya, Uji-Yamada, Ogaki, Uwajima, Nishinomiya, Kurume, Nagaoka, Koriyama, and Hakodate and save your lives."

Although crews were apprehensive, six of the cities were flattened the next night with little opposition.

The awful tide of destruction rose dramatically in July as more cities were warned by leaflets and radio broadcasts beamed to Japan, and the suffering of the Japanese people reached the limits of endurance. Few cities needed more than one attack, and before this campaign was over 43 percent of the built-up area in these smaller cities was destroyed, and production in the bombed cities fell 33 percent. Toyama was engulfed in a fire storm that left crews shaken as 99.5 percent of the city went up in flames. Bomb bays trapped the smell of burning flesh and carried the sickening stench back to the Marianas. In all, 58 of Japan's small- to medium-sized cities succumbed and 23 major aircraft factories, six major army and navy arsenals, and numerous steel, petroleum, and gas plants went with them.

By August 1, B-29s had dropped 147,000 tons of bombs but now that the command was up to full strength LeMay was prepared to drop an equal amount in the next three months.

While the nights were filled with fire bombs falling upon Japan, LeMay sent daytime B-29s against seven targets in the Nagoya and Osaka areas. These strikes were coordinated with two U.S. Navy carrier strikes in the Inland Sea. Despite bad weather, the Sumitoma Metal Company's propeller factory was completely wrecked. It wasn't known at the time that the factory's machine tools had already been removed but fear of such attacks proved equally rewarding because plants all over Japan were being dispersed. The same was true of the Osaka Arsenal. Kawanishi's Takarazuka plant between Kobe and Osaka was thoroughly leveled and the Japanese didn't even attempt to rebuild it. The Nakajima factory at Handa lost its assembly buildings during an attack but the war was coming to an end so quickly that its loss had no effect on production.

Arnold issued orders July 10 to deactivate the XX and XXI Bomber Commands because of a reorganization. General Nathan F. Twining was named to head the Twentieth Air Force and personnel of the XX Bomber Command were transferred to the Eighth Air Force on Okinawa.

Up until now the Pacific War had been fought without a unified command. With the Philippines, Iwo, and Okinawa in American hands, the noose tightened around Japan's home islands, particularly after Japan stood alone following Germany's defeat.

Japan's 2 million-man homeland army remained undefeated and there were 8,000 combat and training planes in the home islands, the latter available for kamikaze attacks. However, lack of fuel was a severe limiting factor to their use. Japan's navy had been practically destroyed. There now were many in the U.S. Navy and the U.S. Army Air Forces who believed it was possible through blockade and airpower to force Japan to surrender without an invasion. Almost without exception the U.S. Army still believed that no such easy victory was possible and plans for the invasion of Kyushu November 1 and Honshu in March 1946 were confirmed by the Joint Chiefs in July; they authorized deployment of invasion units and the accumulation on island bases of huge amounts of supplies.

To the delight of the officers on Tinian, 500 nurses arrived near the end of the war to help run a huge hospital to take care of the thousands of wounded expected following the invasion of Japan.

After MacArthur's forces and Nimitz' Central Pacific forces completed their separate drives toward Japan, these commands intersected for the first time. A unified command obviously was needed for the final assault on Japan's mainland.

Arnold had been convinced of the need for a unified command ever since he had made an inspection trip to the South Pacific in the fall of 1942.

A year later, Admiral King had suggested to the Joint Chiefs that discussions be held with the British about designation of such a commander. Admiral Leahy had squelched that move because he believed the British would never agree to an American supreme commander in both Europe and the Far East.

The Joint Chiefs faced a ticklish decision. The Navy refused to accept MacArthur as such an overall commander, and MacArthur refused to consider an invasion of Japan with an admiral in command of his 50 or so divisions. He told the Joint Chiefs in a letter that "we would be trifling with American lives and it would jeopardize the future of the Army." So, there was a stalemate and both commands went their separate ways. To continue in this manner now was impossible.

Army Air Forces strength in the Pacific had grown in one year to more than 165,000, including almost 3,000 airplanes of which one third were B-29s. Arnold had fought to build up airpower but now these airplanes were congregated in a smaller number of bases with ever-increasing problems of control of their operations.

Arnold argued for a supreme commander with equal status for air, ground, and sea commands reporting to him. Under such an arrangement, all air forces in the Pacific would report to one air commander. Arnold had tried to establish such a command in Europe but succeeded only in gaining a single headquarters for all strategic operations.

In October 1944, Arnold recommended that all strategic bombing of Japan should be under an air commander on the same level as ground and navy commanders.

General Spaatz went further. He said that a commanding general of the Army Air Forces in the Pacific and Far East should be responsible only to Arnold as Commanding General, Army Air Forces, and serve as his deputy. What he was recommending was control by one commander of the Twentieth Air Force, all other bomber units in the Pacific, China, and India, as well as fighter commands. He did recommend that tactical air forces should remain under the control of theater commands although their administration would be under a new strategic air command.

After extensive arguments at all levels, General MacArthur was designated Commander in Chief, Army Forces in the Pacific, with control of all Army units in the Pacific theater except those in the Southeast Pacific and Alaska.

All Navy commands in the Pacific, except those in the Southeast Pacific, were placed under Nimitz. In effect, the Joint Chiefs gave MacArthur control of all land campaigns, and Nimitz all sea campaigns, with problems to be resolved between them by mutual agreement.

Throughout the infighting between the Army and the Navy, Arnold managed to maintain control of the Twentieth Air Force under the Joint Chiefs. In late May 1945, Arnold had recommended that headquarters for the Twentieth be moved to Guam from Washington July 1 with General Spaatz in command of the Army Strategic Air Forces. Admiral Leahy objected claiming that such a move would violate the principle of unity of command, insisting that the Twentieth be placed under MacArthur.

Arnold refused to consider such a move and, after lengthy arguments, a compromise was reached July 10 that gave a measure of autonomy to the new Strategic Air Forces because they would report to the Joint Chiefs with Arnold as their executive agent. Arnold failed to get unified control of all air forces under a supreme commander but three Pacific air forces were combined to form the Far East Air Force. Of great importance to the Twentieth was that no restrictions were placed on where it could operate, and MacArthur and Nimitz were ordered to supply its needs and the needs of the Far East Air Force. In reality, the status of the Twentieth was unchanged.

The organization wasn't completed before the war ended, although Spaatz took over as strategic air commander July 29. General Twining, who had started in the Pacific as Commander of the Thirteenth Air Force, and later the Fifteenth, assumed command of the Twentieth with Giles as deputy commander and LeMay as chief of staff to General Spaatz.

Arnold gave Spaatz broad responsibility for operations and administration of the Eighth and Twentieth Air Forces. Lieutenant General James H. Doolittle took over the Eighth July 19, and his first groups were ready to go into combat when the Japanese surrendered.

Now that the Twentieth was up to strength in aircraft, LeMay appealed again for crews, which were his major limiting factor for continued, high-level operations. He asked that the principle of two crews per aircraft, which had been in effect under Wolfe originally, be reinstated. He was told that crews couldn't be trained that quickly, and the crew shortage lasted until war's end. Somehow all available planes in commission were manned as staff officers did double duty and flew missions in addition to their own work. Such temporary measures worked but if the war had been extended for another three months crew exhaustion would have forced a halt to many operations.

LeMay marveled at Bill Irvine's efforts in keeping airplanes in commission. Few realized, he knew, that it took 12 officers and 73 men on the ground to keep each B-29 flying. He was aware that Irvine had set up his own "airline" to and from Sacramento, California, without any authorization, no table of organization, and no approval by the Air Transport Command. As long as the job was done he never questioned how Bill was doing it. All LeMay knew was that a C-54 transport arrived from Sacramento every day loaded with vitally needed parts. It was an under-the-table operation but LeMay wisely asked no questions.

Each morning at 5 A.M. LeMay would note there were an average of 50 B-29s out of commission because of parts shortage. About ten o'clock an airplane would come in with a load of stuff and Irvine's people were all set to disperse the materials to the fields that needed them so airplanes could take off on a mission that night.

There was a depot on Guam that LeMay had to supply with 500 men every day but he was furious with them because, he said later, "They never fixed an airplane the whole time we were out there. They were absolutely worthless!" That was one organizational problem that he would have loved to resolve but he never found the time.

The pace of the war had accelerated to such an extent by August 1 that deployment of strategic bombers from Europe couldn't catch up with the inexorable march of events in the Pacific.

It was apparent that the actual damage to vital installations in Japan exceeded the most optimistic reports, and that Japan was defeated although she as yet refused to concede. Much of her homeland was a vast wasteland and certainly one of the primary reasons was the increase in numbers of B-29s over her main islands and the greatly increased bomb tonnage dropped on each mission. With lower altitudes, LeMay was able to increase the 2.6-ton load of each Superfortress in November 1944 to 7.4 tons.

# CHAPTER 22

# The Blind Bombers

Air intelligence officers told LeMay in April that Japan's petroleum industry was in a critical state, and that destruction of facilities and storage depots would have an immediate impact on her ability to wage war. LeMay, therefore, decided that the 315th Wing, which would become operational the end of June, should devote its efforts exclusively to oil installations.

Actually, such attacks had already started. The 73rd had hit the Third Naval Depot at Tokuyama, and the 314th struck the Iwakuni Army Fuel Depot, while the 58th was attacking the Oshima oil storage tanks May 10 in support of the Okinawa invasion. Damage was heavy but it would have been even greater except that few tanks had any oil in them. Several other storage areas and refineries had been hit as targets of opportunity.

Japan had always been dependent upon imported oil. Her need for oil precipitated the drive southward at the start of the war, and her quick successes gained her valuable supplies in the Netherlands East Indies. Although she had backlogged 55 million barrels of oil prior to the war, her shipping lanes from the south came under increased attack by airplanes, ships, and submarines so that by August of 1943 oil shipments had declined drastically while expenditures of petroleum products skyrocketed. By April 1945 oil shipments ceased and Japan had to rely upon her limited supplies in storage, which did more to ground her combat planes than anything else. Oddly enough, for a nation so dependent upon oil, Japan had never developed much of a synthetic oil industry.

\* \* \*

Superfortresses of the 315th Wing were equipped with Eagle radar, which was approximately 10 times more efficient than the equipment in other B-29s. Their only armament was in the tail, where two .50-caliber machine guns were installed. The reduction in weight by eliminating gun turrets, gunners, and ammunition permitted a sizable increase in bombs.

The wing was different from other B-29 wings in many ways. Its precision radar-bombing necessitated special crew training, and missions had to be prepared by wing experts so that briefing material could be slanted from the radar point of view. Briefings were held in a blacked-out quonset hut so target material could be displayed as enlarged radar photographs. Most of the photographs were taken by General Armstrong and his Eagle radar-equipped B-29 prior to the first mission. In addition, some of the materials were radar representations of regular photographs. The latter were prepared by the wing's intelligence officer Sy Bartlett, in later years a well-known Hollywood writer and producer, and his staff. Enlargements were made by using special paints and crayons and were illuminated by infrared or black lights.

The wing had been given the job of destroying Japan's oil industry because her refineries were located on or near the coast where the Eagle radar could pick them up effectively. Elements of two groups made the first attack against the Utsube Oil Refinery at Hokkaichi June 26, a target previously hit by the 313th Wing. Total damage from both strikes amounted to 30 percent of the roof area either damaged or destroyed with the 315th claiming responsibility for two thirds of the damage.

On the night of July 9, the wing flew its fifth mission against the same target. This time it was thoroughly saturated with bombs and the Japanese declared the site beyond repair.

Colonel Boyd Hubbard, Jr., commander of the 501st Group, and pilot of the "Fleet Admiral Nimitz," who was ordered by Armstrong to lead the first five missions, led the 315th June 29 against the Kudamatzu plant of the Nippon Company's oil refinery. It had been evident from the first strikes that large and rapidly changing drift corrections were not being applied on the bombing runs, consequently Armstrong sent Hubbard's crew a few minutes ahead of the rest so they could check the wind at the target. Strong wind shifts had been encountered along the coast and sometimes it was difficult, if not impossible, to apply sufficient corrections on the bomb run to hit the target. This procedure was followed on all subsequent missions. Each time, once the drift was ascertained by the mission leaders, the amount of correction for the wind was radioed back to all crews.

For the Kudamatzu mission, they had taken off in late afternoon and climbed slowly to 8,000 feet while behind them the second group, with its planes following at 45-second intervals, climbed to 10,000 feet. Thus positioned, and using the same calibrated indicated airspeed, the second group would arrive at the target at nearly the same time so as to provide compressibility.

Unlike other B-29s, those of the 315th Wing were equipped with ovens so food could be served hot, and they were turned on after takeoff from Guam.

Over Iwo, Hubbard's crew was enjoying dinner with the cockpit lit up as a P-61 Black Widow night fighter came alongside and stared in amazement as the crew dined on steaks. Over the radio, Hubbard called, "Get away, chicken. This is one of LeMay's monsters."

Once they were near Japan, Hubbard climbed to bombing altitude of 15,000 feet through a weather front. He was happy to see the solid cloud bank because zero visibility was an ideal weather environment for them. In the front, electrical activity was high and beautiful colors of St. Elmo's Fire flowed in streams over the windshield while fiery balls played along the winglike antenna vane of the bombing system. The "fire" didn't last long because rain drove it away.

Hubbard turned to his distinguished guest, David T. Griggs from the Secretary of War's office, who leaned on his seat back, his eyes bright with excitement. "Won't be long now," Hubbard said.

Griggs had been an early leader of the Massachusetts Institute of Technology's Eagle radar development group. A year earlier, while Hubbard served with the Operations Division of the War Department's General Staff, Griggs had offered to get him assigned to MIT but Hubbard had declined because he wanted to take a B-29 group to combat.

The crew was quiet as the plane started its run to the target for a distance of 70 miles. Each aircraft flew individually with 200 feet of altitude separation and 10 miles apart as three long lines of bombers converged on the target.

Japanese radar-controlled searchlights probed the clouds and they were momentarily lit up. Aluminum foil, or "rope," was dispensed to throw off the Japanese radar. If the rope was dropped too late, the aircraft would be "coned" by lights and antiaircraft guns could zero in. An aircraft in such a position was allowed to go on maximum power to get ahead of those wicked red flashes.

After bombs were released they turned for home while behind them an average of two aircraft per minute, or 40 bombers in 20 minutes, concentrated their bombs on a two-mile-square target.

Photo reconnaissance showed the plant to be slightly damaged while a locomotive factory adjacent to the target was 40 percent damaged.

A follow-up mission July 15 put the plant out of production.

The third strike July 2 by 40 aircraft accomplished only 5 percent damage to the Maruzen Refinery with only one or two strings of bombs landing on it.

The "Fleet Admiral Nimitz" preceded the main force by 10 minutes when a repeat strike July 16 was ordered against the Maruzen Refinery.

Once on the bomb run, Hubbard followed the pilot's direction indicator as the bombardier, Captain Parker, in the navigator's compartment, corrected the track to the target by maintaining the radar scope's cross hairs on the aiming point. Each time he corrected, an indication went to Hubbard, who made the change in heading. Everything looked good despite 20 degrees of right drift, which the bombardier corrected.

Up front, Hubbard could see the coastline, with a few scattered clouds below and broken clouds above. Then searchlights probed the sky. One swung quickly toward them and hung on while the navigator shoved a bundle of rope out the flare chute, which, aided by the pressurization, shot from the bottom of the cabin. The searchlights wavered, then, to Hubbard's relief, followed the metal chaff away from the plane.

In the nose, the Norden bombsight indicators came together. Hubbard's red light flashed, indicating the bomb-bay doors had snapped open.

"Bombs away!" came the cry and the aircraft lifted as 10 tons of bombs headed for Maruzen.

Hubbard swung right and down away from the target. His copilot, Major Gregory Hathaway, got the best view because he was on the inside of the turn as explosions erupted below and lit up the clouds.

"We've hit pay dirt!" Greg shouted. "Of all the crap I've taken since I've been in the Army, it's paid off tonight. "

Fifty-eight B-29s destroyed 95 percent of the entire plant, which covered an area 2,000 by 1,500 feet. Later, LeMay's staff figured it would have taken 117 regularly equipped B-29s to do a comparable job. LeMay's congratulatory message said it was the most successful precision-radar mission ever flown.

The 315th Wing conducted 15 strikes in the last seven weeks of the war against oil-refinery targets, causing up to 90 percent damage. In that period, 1,095 B-29s bombed the primary target out of 1,200 dispatched on these missions, and over 9,000 tons of bombs were dropped. Opposition was meager and only three bombers were lost while 66 others were damaged. The loss of storage capacity to the Japanese was over 6 million barrels, and Japan's major oil-refining and storage capacity was virtually wiped out.

One of the best examples of the 315th's success was the attack on the Ube Coal Liquefaction Company, one of the few plants that remained in high production in Japan. It was not only destroyed August 5 but when the surrounding dikes were breached it was inundated. A post-strike photograph was sent to Admiral Nimitz with a note. "Target destroyed and sunk!"

While early radar operators were poorly trained, those in the 315th had the best training of all. Premission briefings were so thorough that operators had to spend hours going over radar briefing material, including scope-reconnaissance photos of the target, and they had to prove they could draw the details of the target from memory.

Hubbard's crew prepared for takeoff August 14. When the airplane was out on the runway, a jeep drove up and an officer signaled to cut engines. Once this was done the officer climbed into the cockpit and said, "Admiral Nimitz says the war is over."

Shortly afterward, another jeep rushed up and the driver yelled, "Get going! LeMay hasn't received word that the war is over."

Hubbard headed out for the runway and took off for Akita on northeast Honshu. It proved to be the wing's last and longest combat mission of 3,740 miles that was ever flown by a B-29 with a full bombload. Close to Japan they met hundreds of B-29s en route back. Radio operator James Smith, years later a popular television entertainer, came forward as they passed Tokyo and stared at the destruction in the city below them. With the sky full of American bombers, Hubbard turned on the plane's landing lights because he was afraid of a collision in this aerial traffic jam above Honshu.

By the end of the war most of Japan's refineries were inoperable. Certainly the major credit must go to the 315th Wing because an Air Force Board observer assigned to the wing said that the Eagle radar bombing was 98 percent as good as visual, which was a far cry from the early days when misses by radar bombing frequently were counted in miles.

Through no fault of its own, the wing's effectiveness was reduced considerably because it was learned later that many storage tanks were empty because of the oil shortage, and refinery production had dropped to 4 percent of capacity prior to the time the 315th began its operations.

# CHAPTER 23

# *Operation Starvation*

Prior to World War II, officials of the United States Navy's Mine Warfare Section were almost alone in their belief that the mine was a strategic war weapon of incalculable value. Indifference by most officers in the Navy, and almost total disregard of mine warfare by top men in the War Department despite success of the British mining campaign, prevented serious development of mine warfare.

After war started, the enthusiasm of specialists gradually overcame doubts of mine warfare's effectiveness because of a growing realization of Japan's vulnerability due to her dependence upon sea transportation for raw materials of all kinds.

The superiority of land-based bombers over carrier or amphibious aircraft for mining operations had been recognized for years by the Air Force and some officers in the Navy. As early as the first part of 1944, Navy agencies sought B-29s for mining, with Admiral Nimitz' strong backing, and the recommendation of the Committee of Operations Analysts.

Nimitz agreed to provide and service the mines. He strongly recommended the mining of the Shimonoseki Strait, which served as a funnel through which most of Japan's shipping had to pass to and from the Inland Sea, and also the Sea itself and principal ports on Honshu and Kyushu. In their recommendations Navy advocates said mining these areas would have decisive results because practically all oceangoing traffic to the Empire would be stopped, and the Japanese merchant fleet would be destroyed in a matter of months. After this eventuality, they said, the Japanese would be forced to abandon their overseas empire, which would hasten the war's end due to a cessation in the delivery of war-essential supplies. Further, they said, such action would weaken the home islands and further isolate Japan from her possessions and conquered territories that had been bypassed in the drive up the Central Pacific.

In reply, General Arnold pointed out that only 10 days earlier the Committee of Operations Analysts had recommended top priority should be given to the aircraft industry, urban areas, and shipping and now they were trying to divert a large part of the Twentieth's operations to mining. He refused to go along because, at that time, such a diversion would make it impossible for the Twentieth to perform its primary strategic missions. He assured the Navy that he recognized the validity of their arguments but extensive B-29 mining operations must await a buildup of the Twentieth Air Force.

Nimitz made a formal request to the Joint Chiefs of Staff for employment of the B-29 command for aerial mining. He requested that Arnold authorize 150 sorties a month starting in January 1945, building up to an ever-larger effort in April.

Initially, Hansell agreed to devote one group to the development of tactics and techniques of aerial mining. He resisted Nimitz' proposal to the Joint Chiefs because it would absorb all of the Superfortresses available at the time. He did agree that aerial mining should be carried out in adequate force when the command grew large enough to do so, and directed the 313th Wing to start the preliminary work.

Arnold put his own thoughts in a letter November 28, 1944. He still refused such a diversion of B-29 effort but promised that he would authorize such an effort as soon as more Superfortresses became available and the weather prevented daytime strikes against strategic targets.

In the next few months, Arnold was won over to the proposition and he wrote a letter to Hansell December 22 saying that he should plan for mining operations along the lines recommended by Nimitz but delay the start of such operations until April 1, 1945, instead of January 1 as recommended by Nimitz.

Hansell was having enough problems getting his strategic warfare program in operation and didn't take kindly to such a diversion of his bombers. He firmly believed that his Superfortresses would contribute far more to ending the war by striking at the heart of Japan's strength, which lay in her industrial targets, and gaining aerial supremacy over the Japanese air force prior to the invasion. He had objected to the original date recommended by Nimitz because start of a whole new program of mine laying unquestionably would dilute his force to the point where it would be impossible to do a good job on any targets.

Arnold and Hansell at first agreed to allocate just one bomber group to mine laying. After LeMay took over, he disagreed. In his mind, if his command had to do the job, he wanted it done right, and that meant a larger force than one group. He issued orders January 26 that 1,500 mines would be layed by an entire wing but they would also be available for other operations. The 313th was selected and LeMay set up a training program at North Field, Tinian, in February. Two crew members were eliminated from each aircraft and all .50-caliber ammunition was removed.

LeMay set up the first two mining missions of Operation Starvation between March 27 and April 1, 1945, to mine the Shimonoseki Strait to lend assistance to the invasion of Okinawa.

Early in the war Japanese ship losses became crucial and by late 1942 sinkings exceeded Japan's ability to replace ships. After the war, Admiral King said submarines sank almost two thirds of all Japanese ships. Navy, Army Air Force, and Marine planes also made a contribution. So successful was this interservice attack on Japan's shipping lanes that the Japanese started to close down convoy routes in late 1943, and almost a year later Japan had lost practically all contact with its outposts in the South and Southwest Pacific. Japan's shipping situation was so critical by March 1945 that only 12 of her 47 regular convoy routes were still open. Loss of these routes put an added burden on her railroad system, which was inadequate to begin with, and traffic between the home islands and her overseas holdings was confined to the comparatively shallow and well-protected Yellow Sea, East China Sea, and the Sea of Japan because Japan had withdrawn her 2 million remaining tons of shipping to her inner zone. Therefore, ports on the Asiatic side of Kyushu and Honshu, plus those on the Inland Sea, achieved an importance they had never known now that most shipping was confined to routes between China and Korea and the main islands of Japan. With Pacific ports on Shikoku no longer usable, most shipping was diverted through the narrow Shimonoseki Strait, which divides Kyushu and Honshu islands and provides an entrance to the Inland Sea.

The shallow Inland Sea, with its ring of mountains, was protected by numerous Japanese airfields because through this island-dotted water channel flowed enormous quantities of food and raw materials. Each year about 12,000 ship passages were made through the strait, and Inland Sea ports handled an equal number to provide the Kobe–Osaka industrial areas with the raw materials that were the lifeblood of their existence.

Japan's population during the war was more than half as large as the population of the United States but, by comparison, her arable land amounted to only 3 percent. Shipping, therefore, was vital to bring in the food and raw materials so vital to her economy for the prosecution of the war.

After the invasion of Okinawa was set for April 1, 1945, mining the eastern narrows of the Shimonoseki Strait took on an importance to stop troop reinforcements from being shipped to Okinawa, and to restrict movements of the remaining elements of the Japanese Navy. Of equal importance was the reduction of heavy ship traffic to and from mainland China through the Shimonoseki Strait to industrial ports on the Inland Sea.

LeMay came to the conclusion that it would take 1,500 mines to close the Shimonoseki Strait. He ordered Brigadier General John H. Davies to send three formations of his 313th Wing to drop almost 1,000 acoustic and magnetic mines the night of March 27. The results were good but a three-mile gap remained without mines. Little fighter opposition materialized but heavy flak surrounded airplanes as they moved in singly to their drop zones and cost the command three B-29s.

The strait was closed March 30 when 85 more B-29s dropped mines and the approach to Sasebo was blocked, as well as the southern entrance to Kure and Hiroshima, but the northern approach to these cities remained open because planes assigned to that sector had to abort.

Although the Japanese were caught by surprise at the size of the mine-laying operation, they quickly started mine sweeping to reestablish their lifeline to the Asiatic continent.

LeMay had expected this so he ordered that 2,000 more mines be laid during the month of April. When the 313th got behind schedule in their mine laying because of bombing attacks on Kyushu's airfields, LeMay designated two full wings to drop 1,500 more mines on Shimonoseki and the approaches to Kobe and Osaka. For the first time, small fields were laid in the harbors of Tokyo, Yokohama, and

Nagoya. These missions could not be run until May 3 because of the command's work to keep the airfields on Kyushu out of commission for Japanese bombers, fighters, and kamikaze suiciders. The patterns at Kobe, Osaka, and Shimonoseki were not complete enough to close the areas to shipping, and the drops in harbors of Japan's major cities were even less satisfactory.

On the whole, these early mine-laying operations helped to keep much of Japan's shipping in her harbors. At times, small suicide vessels were used to clear channels but the variety and complexity of American mines made effective sweeps almost impossible.

In late spring, Japan's shortage of food became acute. The fire raids had destroyed 25 percent of her rice stocks, and it became suicidal to send ships through mined areas. Although some ships tried to sneak through, the majority were confined to ports. After the March 27 mine laying of Shimonoseki, no large warship dared to pass through the strait. When the battleship *Yamato* tried to assist the defense of Okinawa, it was forced to leave the Inland Sea April 6 through Bungo Strait between Shikoku and Kyushu and it was detected easily by carrier pilots and destroyed, along with several supporting ships.

A new target directive by command headquarters was issued May 1 that 1,500 mines would be laid in the Shimonoseki Strait and harbors along Kyushu's west shore and the northwest coast of Honshu. These areas were important now that the Inland Sea was bottled up.

The 313th Wing kept the Shimonoseki closed most of the time and, during the month of May, Japanese ship losses to mines exceeded those destroyed by submarines for a total of 85 ships, or 9 percent of all ships remaining in her merchant marine. These losses were hard enough to take, but Japan's repair yards had been destroyed or seriously damaged, which further complicated her shipping problems.

During this period, Japan's cities were fire-bombed, and her industrial targets were under attack every clear day. Just when it seemed that the tempo of operations must be reduced due to crew exhaustion and wear and tear on aircraft, LeMay stepped up the number of missions. Lieutenant Colonel Charles M. Isenhart's 505th Group, which bore the brunt of the mining, flew 14 missions in less than a month starting June 7, planting more than 3,500 effective mines in the Inland Sea and the Sea of Japan.

Often the limiting factor was the supply of mines, particularly different types of mines to give the Japanese sweepers more difficulty in sweeping. The Japanese had an impossible job and assigned 20,000 men and 349 ships to sweep the areas. They found that the magnetic mines posed the most problems.

By the end of July, Japanese shipping was practically immobilized, with her Pacific ports closed down, the Inland Sea bottled up, and most major ports that depended upon water transport for 75 percent of their requirements at a standstill as the crescendo of operations rose daily.

To further complicate the Japanese supply problem, Third Fleet carrier planes struck every ship they could find on the high seas or in port, even attacking railroad ferries between Hokkaido and Honshu.

Shimonoseki Strait was kept mined on a regular basis with new pressure mines that were almost impossible to sweep, and other types that used ship-counting mechanisms and delay features whose ingenious designs were almost incredible. An area could be swept time and time again before these delay mechanisms armed the mine to explode.

Coverage was even extended to Korea, and B-29s used Iwo Jima to refuel for such long missions. These operations cut off one of Japan's few remaining sources of supply in Korea and Manchuria.

As the war neared its conclusion, the Japanese reacted savagely with every weapon at their disposal to stop these dreaded mines from being planted. They used radar, spotters, and interceptor planes to try and pinpoint where each mine was dropped. Japanese efforts at mine sweeping were primitive even though old-style magnetic and acoustic mines, which could be swept more easily, often had to be used. Mines frequently were misdropped on land and their secrets quickly revealed but even then the Japanese seemed unable to establish effective countermeasures.

B-29 losses, while never excessive, started to rise toward the end and altitudes were raised to 12,000 feet.

Just before the Japanese capitulated, her merchant marine had dropped to 1.5 million tons and sea-borne traffic of all types reached a state of virtual paralysis. Operation Starvation had done its deadly work and the Japanese people were living at or below the starvation level. From the beginning, the mining campaign had complemented bombing attacks to reduce Japan's essential supplies and hasten her surrender without an invasion.

U.S. Navy submarines sank 54.7 percent of all Japanese ships during the war, but the Twentieth Air Force accounted for 9.3 percent in just four and a half months, a time period in which it dropped over 12,000 mines. Their losses were 16 B-29s but only nine resulted from enemy action.

Nimitz sent LeMay a letter of congratulations in which he said, "The planning and technical operation of aircraft mining on a scale never before attained has accomplished phenomenal results."

The XXI Bomber Command's work in plugging Japan's arterial waterway through the Inland Sea, and closing the Shimonoseki Strait at the sea's northwest entrance, along with bottling up the other two entrances on the east and south—the Kii and Bungo channels—cost Japan her last vital lines of communication with the outside world.

During this short period more mines were dropped than by all other aircraft in the Pacific during the previous two years. This was possible because of the range and huge load-carrying capabilities of the B-29.

Japanese civilian and military officials were in agreement after the war about the economic impact of mining. Prince Konoye indicated that Japan's economy was strangled and in such dire straits toward the end that all food supplies and critical materials were prevented from reaching the home islands.

There had been many skeptics, including General George Kenney, whose Fifth Air Force was under MacArthur. He had authorized only one mining mission during the entire Pacific War.

Most military leaders failed to understand the potential of aerial mining. In retrospect, it is clear that mining should have been started sooner and on a larger scale. With mine laying held in low esteem not only in the Army Air Forces but in most of the U.S. Navy outside the Naval Mine Warfare Section, it was not possible to do so. Except for General Arnold, the Joint Chiefs regarded blockade and aerial bombing only as contributing to victory but not as war-winning strategies. For the most part, they were not considered substitutes for an invasion. If a vigorous mine-laying program had been begun sooner, with the success it later achieved, it is quite possible the Joint Chiefs might have concluded that a massive invasion of Japan's home islands was not necessary, thereby saving the United States billions of dollars in unnecessary military supplies and equipment.

# CHAPTER 24

# Dawn of the Atomic Age

The eminent scientist Albert Einstein realized in 1939 the potentialities of atomic energy for military purposes, and informed high officials of the U.S. Government. He warned that the Germans were carrying out such experiments, and that the United States should immediately start a program of its own.

President Roosevelt agreed and the Manhattan Project was established. It eventually cost $2 billion, but was successful in winning the race for discovery of an atomic bomb that could be carried in an aircraft.

In September 1943, Arnold recommended that the B-29 be selected as the atomic bomb deliverer because it was the most suitable airplane even though it was just entering production.

Arnold personally picked Lieutenant Colonel John B. Montgomery, Hansell's deputy, to head the 509th Composite Group, which would be trained to drop atomic weapons. Although Hansell wasn't completely aware of the nature of the project, he voiced a vigorous protest to Arnold about losing his ablest staff officer.

Arnold then selected Colonel Paul W. Tibbets, Jr., who was the only one for some time to know the group's true mission, to head it. Tibbets had a fine record of serving with the pioneering 97th Bombardment Group in England and North Africa, and was testing B-29s in the summer of 1944 when he was appointed to head the group. He picked Lieutenant Colonel Thomas J. Glassen, a Pacific war veteran, as his deputy, and handpicked other officers with whom he had fought for their special qualifications to form the nucleus of the 509th.

Montgomery, who did such an outstanding job later as LeMay's operations officer, would certainly have run a more disciplined organization than Tibbets unfortunately was able to do.

Early in 1944, Boeing selected 15 B-29s to be specially fitted for their new role, although no radical changes were needed in the airplanes.

Possible Japanese targets were selected by the end of 1944. Arnold recommended Kyoto, Hiroshima, Niigata, and Kokura, and ordered LeMay not to bomb these cities. They were of medium size with important manufacturing operations. Secretary of War Stimson objected to Kyoto because it was a national religious shrine and a cultural center. LeMay substituted Nagasaki; although he knew it was not an ideal target, it was one of the cities that had suffered little damage.

President Truman learned of the Manhattan Project only after Roosevelt's death April 12, 1945, when he was briefed by Stimson. The Secretary of War recommended that the President appoint a special civilian committee to set guidelines for use of atomic bombs and Truman agreed.

An interim committee report was completed June 1 and it advised the President unanimously that the atomic bomb should be used as soon as possible and against a military target surrounded by other buildings and without prior warning.

Some scientists disagreed, believing that the United States would alienate many peoples of the world who would view use of such a weapon with revulsion. These scientists, who were part of a Committee on Social and Political Implications, told Stimson that the atomic bomb should not be used until after it was demonstrated to members of the Allied nations on a desert or barren island.

The President's advisory panel of scientists, including A. H. Compton, Enrico Fermi, E. O. Lawrence, and J. R. Oppenheimer, told Truman they disagreed with their colleagues. They said they could not foresee an alternative to military use because of the danger that the bomb might prove to be a dud if dropped before officials of the Allied nations. Such an occurrence, they said, might stiffen Japan's resistance.

The President said Stimson agreed with the interim committee's report, and the President's civilian advisers were virtually unanimous that an unannounced test in the New Mexico desert should be held in July, with the first bomb released on a Japanese target in August.

Admiral William D. Leahy, who served President Roosevelt as chief of staff, and now Truman in the same capacity, had been against the atomic program from the start. He called it a "professor's dream." He told Truman, "This is the biggest fool thing we've ever done. The bomb will never go off, and I speak as an ordnance expert."

Leahy was one of those who hoped that an air and sea blockade, and air attacks against the home islands, would end the war without an invasion. He said an invasion couldn't be justified because Japan was already defeated. Arnold and LeMay agreed with him but Japanese troops had often demonstrated their tenacity in battle and the 2 million-man Japanese Army was still a military force to be reckoned with.

Admiral King, chief of naval operations, offered mild arguments to allay Leahy's fear of excessive losses in the invasion during discussions with President Truman. King never opposed the air offensive and believed it was a necessary contribution, but he never specifically expressed the opinion that the war could be won by airpower.

MacArthur wrote to Marshall April 20 in support of an early invasion of Kyushu because such a course would bring the full power of ground, naval, and air forces to bear on Japan whereas a year's delay would make Japan more difficult to invade. He called for a continuation of offensive methods which, he said, had proved so successful in the Pacific campaigns. "Reliance upon bombing alone," MacArthur said, "is still an unproved formula for success." He cited the failure of the bomber offensive against Germany, which had not forced the Nazis to capitulate without a ground invasion. He said that a ring of bases around Japan to intensify air attacks would disperse Allied forces even more, and that seizure of bases on the China coast would only escalate operations on the Asiatic mainland without any military benefit.

Marshall, who had supported Arnold in the hope that a combined bomber offensive against Germany would make an invasion of the continent unnecessary, now agreed with MacArthur's view. Actually, President Truman relied upon Marshall's views about the need for an invasion of Japan following extensive discussions with the Joint Chiefs. The latter had weighed conflicting views and voted unanimously that an invasion of the home islands was necessary. Thereafter, plans to invade Kyushu were adopted with further intensification of the air assault, a tighter blockade, and plans to persuade the Russians to enter the war soon.

General Arnold wasn't present at President Truman's meeting prior to the Potsdam Conference, in which the American position on grand strategy was discussed. He was represented by Lieutenant General Ira Eaker, who queried Arnold while he was visiting bases in the Marianas. Arnold told him not to oppose the position taken by General Marshall because he had been such a firm supporter of the Army Air Forces and he didn't want to risk alienation on such a vital matter.

Inasmuch as Marshall was supporting MacArthur's views for an invasion so strongly, and had already indicated to Arnold that he would support an independent air force after the war, Arnold's decision is understandable. It is possible that Arnold felt that an open insistence that airpower could end the war would be resented, and he certainly didn't want to lose Marshall's support.

After the atomic bomb proved itself at the Alamogordo test site, President Truman and his advisers were at the Potsdam Conference in mid-July. The President asked each of them about use of the bomb. Arnold advised against it on the ground that Japan was already just a hollow shell and could be brought down by continued conventional bombing.

Marshall still disagreed.

There is some evidence to indicate that the war might have ended a month earlier without dropping the atomic bombs if an announcement had been made that the invasion was indefinitely postponed, and that Japan would be subjected to ever-increasing air attacks.

In Japan, the Supreme War Council was divided. Half believed that Japan should seek peace under any conditions, and they had the concurrence of the Emperor and Premier Suzuki.

The premier had two missions. One was to prosecute the war, and the other was to seek peace. The opposition against peace was strong, including the war minister and the two chiefs of staff. They had broken American security and knew about the Kyushu invasion. They believed the armed forces of Japan could defeat the invasion by moving the greater mass of their troops to the site intended for the American landings. This was a vital point because the Japanese Army in the main islands was undefeated and still strong. If the announcement had been made that the invasion was postponed indefinitely, the rug would have been pulled out from under the militarists.

When Marshall told the President that the invasion of Honshu on the Tokyo plain, scheduled for March 1946, would cost at least a quarter of a million American casualties, and probably even more Japanese, Truman decided that he would authorize dropping the atomic bomb to save lives unless Japan agreed to peace terms.

Acting Secretary of State Joseph C. Grew objected although he didn't vote against the decision. He told the President that the Japanese might surrender if we declared that our war aims didn't include the destruction of the Japanese nation or removal of the Emperor. Stimson and Secretary of Navy James Forrestal agreed with Grew so Stimson was ordered by the President to draft a proposal July 2. This proposal offered hope to Japan if she surrendered but promised total destruction if she continued to resist.

A draft of this proposal was prepared at the Potsdam Conference. The American position was that if Japan refused to heed the warning the air and sea war would be stepped up.

Meanwhile, the British agreed to use of the atomic bomb against Japan, and the Combined Chiefs of Staff approved an intensification of the air and sea war while preparations were made for a Kyushu landing now scheduled for November 15.

Marshal Stalin had told Secretary of State Hull in the fall of 1943 that Russia eventually would declare war on Japan, and gave formal notice at the Tehran Conference later that year. In February 1945, at the Yalta Conference, Roosevelt and Stalin had agreed on terms for Russian participation in the war in the Far East, and Americans were led to believe that the Soviets would declare war on Japan three months after Germany's defeat. Unfortunately, most officials felt intervention was necessary because a ground invasion of Japan's home islands was expected to be bitterly resisted.

The majority of Japan's civilian leaders believed their nation had lost the war by July of 1945 because her industries had been crippled by air attacks, the sea blockade had brought the nation to the brink of starvation, and Japan's overseas possessions and conquered territories were isolated from the homeland. Japanese military leaders were convinced they must fight on until more acceptable peace terms could be achieved.

When Prime Minister Tojo was forced to resign after the loss of Saipan, those who favored peace grew in number. The Allied insistence on unconditional surrender thwarted a peace move in September 1944 when the Swedish minister in Tokyo was asked unofficially, supposedly in the name of Prince Konoye, to explore what peace terms the Allies would accept. Another such effort failed the following March for the same reason.

Since April 1945, Emperor Hirohito had indicated he wanted the war to end as quickly as possible. The Suzuki cabinet, which had just come into power, was more than ever convinced that peace had to be obtained somehow—particularly after the Soviets announced they would not renew their neutrality pact. This action, and the German surrender in May, precipitated another peace move and this time the Soviets were asked to intercede with the Allies. Soviet Ambassador Jacob Malik passed along the suggestion to Moscow June 3 but it wasn't acted upon.

By the end of June, with her home islands in a state of siege, Ambassador Sato approached the Soviet Government in Moscow and asked it to serve as mediator with the Allies to end the war. The United States was able to decode the messages from Tokyo and Moscow and American officials believed there was no possibility of the Japanese accepting unconditional surrender terms. This evaluation was correct because Japanese officials were unwilling to accept Allied terms although their nation desperately needed peace. Sato found the Russians of no help because Stalin procrastinated until the Potsdam Conference. He never did have any intention of acting in the role of mediator because it wasn't in line with his long-range goals of gaining new influence on the Asiatic continent.

Acting Secretary of State Grew had long advocated that the Japanese should be assured they could keep their Emperor, believing they would sue for peace on such terms. Truman didn't disagree with Grew but, after consulting with others in his cabinet and the Joint Chiefs, who agreed with the idea, the President delayed such a decision because most of his staff felt it was a matter of timing.

The first bomb was exploded on a tower at Alamogordo, New Mexico, July 16 and proved to be as powerful as the scientists had hoped it would be. Moreover, the bomb proved to be a practical weapon that could be delivered by a B-29.

Truman again called in his chief advisers and asked whether the atomic bomb should be used against Japan. They were unanimous that it should be.

\* \* \*

The Potsdam Conference opened the day after the first bomb was exploded. For the most part, the conference reviewed plans already made and approved them. For planning purposes, the conferees agreed on November 15, 1946, as the date when the war was expected to end.

Stalin told Truman about Japan's efforts to use the Soviets as mediators, a fact that the President was already aware of after the decoding of the cables to and from Tokyo and Moscow.

The Soviet leader also told Churchill that the Russians would attack Japan soon after August 8.

Truman waited until July 24 to tell Stalin casually that the United States had a new weapon of unusual destructiveness. Stalin showed no special interest, saying merely he was glad to hear it and hoped the United States would make good use of it against the Japanese. It wasn't learned until years later that Soviet spies had obtained atomic-bomb secrets and Stalin was well aware of what the United States was doing.

Two days later the Potsdam Declaration signed by President Truman, Prime Minister Churchill, and Generalissimo Chiang Kai-shek was released. Stimson's July 2 memorandum to the President served as the basis for the release but no reference was made about the Japanese keeping their Emperor. Secretary of State Cordell Hull had objected to any such reference because he thought it smacked of appeasement. Neither was there any reference to the atomic bomb. The Japanese were just warned that continued resistance would lead to Japan's prompt and utter destruction.

Arnold requested at the meeting that General Spaatz be given responsibility for delivering the atomic weapons once the President reached his irrevocable decision, and that he be given as much latitude as possible as to choice of target. There was no argument and Arnold's request for such authority was granted.

The Potsdam Declaration caused near panic in Premier Suzuki's cabinet. The military insisted that the government denounce the declaration and Suzuki did so publicly the following day.

The Allies took his statement as a complete rejection of their peace terms and were convinced that the military continued to dominate the Japanese Government.

The 509th Composite Group had arrived at North Field, Tinian,

June 1. LeMay told Colonel Tibbets it had been his experience that every new outfit in a combat theater, although they had been exposed to intensive training in the States, "screwed up" its first mission. He said he wasn't about to let that happen to the 509th.

LeMay had known about the atomic bomb for some time. At first, it hadn't made much of an impression because it had been a long time since he had studied college physics. He knew it would be a big bang, as he said later, but he didn't realize how big a bang it was going to be.

He told Tibbets that his group would go through routine training just like any other coming to combat. At first, the group went on six practice missions to nearby Japanese-held islands, and then took the familiar new-combat-crew runs to Truk and Marcus with regular bombs.

Starting July 20, the 509th carried TNT-filled bombs in cases resembling the atomic bomb to Japan and 12 strikes were made in four days by small formations at high altitude. LeMay had insisted that the final attack with the real thing should be simulated down to the last detail. The 10,000-pound, pumpkin-shaped bombs aroused much interest but only Tibbets, and a few atomic specialists, knew that soon one of those bomb casings would be filled with a small amount of material equal to 20,000 tons of TNT.

LeMay had been briefed by the Manhattan District officer earlier so he would be able to get special bomb-loading pits constructed and alter North Field to the group's particular requirements.

He had a battle with the Manhattan District because General Leslie Groves was impatient to get the first bomb delivered. LeMay understood his feelings because he had proved the bomb and was anxious to drop it. Groves insisted at first that every B-29 in the Marianas should surround the airplane with the atomic bomb in it and escort it to Japan.

"That's not the way to do it," LeMay said stubbornly. "We're running individual planes up there all the time and nobody pays much attention to them. We'll run yours up there like any other and all will be well."

It took Groves some time to be convinced but LeMay was adamant and got his way. At the time, LeMay didn't know Groves but got to know him well after the war and developed great respect for him.

Tibbets was told that the first atomic bomb would be available for use August 6. The cruiser *Indianapolis* had delivered the bomb's components in May to Tinian, but the fissionable material wasn't delivered until after the Alamogordo blast.

General Carl A. Spaatz, as commanding general, U.S. Army Strategic Air Forces in the Pacific, had been given standby authority to select the targets, and the actual time and date, by Stimson and Marshall but subject to final approval by the President. Truman had told Stimson the order to drop the first atomic bomb would stand unless he notified him that the Japanese had changed their stand on the Potsdam Declaration.

August 1 was Air Force Day and Arnold ordered a show of strength over the Empire. Seven hundred and sixty-two B-29s struck four cities and a petroleum center. Certainly a wing to each city was exorbitant but that wasn't the point. There were so few target cities remaining that LeMay didn't have a choice. After fire attacks against Hachioji, Nagasaki, Toyama, and Mito, and the destruction of the Kawasaki Petroleum Center, Japanese radio broadcasts were frank in admitting the terrible destruction and loss of life. Only one plane was lost and the crew was seen to bail out over Japan.

At first, group commanders anticipated that the start of the typhoon season would inhibit missions. LeMay disillusioned them by ordering that bad weather would not serve as an excuse for canceling a mission. Crews were routed around typhoons and everyone prayed that the weathermen had spotted them accurately.

Spaatz had delegated LeMay to pick the date for the first atomic mission. The training was completed, and LeMay believed all was in readiness. When weathermen told him August 5 that weather over the target city of Hiroshima would be clear the next day, he told Tibbets to proceed with the mission as planned for a 2:45 A.M. takeoff.

# CHAPTER 25

# Mission Successful

Tibbets received a report from a weather plane over Hiroshima at 8:15 A.M. that there were only scattered clouds over the city so, if the weather held for another hour, he knew they could hit the primary target at Hiroshima, and not have to go to Kokura or Nagasaki, which had been selected as second and third alternates.

Navy Captain W. S. Parsons and his assistant, Lieutenant Morris B. Jeppson, had assembled the atomic bomb after takeoff, and Parsons told Tibbets that all was in readiness for the historic drop.

Hiroshima, Japan's eighth largest city, was headquarters for the Second Army. LeMay earlier had been instructed not to bomb it, for reasons he didn't learn until later. The city was an important port and contained vital industries.

Seven B-29s of the 509th Composite Group had been assigned to the mission, one as a spare airplane at Iwo in case the "Enola Gay" got into trouble. Three Superforts had taken off first to serve as weather planes, and two others flew with the "Enola Gay" as observation planes. "The Great Artiste" was piloted by Major Charles W. Sweeney, and the other Superfortress was flown by Captain George W. Marquardt. Both were filled with cameras and scientific instruments plus military and civilian observers.

Other B-29s were ordered to fly at least 50 miles from Hiroshima four hours before the scheduled release and six hours after. LeMay scheduled two F-13 photo-reconnaissance airplanes to get post-strike photographs of the city.

The "Enola Gay" reached the initial point at 9:11 A.M. and Tib-

bets turned the airplane over to bombardier Major Thomas W. Fere-
bee, navigator Captain Theodore J. Van Kirk, and radar operator
Sergeant Joe A. Stiborik. After a smooth, tense run at 31,600 feet,
the "Little Boy" bomb went away at 9:15.

Set to explode at 2,000 feet, crew members felt two distinct shock
waves 50 seconds after the bomb left the airplane even though they
were pulling away from the city.

Then a huge mushroom cloud erupted above the city and rose
quickly to 50,000 feet as the crews stared in awe.

Observers on the ground first saw a huge pinkish glare in the sky,
followed by a wave of intense heat and wind that withered everything
in its path. Seventy-one thousand three hundred and seventy-nine
Japanese died instantly, and 68,023 others who were horribly burned
or seriously injured, and suffering from the effects of intense radiation, writhed in agony on the scarred ground. Debris whirled into the
sky as a massive cloud of smoke, fire, and pulverized matter as-
cended thousands of feet in seconds. Fires quickly burned what was
left of the city and only devastated land remained. Here and there on
a pavement was the outline of what had once been a human being,
now completely disintegrated and only a shadow remaining to prove
that the person had ever existed.

Tibbets sent a radio message back to the Marianas. "Mission successful. No hostile fighters, few flak bursts."

Bombing accuracy was hardly up to LeMay's standards because
the aiming point was missed by 800 feet. The new bomb's wide area
of destructiveness, of course, made the error relatively unimportant.

The "Enola Gay" and the observer planes landed at Tinian's
North Field at 2:58 P.M., reporting that smoke from Hiroshima
could be seen for 390 miles.

Five hours after the first atomic bomb exploded, F-13 photo-
reconnaissance planes were over the city. Although smoke and dust
were so heavy over the city that an accurate assessment of the damage would have to wait until later, it appeared that 4.7 square miles
of the city had been destroyed. Later, it was determined that the
number of dead was lower than after the March 9 fire raid on Tokyo,
but the number of injured was higher.

President Truman received news of the bombing on the *Augusta,*
which was en route home from the Potsdam Conference. A few minutes before noon Captain Frank Graham handed the President a

KEY
[⬚] OLD DAMAGE
[⬚] NEW DAMAGE
[⬚] SPARSELY POPULATED

YOKOHAMA

DAMAGE
8.9 SQ. MI.
44 %

*YOKOHAMA—Vertical lines and crosshatched lines indicate extensive damage to the city. Dots indicate areas sparsely populated.*
*(Photo courtesy of T. R. Vaucher.)*

Background: Bomb damage in Hiroshima.
(Photo courtesy of
the National Archives.)

Far left: HSINCHING, CHINA—Natives pulling
roller over new runway.
(Photo courtesy of
the National Archives.)

Near left: Mao Tse Tung about 1945.
(Photo courtesy of
the National Archives.)

Above: XXI BOMBER
COMMAND—A Superfortress
crew chief on Guam tells
General Henry H. Arnold,
commanding general of the
Army Air Forces, how ground
crew keep the B-29s in
readiness for strikes against
Japan. Left to right:
Lieutenant General Barney M.
Giles, commanding general
of the Army Air Forces, Pacific
Ocean Areas; Brigadier
General Thomas S. Power,
commander of the Guam-based
314th Bombardment Wing;
General Arnold; and Staff
Sergeant Leo F. Fliess,
Sturtevant, Wisconsin.
(Photo courtesy of the National
Archives.)

Right: IN THE CLEAR—
Formation of B-29s rides above
the clouds as they head for
target November 3, 1944,
at Rangoon, Burma. These
Superforts were part of the
468th Group.
(Photo courtesy of the U. S.
Air Force.)

Left: VISIT TO THE SOUTHWEST PACIFIC AREA—
After attending the Cairo and Teheran Conferences,
General George C. Marshall, U.S. Army Chief of
Staff, stopped off, on his way home, to visit General
Douglas MacArthur and his command.
(Photo courtesy of the National Archives.)

Lower right: THE HUMP— Formation from the 444th
Bombardment Group rides high above the clouds, and the
Himalayan mountain range, commonly referred to as
"The Hump." (Photo courtesy of the U. S. Air Force.)

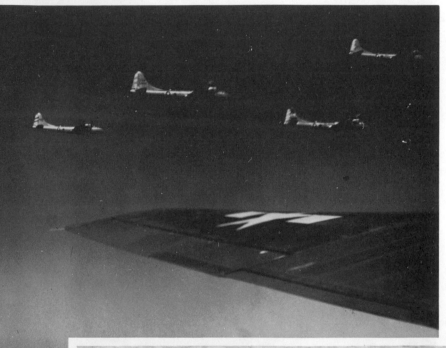

ATOMIC CLOUD rises above Nagasaki, Japan, August 9, 1945, after second atomic bomb is dropped on the city.    (Photo courtesy of the U. S. Air Force.)

OLD FRIENDS—General Curtis E. LeMay, left, and Major General John B. Montgomery reminisce about World War II at a full-dress affair long after the war. (Photo courtesy of J. B. Montgomery.)

radio message he had just received. "Hiroshima bombed visually with one-tenth cover at 052315A. There was no fighter opposition and no flak. Parsons reports 15 minutes after bomb as follows: 'Results clear-cut successful in all respects. Visible effect greater than in any test. Condition normal in airplane following delivery.' "

Then a wire arrived for the President from Secretary of War Stimson. "Big bomb was dropped on Hiroshima August 5 at 7:15 P.M. Washington time. First reports indicate complete success which was even more conspicuous than earlier test."

Truman authorized a press release, which had been prepared earlier, to be released in Washington. It said that an atomic bomb had been dropped on Hiroshima, and warned the Japanese that if they didn't surrender they could expect a "rain of ruin from the air, the like of which has never been seen on this earth."

After the nature of the weapon that was dropped on Hiroshima became known to the Japanese Government, Dr. Yoshio Nishina, the nation's leading nuclear physicist, was ordered to fly to Hiroshima to determine if it was true that an atomic bomb had been dropped. After his visit he told Lieutenant General Seizo Arisue that Hiroshima had been the victim of a uranium-type bomb.

Japanese Army officials refused to allow the press to mention that an atomic bomb had been dropped. All they were allowed to say was that a new type of bomb had caused considerable damage. There had been some confusion over reports that several parachutes had been seen just prior to the explosion. What they didn't release was that special instruments were attached to these parachutes to record data on radiation, blast effect, etc.

Premier Kantaro Suzuki and Tojo again advised the Emperor that Japan should accept the Potsdam formula for ending the war, but the Army stubbornly resisted such a move.

LeMay followed up the atomic attack by sending three formations to hit the Toyakawa Arsenal near Tokyo the next day. Other Superfortresses struck the Nakajima Aircraft Plant in the same area and both were knocked out. The 58th was assigned Yawata to fire-bomb the city. Two B-29s, one on each runway, crashed on takeoff and blocked the runways so only a few planes got over Yawata. Unlike earlier missions when this had been a hot corner of Japan, no fighters rose to challenge the veteran crews and there was only moderate flak.

Eleven groups went out with mixed loads of incendiaries and general-purpose bombs on the eighth and in the early-morning hours of August 9 destroyed four more cities, including Fukuyama, whose horrors were enlivened by the explosion of a huge dye works.

Ambassador Sato in Moscow got word the previous day that Molotov would see him in the Kremlin. He went there hoping that his previous overtures for Russian mediation now would be realized. Instead, he was handed a declaration that the Russians had declared war on Japan, and he now knew there was no hope for a negotiated peace.

Some Japanese leaders had been searching for a way to end the war for months. Emperor Hirohito, who had earlier tried to get the military to agree to a cessation of hostilities, called a meeting of his inner cabinet. Although he had little authority, he used his vast prestige with the people as Emperor to insist that the war be stopped.

The cabinet sent messages to the Allies that Japan would accept the Potsdam terms if they didn't threaten the prerogatives of the Emperor. The United States received word through Switzerland, and the British and Russians through Stockholm.

The United States didn't reply immediately because it was felt that any Japanese qualifications might be construed as a lessening in the terms agreed to at Potsdam. Truman and his cabinet had never insisted that the office of Emperor should be abolished, but the whole matter needed a thorough review.

While Japanese militarists talked about taking over the government, President Truman authorized release of the second and last atomic bomb, with Kokura, on the northern tip of Kyushu, as the primary target because of its huge Army arsenal, and Nagasaki as secondary target.

LeMay had stepped up the propaganda campaign as hundreds of thousands of leaflets were dropped over Japan, detailing the terms of the Potsdam Declaration, describing what atomic bombs would do to Japan, and announcing that the Russians had entered the war.

Major Sweeney's "Bock's Car" ran into foul weather August 9 over Kokura, and despite three separate runs looking for a hole over the target, bombardier Captain Kermit K. Beahan had to admit failure.

Sweeney noted that fuel was running low so he turned the B-29 toward Nagasaki on Kyushu's west side. Although the city of Nagasaki had been bombed several times, it was not appreciably damaged and its Mitsubishi plants had hardly been touched. It was not a good target because the city's valleys were deep within hills across an up and down terrain.

Beahan sought the aiming point frantically because the countryside lay under an eight-tenths cloud cover and he hoped that radar was bringing them in properly. During the last few seconds, he found a hole and "Fat Boy" left the airplane at 10:58 A.M. Nagasaki time. The bomb missed the aiming point by three miles this time.

Sweeney racked the airplane sharply away from the city but the explosion was worse than over Hiroshima and the plane was pummeled by shock waves and for a moment they thought they would become part of the tragedy unfolding beneath them as 35,000 Japanese died instantly while 60,000 others were injured. An area of 1.45 square miles, or more than 43 percent of the city, was obliterated, including more than two thirds of the industrial section. Due to the hilly terrain, destruction spread laterally through the valleys, and was less than a normal fire raid with incendiaries.

Due to a fuel-transfer malfunction, "Bock's Car" was short of fuel so Sweeney headed for a base on Okinawa. He didn't arrive back on Tinian until late that night and Sweeney learned that his bombs-away message had not been received.

An imperial conference was held in Japan the next day. Although no agreement was reached, the Emperor made it clear that he wanted the war brought to an end. He said Japan's only course was to accept the Potsdam Declaration.

After the second atomic bomb was dropped, Colonel Montgomery went in to see General Twining, telling him he thought it was foolish to send out any more missions because Japan was trying to settle the war. He told the new head of the Twentieth, "It will simply play into the hands of the militarists who keep telling their people that we're trying to destroy them and not just defeat them."

Twining was impressed with Montgomery's arguments and stood the command down for maintenance.

It wasn't long before Twining received a message through Spaatz from General Marshall ripping him to pieces for such an act. A badly shaken Twining ordered renewal of attacks.

Just before resumption of missions, a pilot got up in a Saipan mess hall. "Men," he said loudly, "I've just heard that Premier Suzuki has asked LeMay to provide him with air transportation back to the States to try and end the war."

That got their attention, but the pilot just stood there without saying another word.

Finally, someone yelled, "What happened?"

"LeMay said 'no,' " the pilot said.

An anguished roar went up from the group. "Why?" came a chorus of voices.

The pilot grinned. "Because Suzuki hasn't flown his thirty-five missions."

They laughed appreciatively because they were all sorcly in need of a good joke.

Meanwhile, Arnold recommended that the Tokyo area be hit by 1,000 B-29s to prod the Japanese militarists into an early surrender.

Instead, a mission was scheduled for August 11 to bomb the Hikari Naval Arsenal on the Inland Sea. It was scratched at the last minute by President Truman when he ordered a cessation of all operations that day. This action was taken because the Big Four had agreed to the Japanese surrender offer but with the provision that the Emperor must carry out the orders of the Supreme Allied Commander.

When the Japanese were not immediately responsive to this provision, daylight precision strikes were scheduled for August 14. LeMay split his command so that B-29s would be over Japan every hour of the night and day.

The veteran 58th Wing, rescheduled to hit the Hikari Arsenal, destroyed it with three formations by placing 95.6 percent of its bombs on the target. Group Commander Kalberer led a formation in one of the most spectacular bombing feats of the war. LeMay termed the bombing the best of any flown by the 58th during the war, and among the best ever flown by any heavy-bomber outfit. For those who remembered the early chaotic missions, the 58th's last was a source of pride, and they gave full credit for their professionalism to one man—Curtis E. LeMay.

Three hours after they dropped their bombs, the word was flashed to all B-29s that the war was over. The Japanese had finally agreed to call it quits.

The Emperor had called his cabinet together that morning and insisted on an end to the war, saying there was nothing objectionable in the United States proposal. He asked his minister to prepare for his signature a statement that Japan accepted the Potsdam Declaration. The cabinet agreed and it was sent out.

In response, the United States insisted on an immediate end to all hostilities. The Japanese Government was advised to send emissaries to General of the Army MacArthur, who as supreme commander for the allied powers would arrange for a formal surrender.

Nimitz and MacArthur had been kept abreast of developments and had been directed to make plans for Japan's collapse.

Later, it was learned that both Hirohito and Suzuki had agreed to accept the Potsdam terms as early as July 26, and that most leaders outside the Army had long since conceded they had lost the war and had been seeking some means by which to end it gracefully since early spring.

The last combat mission had seen 828 B-29s over Japan and 186 American fighters for a total of 1,014, and not one airplane was lost.

B-29s were sent on daily reconnaissance over the home islands until the occupation forces could take over. And, in one of the more pleasant tasks assigned to the Twentieth Air Force, hundreds of B-29s headed for Japan with bomb bays filled with food and clothing for the thousands of starving prisoners of war of many nations. They were air-dropped at sites marked by the Japanese, and it was the first time in many years that most prisoners had a chance to eat an adequate meal. One hundred and fifty-four camps were supplied in August and September but even these mercy missions proved dangerous because eight bombers were lost and 77 men were killed in operational accidents.

General LeMay was invited to attend the surrender ceremony September 2 aboard the battleship *Missouri*. He landed on an airfield near Yokohama and was assigned a seat in one of the 200 automobiles the Japanese had been ordered to furnish for the Americans.

After they started off for Yokohama, he was surprised to see at least half of these automobiles abandoned alongside the road. They were so decrepit that they couldn't make those few miles into town, although the Japanese assured the Americans they were the best available.

He thought of the mountains of supplies piled up on Guam and the other islands awaiting an invasion that now was no longer needed. To himself, he wondered how much money and resources the United States might have saved if it had been recognized earlier that an invasion would not be necessary because the Japanese could be forced to surrender by sea and air power. These wrecks of automobiles epitomized for him the fact that the Japanese had run out of everything.

On the *Missouri,* he stood silently as the formalities for ending the war were completed. Then, he and others looked up as hundreds of airplanes roared overhead in salute, including tight formations of B-29s, which had done so much to bring about the events of this day.

A few days after LeMay returned to Guam, he was visited by General Stilwell, who had attended the surrender ceremony and was on his way home.

"LeMay, I just wanted to stop and tell you that when I went through Yokohama for the ceremony, I understood for the first time what you were trying to tell me up in the Chengtu Valley. I knew Yokohama well because I was a language student there when I was a second lieutenant. I remember its size and what it was like. When I saw what's there now—nothing but ashes and rubble—I understand what you were trying to tell me about strategic bombing."

# Epilogue

Japanese militarists had hoped for a quick victory over the United States because Japan's industrial and military power was inadequate to sustain a long war. Once American industry, with 10 times the production capacity of the Japanese, was geared up for war the end was inevitable.

The Twentieth Air Force had flown more than 100 million miles on 380 combat missions, which didn't include training, reconnaissance, or weather missions. Its Superfortresses released 91 percent of all bombs dropped on Japan's home islands for a total of 147,000 tons. Nine times as many tons of bombs were dropped on Germany but total damage was about the same in both countries.

Superfort losses overseas totaled 512, and 576 fliers were killed while over 2,400 were missing in action. Many of the latter were killed by the Japanese after bailing out over Japan. Crew losses amounted to only 1.38 percent of all sorties. Training losses in the States were high and claimed another 260 B-29s.

Toward the end of the war, Japanese fighter attacks dwindled but there were times when formations had to fight their way through to the targets. Although claims often were exaggerated unintentionally, 714 Japanese fighters were destroyed, and another 456 probably destroyed.

B-29s leveled about 40 percent of the built-up area of 66 principal cities, and 602 major war factories were destroyed. This was a catastrophe for Japan at the time but new plants were built with American aid with the most modern equipment in the world, thereby giving

Japan after the war an economic advantage over other nations that she was quick to exploit by producing goods at a cheaper rate.

Fire raids brought destruction to 2.3 million homes and 330,000 Japanese civilians were killed and another 476,000 were injured. These figures tell only part of the tragedy because 8.5 million civilians were made homeless and 21 million were displaced. Civilians actually bore the brunt of war losses because B-29 attacks caused more casualties than Japan's armed services suffered.

Attacks against the aircraft industry proved effective and postwar analysis indicated that 7,200 combat planes were denied to the Japanese as a direct result of attacks against aircraft and engine factories, which, respectively, lost 75 and 60 percent of plant capacity.

Prince Nauhiku Higashi-Kuni told the Japanese Diet September 4, "The general conditions of the country began to show marked signs of impoverishment and exhaustion. So much so that in the days just preceding the termination of the war it seemed almost impossible to carry on modern warfare further for any long period of time. The production methods such as we had adopted before would shortly have to face insurmountable difficulties as a result of the destruction of transportation and communication facilities caused by air raids. Our losses in naval and aerial strength were so enormous as to obstruct seriously the prosecution of the war. Moreover, various industries suffered directly from air raids which caused huge damage to plants and lowered the efficiency of the workmen.

"Frequently air raids together with depreciation of rolling stock and equipment brought about a steady lowering of its capacity and a tendency to lose unified control. Despite the exertion of all possible efforts the carrying capacity of railways would have had to be reduced to less than one-half as compared with last year."

Prince Konoye said, "Fundamentally the thing that brought about the determination to make peace was the prolonged bombing by the B-29s."

Premier Suzuki voiced similar views. "It seemed to me unavoidable that, in the long run, Japan would be almost destroyed by air attack so that merely on the basis of the B-29s alone I was convinced that Japan should sue for peace."

It is apparent that the atomic bombs gave the Japanese an excuse to surrender when they did, although airpower would have forced them to the same conclusion in a few more weeks or months.

Arnold was emphatic in his opinion that the atomic bombs did not bring about Japan's defeat, although he conceded that the bombs had precipitated her earlier surrender. He said the efforts of the Twentieth Air Force had been directed to Japan's defeat without an invasion of her home islands and that objective had been reached.

LeMay believed there was no doubt but that Japan had been defeated mainly by airpower but he also gave credit to the contributions of all other services.

The United States Strategic Bombing Survey reported that Japan would have surrendered before the end of the year regardless of the atomic bomb and without an invasion.

Others disagreed. Dr. Compton said the war would have continued for many months and that the atomic bomb forced Japan's surrender. Admiral Nimitz stated his belief that the decisive factor was the ability of the Pacific Fleet to attack Japan against only limited opposition.

After the war LeMay got a half-dozen letters from families who castigated him because their son, husband, or brother had been killed as a result of his decision to make low-altitude fire raids on Japan.

He answered each letter personally, and enclosed a copy of a service magazine called *Impact* that reported on new developments in war theaters. One of the articles in that issue stated that in the last three months of the war it was safer to fly a combat mission over Japan than it was to fly a B-29 on a training mission in the States. In the last month alone, when his command had over 1,000 B-29s, only four bombers were lost to all causes.

Generals Eisenhower and MacArthur, both of whom considered themselves staunch advocates of airpower, had narrow visions when it came to employment of strategic bombers. Four years of war hadn't changed the dogma of the joint Army–Navy Board, which still believed that navies and air forces can render valuable support, but that it can be accepted as an almost invariable rule that only armies can win wars. Both generals considered bombers primarily for support of ground troops.

In MacArthur's case, he may have considered his return to the Philippines a "sacred duty" but this unnecessary operation caused the deaths and injuries of thousands of Americans and Filipinos. With the U.S. Navy in command of the seas, the Philippines should have been bypassed. The Philippine Islands weren't needed even if an invasion had been necessary.

\* \* \*

In retrospect, there was no need to spend millions of dollars to train the 509th Composite Group, an organization that proved itself singularly lacking in discipline for such a grave responsibility. At a time when they continued to fly training missions month after month, replacement crews were desperately needed in the Twentieth Air Force for conventional bombing. There were sufficient trained professionals among the oldtimers in the field who, with a few weeks special training, could have done a far better job of dropping those two atomic bombs.

The strategic bombing survey's report said that the overall effect of the Twentieth's air offensive had been devastating and decisive before the atomic bombs were dropped.

For some strange reason, nothing was said in the survey about the Twentieth's basic purpose of undermining the industrial, economic, and social structure of the state to the point where it would be fatally weakened and the Japanese would be compelled to surrender.

How effective was the original AWPD-1 plan that General Hansell had helped to draft before the war? First, the forecast of the number of combat groups that it would take to do the job was predicted within 2 percent, and the total number of officers and men within 5.5 percent.

Hansell has concluded that the effects of the air offensive were catastrophic and decisive and they were caused by the direct damage from bombing; the indirect effect of bombing resulting from the frantic efforts of the Japanese to disperse their industry; the loss of essential raw materials through blockade, including aerial mining by the B-29s and the absenteeism of destitute workers.

In Hansell's opinion, Japan's economic system had been shattered by July 1945. Production of civilian goods was below the level of subsistence, he says, and munitions output had been curtailed to a level that could not sustain military operations. In other words, he says, the economic basis of Japanese resistance had been destroyed.

"This economic decay resulted from the sea-air blockade of the Japanese home islands, and direct bombing attacks on industrial and urban-area targets," Hansell says. "The urban incendiary attacks had profound repercussions on civilian morale and Japan's will to stay in the war. Sixty-six cities, virtually all those of economic significance, were subjected to bombing raids and suffered destruction ranging from 25 to 90 percent."

Most knowledgeable officials credit the bombing offensive as the major factor that secured agreement to unconditional surrender without an invasion, an invasion that undoubtedly would have been extremely costly in American lives. Long before the Japanese surrendered, the lack of adequate defenses against B-29 attacks brought home to civilians that further resistance was futile.

In the opinion of those who conducted the bombing survey, Japan would have surrendered prior to December 31, 1945, and in all probability by November 1 even if the atomic bomb had not been dropped, without Russian intervention, and even if no invasion had been planned or contemplated.

The continued efforts during the war to get Soviet Russia to declare war on Japan were unnecessary, and may have helped to give the Soviets a stronger foothold in the Far East. However, it must be recognized that Russia would undoubtedly have moved as she did at the end of the war without any prodding from the United States.

President Roosevelt, and later Truman, sought Soviet intervention because they both were appalled by the prospect of huge casualties if Japan's islands were invaded. Such a thought was uppermost in Truman's mind when he agreed to drop the atomic bombs. When the counsel of his advisers is considered, and everything the President was told at the time, there's no doubt that Truman made the correct decision even though it has led to countless misunderstandings.

Unfortunately, vulnerability of the Japanese electric-power systems was not understood. By destroying 54 switching stations and 13 generating plants Japan would have lost essential power for its industrial and urban areas. This was a job that the 315th Wing could have handled easily.

In summary, Hansell says that airpower was the primary but not the sole reason for Japan's surrender. "The long and costly drive across the Central Pacific to secure the Marianas as air-base sites was a prerequisite to the final air offensive against Japan," he says. "Japanese capability to sustain her armed forces, particularly those abroad, was undermined by the war at sea. One must remember," Hansell says, "that Japan as an island empire was entirely dependent upon sea transportation and was particularly susceptible to sea power. The Navy played a vital role by cutting off sea commerce."

Hansell has a word of caution about drawing conclusions from the switch from precision bombing of selected targets to urban-area incendiary attacks. "Japan was peculiarly vulnerable to incendiary bombing. The weather and winds made precision bombing by visual means extremely difficult, especially for ill-trained crews. The decision to turn to the easier task of incendiary bombing," he says, "was reluctantly but wisely taken. The tactical method selected by LeMay was a superb decision."

In the event of a future war, which Hansell fervently hopes will never occur, he says that not all situations will have these same characteristics.

"In my judgment, selective destruction of vital industrial, logistical and military targets is a better method of waging strategic air war than area destruction of population centers." He still believes it was the better method against Germany.

"Towards the last of the strategic air offensive against Japan selected targets were frequently demolished. Today, selective destruction is much more feasible with modern strategic air operations due to superior all-weather bombing equipment and superior training. The method selected should fit the situation, and the capabilities of the force. Accuracy is still a priceless asset."

Airpower as a primary war-winning force came of age in 1945. Japan's ability to sustain her armed forces, particularly those abroad, were undermined by the war at sea. The flow of raw materials from Southeast Asia had been cut off early in the war, but the flow from China and Korea continued until mines dropped by Superfortresses cut off the last commercial contact with the outside world.

General Marshall's support of Arnold was vindicated by the sudden ending of the war. His comment on the first presentation of AWPD-1, which called for a strategic bomber offensive, that "this plan has merit," was more than justified by the final course of events.

In the fall of 1977, LeMay, his once jet-black hair now gray and at 71 trimmer than he ever was during his younger years, said, "To me the greatest victory during the war was getting an Air Force built, and training 2.4 million people to do the job. To do this in peacetime would be a tremendous undertaking. To accomplish it in wartime, and fight at the same time, was a miracle.

"Few people understand that airpower couldn't demonstrate its potential early in World War II because we had too few airplanes and untrained people. Towards the end of the war, more and more damage was done because of the increase in the size of the force and the increased efficiency of operations."

He paused a moment, his hazel eyes shrouded in the past. "Think what the early missions would have been like if they had operated as efficiently as those at the end of the war. We can thank people like Colonel Joseph Preston whose lead-crew school turned out professionals. Then, there was the reorganization of the maintenance system that kept an underdeveloped airplane flying. No other command during the war even approached the flying time per airplane achieved by the Twentieth Air Force."

Then, in the familiar free-swinging, let-the-chips-fall-where-they-may style of old, he let go at his critics. Despite the usual pipe in his mouth, his voice was firm when he said, "Any time anybody writes about the Air Force, particularly the swivel-chair, intellectual types in Washington who think they know all there is to know about war, they downgrade strategic bombing as no good. They point to failure of the Eighth Air Force in England to prevent an invasion of the continent, and the inability of B-29 operations in China to be more effective. They don't take into account that we didn't have the airplanes! Germany could have been defeated by air if our leaders would have waited until bomber forces were strong enough to be decisive.

"When I came back from Europe after the war to take command of the Strategic Air Command, most people thought we had just been through a war so there were plenty of trained crews available. That wasn't true. By and large, those who had fought the war had gotten out or were in staff positions. We had a bunch of men who had not been through the war, or if they had, had served in fighters or some other segment of the Air Force. There wasn't one single crew ready to fight if necessary. So, starting from that level, we were still improving when I left SAC nine and a half years later.

"It takes years to assemble and train people to form a combat outfit."

Unspoken was his hope that the American people would never forget.

# Bibliography

Arnold, H. H. *Global Mission.* New York: Harper & Bros., 1949.

Baxter, James Phinney 3rd. *Scientists Against Time.* Boston: Little Brown and Company, 1945.

Craven, W. F., and Cate, J. L. *The Army Air Forces in World War II,* Vol. 5, *The Pacific—Matterhorn to Nagasaki.* Chicago: University of Chicago Press, 1945.

Hansell, Maj. Gen. (Ret.), Haywood S. *The Air Plan that Defeated Hitler.* Atlanta: Higgins-McArthur Longino and Porter, Inc., 1972.

Mansfield, Harold. *Vision—A Saga of the Sky.* New York: Duell, Sloan and Pearce, 1956.

Marshall, General of the Army, George C.; Arnold, General of the Army, H. H.; and King, Fleet Admiral, Ernest J. *War Reports.* Philadelphia and New York: J. B. Lippincott, 1947.

General Marshall's Reports, "The Winning of the War in Europe and the Pacific." The Biennial Report of the Chief of Staff of the United States Army to the Secretary of War. New York: Simon and Schuster, 1945.

Morrison, Wilbur H. *The Incredible 305th: The "Can Do" Bombers of World War II.* New York: Duell, Sloan and Pearce, 1962.

Morrison, Wilbur H. *Hellbirds: The Story of the B-29s in Combat.* New York: Duell, Sloan and Pearce, 1960.

Morrison, Wilbur H. *Wings over the Seven Seas: U.S. Naval Aviation's Fight for Survival.* Cranbury, New Jersey: A. S. Barnes, 1976.

Pogue, Forrest C. *Organizer of Victory, 1943–1945, George C. Marshall.* New York: The Viking Press, 1973.

Potter, E. B. *Nimitz.* Annapolis, Maryland: Naval Institute Press, 1976.

Smith, Robert R. *Command Decisions.* New York: Harcourt, Brace and Company, 1959.

Sallagar, F. M. "Lessons from an Aerial Mining Campaign." Rand Corporation Report No. R-1322PR. Santa Monica, Calif.: 1974.

Truman, President Harry S. *Years of Decision*. New York: Doubleday & Co., 1955.

United States Strategic Bombing Survey, U.S. Government Printing Office. Washington, D.C.: 1946–47.

# Index

Hsinching, 53, 89, 114, 165
Hubbard, Col. Boyd, 249, 264–268
Hubbard, Lt. Col. Harry, 63
Hull, Maj. Carl T., 243, 244
Hull, Secretary of State Cordell, 281, 283
Hump, 37, 40, 41, 70, 84, 96, 122, 123, 135, 151
Hurley, Brig. Gen. Patrick, 139, 140–141
Hwangoo River, 162

Iki Island, 110
Imperial Iron and Steel Works, 88, 109
Imperial Palace, 233
*Indianapolis*, 285
Inland Sea, 225, 269, 271–274, 292
Insein, 81
Irish Lassie (B-29), 205
Irvine, Col. C. S., 62, 200, 205, 221, 261
Isenhart, Col. Charles M., 273
Isley Field, 176–177, 179, 189
Iwakuni Army Fuel Depot, 263
Iwo Jima, 179, 181, 184, 189, 195, 202, 207, 210, 211, 220, 231, 233, 242, 244, 256, 259, 265, 274

Jack II (fighter), 134, 205
Japanese Army, 279, 289
Japanese Diet, 296
Japanese Navy, 19
Jarman, Maj. Gen. Sanderford, 177
Jeppson, Lt. Morris B., 287
Johnson, Maj. Harvey, 133
Johnston Island, 202
Johore Strait, 131, 162
Joint Chiefs, 30, 41, 43, 52, 55, 63, 73–76, 78, 80, 83, 88, 95, 118, 123, 127, 138, 141, 148–151, 159, 174–177, 180, 191–192, 228, 248, 249, 251, 259, 260, 261, 270, 275, 282
mainland targets assigned to coordinate invasion of Saipan by, 88

overall war plans for defeat of Japan considered by, 95
withdrawal of XX Bomber Command to Tinian ordered by, 150
Joint Intelligence Committee, 30
Joint Logistics Committee, 39
Joint Planning Staff, 74–77
Joint Plans Committee, 44
Joint Strategic Committee, 30
Joint Target Group, 235, 255, 256
Joltin' Josie, the Pacific Pioneer, 113, 175, 176, 200
Jones, Lt. Louis M., 82
Joyce, Capt. Charles, 131–133

Kagi, 149
Kagoshima, 257
Kalaikundi, 55, 123
Kalberer, Col. Alfred F., 111
Kamikaze, 229, 230, 237, 238
Kandy, 163
Kawanishi Aircraft Company, 234, 255, 256, 258
Konan plant, 234
Narao plant, 255, 256
Takarazuka plant, 258
Kawasaki, 180, 199, 226, 233, 235–236, 256, 285
Akashi plant, 256
Petroleum Center, 285
Keller, Maj. John B., 81
Keller, Lt. Ray, 194
Kennerson, Lt. Col. Waldo I., 53, 55–56
Kenney, Maj. Gen. George C., 38, 78, 182, 275
Kesekes, Lt. John, 246
Khabarovsk, 111
Kharagpur, 55, 70, 78, 94, 158, 161, 165
Ki-84 (Frank fighter), 211
Kii Channel, 275
Kilner, Brig. Gen. W. G., 22
King, Admiral Ernest J., 74, 75, 127, 128, 148, 164, 176, 210, 230, 252, 259, 271, 279
King, Col. Richard T., 192–193